FOLK RELIGION IN JAPAN

Continuity and Change

HASKELL LECTURES ON HISTORY OF RELIGIONS

NEW SERIES
No. 1

JOSEPH M. KITAGAWA, General Editor

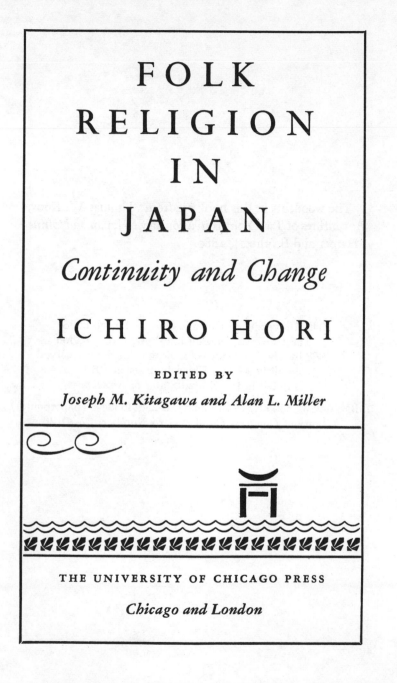

FOLK RELIGION IN JAPAN

Continuity and Change

ICHIRO HORI

EDITED BY

Joseph M. Kitagawa and Alan L. Miller

THE UNIVERSITY OF CHICAGO PRESS

Chicago and London

The woodcuts in this book are from: Thomas W. Knox, *Adventures of Two Youths in a Journey to Japan and China* (Harper and Brothers), 1880.

The University of Chicago Press, Chicago 60637
The University of Chicago Press, Ltd., London
© 1968 by The University of Chicago. All rights reserved
Published 1968. Third Impression 1974
Printed in the United States of America

ISBN: 0-226-35333-8 (clothbound); 0-226-35334-6 (paperbound)
Library of Congress Catalog Card Number: 67-30128

Foreword

Some time ago, H. I. H. Prince Takahito Mikasa characterized Japan as a "living laboratory and a living museum to those who are interested in the study of history of religions." Visitors to Japan will find the countryside dotted with Shinto shrines and Buddhist temples. In the big cities, too, one finds various kinds of Shinto, Buddhist, and Christian establishments, as well as those of the so-called new religions, which have mushroomed since the end of World War II. Indeed, even in the modern industrialized Japan, colorful religious festivals and pilgrimages play important parts in the life of the people.

Historically, the Japanese archipelago, being situated off the Asiatic continent, was destined to be influenced by a number of religious and semi-religious traditions from abroad, such as Confucianism, Taoism, Yin-yang school, Neo-Confucianism, various forms of Buddhism and Christianity, as well as all kinds of magical beliefs and practices. This does not imply, however, that these traditions have been preserved intact in juxtaposition. In this respect, James B. Pratt once stated that the Japanese people have accepted Buddhism "simply, humbly, in sincere and almost childlike fashion, and they have laid the stamp of their transforming genius upon it." Similarly, they have interpreted and appropriated other religious and semi-religious systems in terms of their particular religious outlooks and experiences.

The complexity of the religious heritage of Japan is such that it can be viewed, as indeed it has been, from different perspectives and with different assessments. Thus, some hold that Shinto is the Japanese religion par excellence, while others would argue that Buddhism is at least the "half-creed of Japan." Those who are impressed by Zen would stress the decisive, though nebulous, influence exerted by Zen on all aspects of Japanese culture. Still others would assert that Confucian tradition, despite its reluctance to be classified as a religious system in the usual sense of the term, has nevertheless provided the most enduring framework for the Japanese world view. These opinions have been advocated and affirmed by many both Western and Japanese scholars, and be it noted that each one has a great deal of truth. On the other hand, few attempts have been made thus far by scholars, Japanese or Western, to delineate the nature of the total pattern of religious development in Japan. In this sense, the present volume by Professor Hori is an important contribution to the study of Japanese religion because of his serious endeavor to portray significant characteristics which have been shared by different religious traditions on the folk level throughout the history of Japan. For this task, the author is enviably equipped by his training in Buddhology, history of religions, and folklore studies—all of which are essential for the understanding of Japanese religion.

We may recall in this connection that scholarly inquiry into Japanese religion and culture was pioneered in the latter part of the nineteenth century by a number of talented Western scholars. Some of them—for example, Basil Hall Chamberlain, Karl Florenz, and Ernest Fenollosa—were academicians by profession, while others were what George B. Sansom called "scholarly amateurs"—for example, William G. Aston, Ernest M. Satow, Charles Eliot, John Batchelor, and Sansom himself. These men, undaunted by linguistic jungles, worked out the chronology of Japanese history, translated texts, and analyzed unfamiliar concepts, beliefs, and practices of the Japanese according to the canon of Western humanistic disciplines. Meanwhile, many able Japanese scholars studied abroad and were trained in modern scholarly disciplines and methodologies. For instance, as early as 1873, Bunyū Nanjō studied Sanskrit under Friedrich Max Müller at Oxford, and published in 1883 A *Catalogue of the Chinese Translations of the Buddhist Tripitaka*. Following him, other Japanese scholars studied Indology, Buddhology, Sinology, philology, philosophy, ethnology, and history of religions in Europe, England, and America. In a real sense, it was the combined effects of the dedicated labors of the Western Japanologists and of the Western-trained Japanese scholars which established in Japan during the first three decades of the present century the various scholarly disciplines dealing with Japanese religion and culture, as exemplified by the works of Masaharu Anesaki in the science (history) of religions, Kakuzō Okakura in Japanese art, Junjirō Takakusu in Buddhology, D. T. Suzuki in Zen study, Genchi Katō and Tsunetsugu Muraoka in Shinto study, and Kunio Yanagita in folklore study, to name only the most obvious. Thanks to the research of these men and their disciples, the study of Japanese art and culture, philosophy and religion attained a high standard before World War

II. Owing largely to historic factors, however, Japanese scholars of different disciplines tended to work more or less independently of each other without much cross-fertilization. Also, most of their works were almost unavailable to Western scholars, except a small number of specialists, because of the barriers of language and thought pattern.

Happily, the picture has changed considerably since the end of World War II. Not only have scholars of various disciplines in Japan begun to develop methods of cooperative inquiries, but also Western and Japanese scholars have begun to be engaged in meaningful dialogue and collaboration on various levels. In this atmosphere, the culture and religion of Japan, for example, have come to be reexamined and reassessed from broader perspectives. While experts in specialized areas continue their researches, they too are aware of the necessity of relating their findings to those of others, including those of Western scholars. I might add that this sentiment is warmly reciprocated by many Western scholars who are concerned with the significance of Japanese culture and religion.

It is therefore most appropriate and timely that the present volume be published by the University of Chicago Press at this time. Hori was Visiting Professor of the History of Religions at the University of Chicago, 1957–58. At that time we explored the possibility of his returning to Chicago at a later date. In the fall of 1965, he was invited to deliver the six lectures sponsored by the Haskell Lectureship on Comparative Religions. It is through this lectureship, which was established in 1895, that many distinguished scholars on the history of religions have been invited from abroad to the campus of the University, including J. J. M. DeGroot of Berlin, Franz Cumont of Brussels, Carl Bezold of Heidelberg, Christian Snouck Hurgronie of Leiden, Sarvepalli Radhakrishnan of India, A. R. Gibb of Oxford, Louis Massignon and Mircea Eliade of Paris, and Friedrich Heiler of Marburg, as well as Masaharu Anesaki and Hideo Kishimoto of Tokyo. Hori's manuscript was gone over initially by H. Byron Earhart, who was then engaged in research under Hori at Sendai, and Robert S. Ellwood, who later spent a year in Tokyo to work with Hori. After delivering the Haskell Lectures, Hori entrusted his manuscript to me and to Alan L. Miller, and we took the responsibility of preparing it for publication. We are grateful to the Committee on Far Eastern Civilizations at the University of Chicago for its financial assistance toward the preparation of the manuscript. In our editorial work, we have shifted, with the consent of the author, some of the texts into the notes and changed some of the phrases and expressions. We sincerely hope that our efforts did not unduly distort the original intent of the author.

JOSEPH M. KITAGAWA
For the Committee on Haskell Lectures

Preface

༄༄༄ The present book is based on the Haskell Lectures given in 1965 at the University of Chicago. While I have added notes, glossaries, and bibliographic references, I have attempted to retain the oral style of the lectures as much as possible. The aim of this book is to delineate the main features and characteristics of Japanese folk religion, which has been transmitted from the early phase of Japanese history. Folk religion in Japan, like its counterparts in other parts of the world, has many similarities with archaic and primitive religions. It is significant to note, however, that Japanese folk religion has greatly conditioned the political, economic, and cultural developments historically. To be sure, we are aware of the important roles played by more self-conscious religions and semi-religious systems such as Shinto, Buddhism, Confucianism, Taoism, and Christianity in the religious history of Japan. But on the folk level, various features of these religious and semi-religious systems were blended to meet the spiritual needs of the common people, who had to find religious meaning in the midst of their workaday life. Thus, throughout this book no attempt is made to portray Shinto and Buddhism, for example. Rather, they are viewed from the perspective of folk religion and are discussed only to the extent that they contributed to the development of the folk religious tradition.

It has been my intention to depict some of the important facets of the phenomenon of Japanese folk religion. With this in mind, I have discussed the main characteristics (Chapter I), the relation between social structure and folk religion (Chapter II), the popular Pure Land Buddhist practice, called Nembutsu in the context of folk religion (Chapter III), the importance of the mountains for the idea of the other world (Chapter IV), Japanese Shamanism (Chapter V), and the survival of Shamanistic tendencies in the contemporary new religions in Japan (Chapter VI). Some of the materials used here have been published previously; "Japanese Folk-beliefs," *American Anthropologist*, 61: 3 (June, 1959), which became the basis of Chapter II; "On the Concept of Hijiri (Holy-man)," *Numen*, V, Fasc. 2–3 (April–September, 1958), a portion of which is used in Chapter III; "Mountains and Their Importance for the Idea of the Other World in Japanese Folk Religion," *History of Religions*, 6: 1 (August, 1966), which constitutes Chapter IV; and "Penetration of Shamanic Elements into the History of Japanese Folk Religion," dedicated to the *Festschrift*, Vol. 2 (Frankfurt am Main, 1965), in honor of Adolf Jensen's sixty-fifth birthday, parts of which are used for Chapters V and VI. I hereby thank these journals and publishers for granting me permission to use these materials.

It is my pleasant duty to express my gratitude to the President and the members of the Committee on the Haskell Lectures of the University of Chicago for the honor of appointing me the 1965 Haskell Lecturer, and to the Dean of the Divinity School for inviting me as Visiting

Professor of History of Religions during the autumn quarter, 1965. I am greatly indebted to my colleagues at Chicago, especially Mircea Eliade and Joseph M. Kitagawa, for their kindness and encouragement. The publication of this book would not have been possible without the assistance of a number of my friends who have made stylistic corrections and suggestions, especially H. Byron Earhart of Western Michigan University, and Robert S. Ellwood, Jr., of the University of Southern California, as well as Joseph M. Kitagawa and Alan L. Miller, who have edited the manuscript and prepared it for publication.

ICHIRO HORI

TOKYO

Contents

CHAPTER

I

Main Features
of Folk Religion
in Japan

ぴぴぴJapanese folk religion, unlike Buddhism or
Confucianism, is extremely diverse in character and difficult to define precisely. It is made up of vague magico-
religious beliefs, many of which are survivals or successors
of archaic and primitive elements; these beliefs or primitive elements themselves remain unsystematized theoreti-
cally and ecclesiastically but in many ways have penetrated and become interrelated with institutionalized religions.[1]

In fact, this folk religion consists mainly of natural religion, and includes various magico-religious or even superstitious elements. Therefore, from the standpoint of
organized religion or orthodoxy, some aspects of folk re-

[1] Ichirō Hori, *Minkan-shinkō (Japanese Folk Beliefs)* (Tokyo: Iwa-
nami-zensho No. 151, 1951), pp. 8–10.

1

ligion are not necessarily legitimate religious practices. Moreover, sometimes they are harmful to society, and often hinder the process of modernization in Japan. The significance of the phenomenon of Japanese folk religion cannot, however, be limited to its religious content or quality. It should be pointed out that folk religion means a group of rites and beliefs which has been deeply felt by the common people, and supported and transmitted by them from generation to generation. Therefore, folk religion not only has historical and traditional significance but, what is more important, it defines the social raison-d'être in contemporary Japan. Folk beliefs might be criticized as vulgar magico-religious phenomena, especially since they are not under the direct control of the institutionalized religions such as Buddhism, Shinto, Confucianism, and Christianity. Nevertheless, it should not be forgotten that even today the majority of the Japanese people are dominated by folk religion in its social, family, and individual life as well as in its productive activities. Either consciously or unconsciously, the people feel that their daily lives require several kinds of rites, festivals, ceremonies, and their connected magic and taboo.

The old established religious bodies as well as the new religions are forced to regard the existence of folk religion as important. Some of these religious groups have originated out of folk or natural religion. This is true of Shrine Shinto, Sectarian Shinto, and religious Taoism. On the other hand, Confucianism and Buddhism were established in opposition to folk religion or superstitions. However, not one of them has failed to be intimately related to folk religion or to utilize folk religion in the course of evangelizing the masses. In fact, the temptation to accommodate folk religion has really been the weak point of institutionalized religion in the history of Japanese religion from ancient times to the present.

(*The Characteristics
of Japanese Folk Religion*

In Japan, as elsewhere, there are several kinds of rites and magico-religious customs that are thought to have originated in antiquity, before human memory or records. According to the inferences of Japanese physical anthropologists, the proto-Japanese were made up of nine different racial stocks, or at least three major stocks—namely, the Mongolian, Malayo-Polynesian, and the Ainu. It is still unclear which stock was predominant and when and where it originated. The famous physical anthropologist Kenji Kiyono has designated as one distinct race the so-called stone age man in Japan (*Nihon sekki-jidai jin*), who inhabited nearly all districts of the Japanese islands. It is clear that since then various stocks have immigrated from the South Sea islands or the Asian continent and mixed with each other.[2]

The traces of such complicated racial mixture may be inferred from the formation of the Japanese language, which has a distinctive structure absent in the cognate languages.[3] Ōbayashi, in a recently published work,[4] ana-

[2] Kenji Kiyono, *Kodai-jinkotsu no kenkyū ni motozuku Nihon-jinshu-ron* (*A Study of the Japanese Race Based on the Researches of Human Bones by Japanese Antiquarians*) (Tokyo, 1949).

[3] Susumu Ōno, *Nihon-go no kigen* (*Origin of the Japanese Language*) (Tokyo: Iwanami-shinsho, 1957).

[4] Taryō Ōbayashi, *Nihon shinwa no kigen* (*Origins of Japanese Mythology*) (Tokyo, 1961); see especially pp. 21–52. Cf. Takeo Matsumura,

3

lyzed the structure of Japanese myths found in the *Kojiki* and *Nihongi*. His comparison of these myths with those of the East Asian and the Oceanic peoples brought to light the existence of several Altaic, Southeast Asian, and Polynesian motifs or types in Japanese mythology. Since the appearance in 1798 of Motoori's *Kojiki-den* (44 volumes of commentary on the *Kojiki*), the part of the creation myth known as the Seven Divine Generations[5] has

---

Nihon shinwa no kenkyū (Studies of Japanese Mythology) (Nagoya, 1956); Shōei Mishina, *Shinwa to bunka-kyōiki (Mythology and Cultural Areas)* (Tokyo, 1948); Takeshi Matsumae, *Nihon shinwa no shinkenkyū (A New Study of Japanese Mythology)* (Tokyo, 1962); Nobuhiro Matsumoto, *Nihon no shinwa (Japanese Mythology)* (Tokyo, 1956).

[5] The creation myth at the beginning of the *Kojiki* is as follows:

(1) The names of the deities that were born in the Plain of High Heaven (Takama-no-hara) when the Heaven and Earth were formed, were the Deity Master-of-the-August-Center-of-Heaven (Ame-no-minaka-nushi), next the High-August-Producing-Wondrous Deity (Taka-mi-musubi), next the Divine-Producing-Wondrous Deity (Kami-musubi). These three deities were all deities who were born alone, and hid themselves. (2) The names of the deities that were born next from a thing that sprouted up like a reed-shoot when the Earth, young and like floating oil, drifted about medusa-like, were the Pleasant-Reed-Shoot-Prince-Elder Deity (Umashi-Ashikabi-hikoji), next the Heavenly-Eternally-Standing Deity (Ame-no-tokotachi). These two deities likewise were born alone, and hid themselves. (The five deities in the above list are separate Heavenly Deities [*Koto Amatsu-kami*].) (3) The names of the deities that were born next were the Earthly-Eternally-Standing Deity (Kuni-tokotachi), next the Luxuriant-Cloud-Moor Deity (Toyo-kumonu). These two deities were likewise deities born alone and hid themselves. The names of the deities that were born next were the Deity Mud-Earth-Lord (U-hiji-ni), next his younger sister the Deity Mud-Earth-Lady (Su-hiji-ni), next the Germ-Integrating Deity (Tsunu-gui), next his younger sister the Life-Integrating Deity (Iku-gui), next the Deity Elder-of-the-Great-Place (Oho-tonoji), next his younger sister the Deity Elder-Lady-of-the-Great-Place (Oho-tonobe), next the Deity Perfect-Exterior (Omo-daru), next his younger sister the Deity Oh-Awful-Lady (Aya-kashiko-ne), next the Deity Male-Who-Invites

4

been recognized as the most difficult to interpret coherently, both for scholars of mythology and for scholars of the Japanese classics. Ōbayashi has offered an hypothesis from the viewpoint of comparative mythology. He theorized that the first group of deities originated in the Altaic nomadic culture, because of the idea of the creator and ruler who were born at the center of heaven. The bearers of this part of the myth were probably the ancestors of the imperial family and the accompanying shamanic priest clans. The second part of the myth Ōbayashi assumed to have originated in Southeast Asia, as evidenced by the idea of a cosmic tree and the motif of the appearance of the first human being or deity from vegetation. The bearers of this part of the myth were probably the wet-rice cultivators of the lowlands. The third group of deities is characterized by the idea of an appearance of the cosmic giant between primordial heaven and earth or a primordial chaos or vacuum and of the appearance of the deities that manifest the several stages of cosmic evolution. This type of creation myth is similar to those of Polynesian mythology, and the bearers were probably the Ama tribes (seamen) in ancient Japan.

For our purposes Ōbayashi's hypothetical analysis of mythical elements in the *Kojiki* serves to show the complexity of the Japanese people and their culture and life

(Izanagi), next his younger sister the Deity Female-Who-Is-Invited (Izanami). (From the Earthly-Eternally-Standing Deity down to the Deity Female-Who-Is-Invited in the previous list are what are termed the Seven Divine Generations.)

Chamberlain's translation of the *Kojiki* is quoted here, with several adaptations by the writer. The English renderings of Toyo-kumonu and Izanami have been slightly changed. See B. H. Chamberlain, *Translation of "Kojiki" or "Records of Ancient Matters"* (2d ed.; Kobe, 1932).

in prehistoric times. A similar inference could be made in the area of Japanese folk religion. In fact, we can find many elements of folk religion which supposedly originated from, or at least are similar to those of, other cultural areas. For example, certain practices originated in or resemble those of ancient food-gathering or hunting, nomadic cultures in Northern and Central Asia, those of the rice culture in Southeast Asia, and the customs and magical techniques in Melanesian and Polynesian culture.[6]

As I shall discuss in detail later, Japanese popular religion has been greatly influenced by shamanic elements. It is commonly known that the typical forms and functions of shamanism are seen now in Northern and Central Asia, Mongolia, Manchuria, Korea, Saghalien, and Hokkaido as well as among Eskimos and North and South American Indians. Among the ancient Japanese also, great shamanesses seemed frequently to play important roles in political or social crises. In the course of history the descendants of these shamanesses, in the process of mixing their religious forms with others, underwent various transformations, and thereby exerted diverse influence, not only on folk religion and folk arts, but also on the institutionalized religions. Moreover, we can find several shamanic forms and functions in some new popular religious sects appearing from the beginning of the Meiji era to the present, as well as in magicians, seers, and healers in the rural communities.

In Japan today there exist two different kinds of shamanesses: the "arctic hysteria" type, borrowing Czaplicka's term; and the Polynesian type. Shamanesses of the

[6] See, for example, Enkū Uno, *Mareishiya ni okeru tōmai girei* (*Rice Rituals in Malaysia*) (Tokyo, 1944).

6

first type live in Hokkaido as well as such small isolated islands as Hachijo-jima, Ryuku, and Amami. As we shall see later, several founders of the newly arisen religious bodies (*Shinkō-Shūkyō*), such as the Tenri or Ōmoto sects (which appeared in the nineteenth century), seem to have been typical shamanesses of the arctic hysteria type. At the same time, many shamanesses in the ancient *Shinanomiko* were of the second type, as are the contemporary *itako* who live mainly in northeast Honshu. They do not display any physical illness or neurotic symptoms before initiation, such as exist among the shamans of the arctic hysteria type of which the Ainu *tsusu* is an example. Because her ecstasy and possession are learned techniques, inevitably they tend to be stereotyped and to follow the path of folk arts more than of pure shamanic functions.[7]

The style of architecture seen in the Ise and the Izumo shrines, thought to preserve vestiges of ancient residential buildings, suggests some tropical area and may be a clue to the problem of cultural diffusion. Likewise, we can see similarities and connections between some folk customs and annual festivals in present-day Japan and the customs of so-called primitive neighboring peoples or of the ancient Chinese.[8] The seasonal rites featuring visits by masked

[7] Most of them are blind or partly blind women who become apprentices of their master shamaness in order to learn the rituals and techniques of ecstasy. After several years' training, an apprentice becomes an independent professional shamaness, having undergone the ordeals and ceremony of initiation. See M. Czaplicka, *Aboriginal Siberia: A Study in Social Anthropology* (Oxford, 1914); Mircea Eliade, *Shamanism: The Archaic Techniques of Ecstasy* (New York, 1964).

[8] For an interesting attempt to discover similarities between two widely separated peoples, see Alexander Slawik, "Kultische Geheimbünde der Japaner und Germanen," *Wiener Beiträge zur Kulturgeschichte und Linguistik*, Vol. IV (Salzburg-Leipzig, 1936).

persons, the *tsuina* (demon-expulsion) festival at the end of the year, and the *tanabata* (star festival) at the seventh night of the seventh month of the lunar year are only a few Japanese examples of such customs, even though they have been greatly transformed and reinterpreted in the course of history.[9]

It is clear, however, that the actual contents of Japanese folk religon are not exhausted only by these archaic elements. Japan has never been isolated from political, economic, and cultural changes on the Asian Continent, but has reacted sensitively to these changes. Thus to the northern, western, and southern routes of cultural diffusion in prehistoric Japan must be added the introduction of rice culture (Yayoi culture), which penetrated into western Japan about the third century B.C. It is thought that at this time a revolutionary change took place in the socio-cultural systems which eventually brought about the formation of a unified empire, first in the form of village-states, and then of federated village-states. These village-states were quite different from the former food-gathering or shell-mound (*kai-zuka*) culture complex (Jōmon culture). Corresponding to this social change as well as to the technological changes caused by the introduction of bronze and iron tools and arms, there occurred a fundamental change in natural religion—a transformation from the small-scale magic and religion of isolated clans to large-scale state religion with agricultural magico-religious forms. Perhaps proto-Shinto was formed gradually during the period from the introduction of agriculture to the early Yamato dynasty of the Kofun

[9] Hori, "Rites of Purification and Orgy in Japanese Folk Religion," an unpublished paper read before the XIth International Congress for the History of Religions held in Claremont, California, in 1965.

(Tumulus) age from about the fourth to sixth centuries A.D.

After the first century A.D.[10] the current of Chinese civilization seems to have flowed mainly into northern Kyushu through the Korean peninsula, and on a rather large scale. From then until the seventh century, and especially in the sixth century under the leadership of the Yamato dynasty, the exchange between Japan and Korea and North and South China resulted in a remarkable number of immigrants from these areas. They settled not only in western Japan, but also in the eastern provinces, until they made up more than one-fourth of all the clans at the end of the eighth century. As a result of the new civilization and technical skills which the immigrants brought with them, Japan became the site of industrial and technological innovations, and their collective power and wealth have left extensive traces.

It is still unclear precisely what beliefs, rituals, and customs these immigrants brought with them from their homelands. However, from the fragmentary materials handed down, we may infer that they introduced among the ruling classes the Confucian ethics and the philosophy and religion of Lao-tze and Chuang-tze. At the same time, they introduced among the lower classes some beliefs, rituals, and techniques of Taoism and Yin-yang magic, as well as Korean shamanism, all of which still survive

[10] The discovery of a buried golden seal in 1784 in Shiga-no-shima near Fukuoka in northern Kyushu verified the record in the *Hou-Han-shu* of A.D. 57 that a local king of Na state of Yamato (or Wo-jen) sent his messengers to the imperial court of the later Han dynasty, at which time the first Emperor Kuang-wu gave the king of Na a golden seal. See Seita Tōma, *Uzumoreta kin-in* (*Buried Golden Seal*) (Tokyo, 1950); Mitsusada Inouye, *Nihon kokka no kigen* (*Origin of the Japanese State*) (Tokyo, 1965).

9

in the rural communities of China and Korea. Moreover, Buddhism, having been transformed in various ways during its long journey from India to Korea through Central Asia and China, came to Japan in the middle of the sixth century under the auspices of the imperial family, noble families, and the naturalized clans.[11]

These borrowed ethical, magical, and religious elements were blended, reinterpreted, and resystematized into Japanese religion as one entity, through the processes of cultural contact and interchange with the indigenous beliefs, rituals, and customs of primitive Shinto. They intermingled so completely that they lost their individual identities, and they have actually played the traditional roles of state religion and/or family religion. Confucianism and Shinto have borrowed Buddhist metaphysics and psychology; Buddhism and Shinto have borrowed many aspects of Confucian theory and ethics; and Confucianism and Buddhism have adapted themselves rather thoroughly to the indigenous religion of Japan instead of maintaining their particularity, though of course their manifestations are many and varied.[12]

In this context, we may point out that there is good reason to speak of Japanese religion as an entity. Throughout there are several significant common tendencies: emphasis on filial piety (*kō*) and ancestor worship connected with the Japanese family system; emphasis on *on* (debts or favors given by superiors) and *hō-on* (the return of

[11] See Hori, *Wagakuni minkan-shinkō-shi no kenkyū (A Study of the History of Japanese Folk Religion)* I (Tokyo, 1955), 79–143, especially pp. 117–31; see also Akira Seki, *Kika-jin (Ancient Immigrants)* (Tokyo, 1956).

[12] Robert N. Bellah, *Tokugawa Religion: The Values of Pre-industrial Japan* (Glencoe, 1957), p. 59.

on); mutual borrowing and mixing of different religious traditions (or syncretistic tendency); belief in the continuity between man and deity, or easy deification of human beings; coexistence of different religions in one family or even in one person; strong belief in spirits of the dead in connection with ancestor worship as well as with more animistic conceptions of malevolent or benevolent soul activities.

❲ *Institutionalized Religion and Folk Religion*

As Ralph Linton has pointed out, borrowing is an indispensable condition for the progress of culture. None of the contemporary highly developed peoples has built up its total culture by itself. They all reached a high level of culture after passing through the two stages of borrowing and reintegration. Needless to say, there is a significant disparity between material culture and spiritual culture in the case of borrowing and reintegration: material culture or technology can be transplanted just as it is, but it is difficult to borrow spiritual culture, which is accompanied by complicated inner associations or emotional responses. According to Linton,

> Such things as religious or philosophical concepts can be communicated after a fashion, although probably never in their entirety. Patterns of social behavior can also be transmitted in the same uncertain way, but the associations which give them genuine potentialities for function can not be transmitted. A borrowing group

13

may imitate their outward forms, but it will usually be
found that it has introduced new elements to replace
those which could not be genuinely communicated to
it.[13]

The magico-religious needs and emotional associations
of the Japanese people are important factors of receptibility in the process of borrowing or selection of foreign
religions in Japan. Not only has folk religion played an
important role with respect to the receptibility of foreign
religions, but folk religion has also borrowed from foreign
religions for its own uses and devices. Actually, folk religion has swallowed up foreign religions with an insatiable
appetite.

For example, philosophical and religious Taoism is
thought to have been introduced before the Nara period
(seventh and eighth centuries). On the other hand, religious Taoism had flourished at its peak in T'ang China
and acquired the ardent support of successive emperors,
which led to the severe anti-Buddhist persecution of Emperor Wu-tsung in A.D. 845. Though there was intimate
intercourse between T'ang China and Japan during this
period, religious Taoism could not succeed in establishing
an independent religious order, in building any temple,
or in converting any priest. The Yin-yang magic and
techniques (Japanese, On-myō-dō) had been controlled
and monopolized by the Kamo and Abe families since
the Heian period (A.D. 782–1185). However, the same
Yin-yang techniques were adopted in the Shinto rituals at
the imperial court by Shugen-dō and other religious sects,

[13] Ralph Linton, *The Study of Man: An Introduction* (New York,
1936), pp. 337–40; Hori, "Sho-shūkyō no uketorare-kata" ("Japanese
ways of acceptance of foreign religions"), *Nihon shūkyō-shi kenkyū*
(*Studies on the History of Japanese Religions*), II (Tokyo, 1963), 31–48.

and other aspects of Yin-yang were absorbed by folk religion.

As I shall discuss in detail in Chapter VI, the so-called *Shinkō-Shūkyō* (newly arisen religions) have originated from these syncretistic strata of ancient folk religion. The newly arisen religions are especially characterized by shamanistic leaders and the attempt to obtain divine favor in this world, based on primitive magical forms as well as on the syncretistic but simplified or popularized theology of various religions. It is not exaggerating to say that we can find here the historical remains of ancient Japanese religions which have penetrated to the level of the common people.

The hidden Christians (*Kakure-Kirishitan*) in the isolated seashore areas and small islands in northern Kyushu are another example of acculturation. They have formed a kind of secret society since the Tokugawa shogunate strictly prohibited Christian missions and converts in 1614. They are descendants of Christians converted through the missionary activities of the Jesuits led by St. Francis Xavier between 1549 and 1614. They have continued to maintain their ardent faith from generation to generation for more than three hundred years without priests or any communication from Rome and in spite of frequent martyrdoms and severe oppression by the shogunate and the feudal lords. Nevertheless, the contents of their faith have been radically transformed and reshaped by folk religion and indigenous elements, so that it has lost almost all its Catholic characteristics. As Kiyoto Furuno has pointed out,[14] their present faith should no

[14] Kiyoto Furuno, *Kakure-Kirishitan* (*Hidden Christians*) (Tokyo, 1960); see also Kōya Tagita, *Shōwa-jidai no senpuku kirishitan* (*Hidden Christians in the Shōwa Era—1926 to the Present*) (Tokyo, 1954).

longer be called Catholicism. Instead, the movement should be called Kirishitan-ism, according to the common Japanese term Kirishitan for "Christian" in the Tokugawa period (1603–1868), even though they still believe that they transmit the authentic Catholicism of Xavier. This makes us feel all the more keenly the regulating power and ability of folk religion to permeate all areas of folk life.

Even though this acculturation phenomenon of the hidden Christians (*Kakure-Kirishitan*) represents the most extreme example, the same tendency can be seen among Japanese Buddhists. Of course, Buddhism, unlike Christianity, is characterized by weakness of authoritarian structure in both theology and organization. The so-called eighty-four thousand varieties of the Buddha's teachings contrast sharply with the authority of the Old and New Testaments; also, Buddhism has nothing to compare with the strong centralized authority of the papal see. Therefore, Japanese Buddhism has naturally tended to commingle with the folk religious elements, reinterpreting and systematizing them in various ways. The best example of this tendency is the fact that the most significant social function of present-day Japanese Buddhism, regardless of sect, is the funeral ceremony and memorial services for the spirits of the dead. Sir Charles Eliot wrote:

> Until the Meiji era all funerals were performed by Buddhist priests, and even now many Japanese who have little to do with Buddhism during their lives are buried according to its rites. . . . In Buddhist families the mortuary tablets are placed before the household shrine which occupies a shelf in one of the inner apartments and the dead are commonly spoken of as buddhas

(hotoke-sama). . . . *This bold language is, so far as I know, peculiar to Japan and is an imitation of Shinto. The Shinto dead become (it is not explained how) Kami or superhuman beings, for the translation "gods" is an exaggeration: it could hardly be allowed that the Buddhist dead had an inferior status and they were therefore termed Buddhas, Buddhas and Kami being, according to popular ideas, much the same.*[15]

To put it in the extreme, it seems to me that what gave Japanese Buddhism a form and character so markedly different from that of Indian or Theravāda Buddhism is Japanese folk religion or popular Shinto. This latter was based on the cultural and value systems of Japan, and originated from the religious consciousness, magico-religious needs, and social system of the people. Generally speaking, the universal religions, such as Buddhism or Christianity, insisted on attitudes of negation, separation, and transcendence in opposition to secularism. They usually tried to actualize an ideal community either in this world or in the other world, based on the principle of communion or union with the sacred or the absolute reality. However, once an ecclesiastical order was established on earth, it was not able to stand aloof from the mundane world. It pursued a course of secularization under the application of social, political, and economic rules. As Talcott Parsons has pointed out, no institutionalized or systematized religion can escape this kind of dilemma.[16] The so-called universal religions started without

[15] Sir Charles Eliot, *Japanese Buddhism* (London, 1959), p. 185.

[16] Talcott Parsons, *Religious Perspectives of College Teaching in Sociology and Social Psychology* (New Haven, 1952); see also Hori, "Shakai-henkaku to Bukkyō" ("Social Innovation and Buddhism"), *Nihon shūkyō-shi kenkyū*, II (1963), 7–30.

exception as minorities that were suppressed by the worldly authorities. Thus they began with anti-social, anti-secular, and anti-authoritarian tendencies. However, their worldly authority and power tended to grow apace with their ecclesiastical power. This meant that religion could not escape from the direct influences of political and economic fluctuations of the ruling classes of society. Moreover, it was easily overcome by temptations to worldly power, wealth, or extravagance. On the one hand, there was frequently an opposition between ecclesiastical authority and worldly authority, or between ecclesiastical wealth and worldly wealth; on the other hand, they frequently intertwined on the historical stage. Many of the religious elite and scholars established vast systems of theology or metaphysics, and much effort was given over to the study of mythology, ethics, and philosophy, but this religious scholarship was dominated by the humanities.

Folk religion has never faced the kind of dilemma of secularization which has been experienced by Buddhism or Christianity. Folk religion always preserves the strong enduring power which perseveres in the lower structure of society and religious institutions. In spite of bewildering changes in the superstructure, the substructure is comparatively stable and follows a course of rather slow changes. It has a strong digestive power that enables it to hold together the homogeneous and heterogeneous elements. These elements, mutually linked and fused together, form all possible phenomena of syncretism, which continue to function among the people to satisfy their emotional and religious needs. For this reason folk religion has great social significance, in spite of its vulgarity.

The analysis of folk religion, then, is important not

only historically, that is, for understanding its own original meaning or the historical processes of its transformation; folk religion is also important for understanding the spiritual life of the people, as well as their social psychology from the viewpoint of its contemporary social functions.

⟦ *Folk Religion as Natural Religion*

In folk religion, as I have already described, there survive several elements firmly based on ancient natural religion which take root in the beliefs and rituals common to all human beings.

The appearance of religious behavior is thought to be as old as human society. There are several archeological remains which suggest the existence of rites for the dead even in the paleolithic age. The discovery of death by human beings gradually gave rise to the ideas of life and existence. There is an essential anxiety unique to the human being, so that he lives in the consciousness of self-existence. Various activities are created in order to remove this kind of anxiety.[17] These seem to be the most direct factors in the appearance and the development of magic and religion, though such motivations function strongly at the basis of all human culture.

The basic themes of beliefs, rituals, and customs which have controlled the life of the Japanese people for a long time are thought to have emerged gradually with the appearance of agriculture. If the various hereditary elements

[17] Hori, "Fuan ni okeru Kakujitsu-sei no tankyū" ("Inquiry into Certainty within Anxiety"), *Nihon shūkyō-shi kenkyū*, I (Tokyo, 1962), 115–40.

from the pre-Jōmon (paleolithic) and Jōmon (neolithic) cultures have been preserved, they seem to have been reorganized and reinterpreted by the elements of the agricultural culture complex. As I have discussed elsewhere,[18] the fundamental form of agricultural life is stationary. Stationary life, which implies that man occupies space as well as lives in time—a fact which inevitably brought about the self-consciousness of limitation or finitude—made possible the man-plant homology in which variation or change is felt in one's own life. Agriculture involves the dynamic cyclical course from sowing to the harvest, through germination, growth, and maturity. The cyclical idea of life and cosmology was based on this understanding of agriculture, although an additional element was the discovery of meaning in the waxing and waning of the moon, which is generally held to have originated in the more ancient nomadic or hunting culture complex. At the same time, the discovery of the seed as the source of the continuity of plant life strengthened the consciousness of tradition and increased the importance of the ancestor in human life. Furthermore, immobility and deterministic control of both plants and farmers by nature seem to have led to the consciousness of solidarity of destiny between plants and human beings, and to have given rise to the fatalism and feeling of dependence peculiar to an agrarian community. The primitive or naïve self-consciousness of depending upon the other and of helplessness and limitedness should be seen as forming the basis of magic and rituals among the agrarian peoples.

18 *Ibid.*; originally this paper was published in *Nihonjin* (*The Japanese*) (Tokyo, 1954) under the title of "Anxiety and Hope" ("Fuan to kibō").

There are, therefore, significant coincidences between the beliefs, rituals, and customs centering in the agricultural productions of all agrarian peoples. However, there exist great differences of race, social structure, modes of life, ways of thinking, linguistic representations, and so on. In both wheat culture and rice culture, the staple farm products are regarded as sacred in themselves or as the gift of a superhuman being. Therefore, farm work is also regarded as a sacred action or rite and not merely productive labor. At the end of each agricultural task, various magico-religious rituals are performed in order to ensure the favorable course of the ripening of wheat or rice plants.[19] For example, in Japanese agrarian communities, before the seeding, several praying services for good crops are performed which are usually rich in magical elements; then come the rites for seeding; ceremonies for transplanting; praying for rain, for stopping storms or long rains, for frightening or driving away injurious birds and noxious insects; the offering of the new harvest and various customs accompanying it; and, finally, various harvest festivals for each family and community as well as official ceremonies at the imperial court.

We can find some marvelous coincidences of ideas and ritual performances between Japanese folk religion and those of other peoples. For instance, both in Japan and other countries, there are magico-artistic and orgiastic elements including sexual excesses, especially in the festivals of early spring, to celebrate the coming of spring and to pray for a good harvest in the coming autumn.[20]

[19] Mircea Eliade, *Patterns in Comparative Religion* (London–New York, 1958), Chapter IX, "Agriculture and Fertility Cults," pp. 331–66.

[20] Since it is presumed that no astrological calendar system existed in Japan before the third century A.D., the people must have employed

Other examples are: the memorial services for the dead or ancestors at the first crop offering; the death and resurrection of the rice soul manifested as the rice child together with the idea of the Great Rice Mother; and the ceremonial divine marriage of the Great Rice Mother and a human emperor to reproduce the sacred child of the rice.[21] (I shall leave more detailed discussion to the following section.)[22]

There are of course many variations from the common primitive ideas according to the ethos, social structure, and value system of any particular race or tribe. That is to say, although the motifs and ideas may be universal, the actual details have their particular nuances based on the particular folk mentality. Moreover, these variations are all the more colorful according to the individuality of the religious specialists who engage in these ceremonies and rituals. The myths and legends, rites and customs found in agrarian societies concerning particular deities, spirits, and heroes function within this general world view as the particular types which have emerged from the characteristic system of each society.

---

a natural year, which means that the year was reckoned from seeding in spring to harvest in autumn. The period from harvest to seeding was regarded as the season of rigid abstinence for assuring the rest of the rice seed or rice soul and praying for vigorous germination in the coming spring. *Gishi Wajin den* (*Wo-jen Chuan in the History of the Wei Dynasty*), translation with annotations by Kiyoshi Wada and Michihiro Ishihara (Tokyo: Iwanami-Bunko, 1951). It relates that the Japanese (*Wo-jen*) do not know the calendar and reckon the year by seeding in spring and harvest in autumn.

21 Cf. James G. Frazer, *The Golden Bough* (London, 1924).

22 See Hori, "Mysterious Visitors from the Harvest to the New Year," *Studies in Japanese Folklore*, edited by Richard M. Dorson (Bloomington, 1963), pp. 76–103.

To delineate the religious attitude common to agrarian societies in Japan, I shall consider several particular examples. For instance, it is significant that there are few real local heroes in Japan. On rare occasions, we can find some legends concerning local heroes, but even then they are linked almost without exception with the political center of that time. In all cases, the local chiefs or braves were overthrown by the heavenly deities, princes, or military commanders from the mikado's capital. The local people invite and greet these strange deities or heroes from outside their village and enshrine them as village guardians or transmit their legends from generation to generation in place names and monuments. Prince Yamatotakeru in the mythical age, the generalissimo for the subjugation of eastern barbarians, Tamuramaro of the Sakanouye in the tenth century, Yoshiiye and Yoshitsune of the Minamoto family in the twelfth century—all were cordially invited to be village guardians or revered heroes by the local people who are supposed to have been the descendants of the defeated eastern barbarians called Ezo.

Another interesting example is the large-scale distribution of legends concerning the tombs of such emperors as Antoku (reigned 1180–83), who was reported missing in the battle between the Taira family and the Minamoto family in 1185, and Chōkei (reigned 1368–83) of the Southern dynasty. Even today, local people identify many sites as the imperial tomb of either Antoku or Chōkei, fervently believing in the authenticity of their claims.[23]

[23] The so-called tombs of Emperor Antoku are widespread throughout western Japan as far as the islands of Iwo-jima and Tsu-shima. The supposed tombs of Chōkei are widespread, mainly in eastern Japan as far as Aomori prefecture at the northern tip of Honshu. In the latter case, the tomb of Emperor Chōkei was formally decided by the present emperor in order to perform memorial services, because Chōkei was

We can infer several factors which made possible the widespread distribution of this type of legend and belief. First, there is the socio-psychological situation of the interpreters or bearers of such legends. Second, there is the socio-psychological situation of the local inhabitants who have voluntarily accepted them. Third, we realize that there exists a strong political value system which penetrated deeply into the hierarchy of Japanese society, influencing the family system as well as the religious psychology of the people. This exclusive society manifests belief in authority from without, based on the idea of hospitality. Religiously speaking, this kind of motif is thought to have originated in the ancient Japanese belief symbolized by the myth of the descent from heaven of the august grandchild (*Tenson-kōrin*), which relates the origin of the imperial family in the *Kojiki* and *Nihongi*. According to Shinobu Orikuchi,[24] this motif is widespread in Japanese folklore. For example, it can be seen in the myths of combat between the visiting or descending god or spirit and the local god or spirit, with the final victory of the former. This motif is seen also in the fact that magico-religious or magico-technical strangers are usually welcomed by villagers, even though there is some

---

first officially added to the imperial line in 1926. The Department of the Imperial Household was under great pressure by many ardent petitioners who insisted that the real tomb was in their village. In 1926, the Department of the Imperial Household received 123 petitions concerning the site of Emperor Chōkei's tomb, and in the 1940's there were more than two hundred petitions from northeast Honshu to northern Kyushu. See Hori, *Wagakuni minkan-shinkō-shi no kenkyū* I, 500–565.

[24] Shinobu Orikuchi, "Tokoyo oyobi Marebito" ("The Eternal Land and the Sacred Guests"), *Kodai kenkyū (Studies in Japanese Antiquity)* (Tokyo, 1929). Originally this paper was published in *Minzoku*, IV, No. 1, 1–62.

ambivalence of attitude toward them: awe, fear, respect, and contempt. We can clearly observe here the Japanese people's respect for authority based on their social value systems as well as on the exclusiveness of their agrarian life and personality.

In this connection I shall discuss puberty rites as an example which seems to symbolize more clearly such an authoritarian attitude. As is well known, there are three general kinds of these rites: periodic or seasonal, such as the annual festivals based mainly on the annually repeated phenomena of nature or agriculture; temporal or extraordinary, for protection and opposition against the threats of unforeseeable natural disasters, epidemics, wars, fires, and so on; the group generally called rites of passage after Van Gennep,[25] and which seek to resolve the anxiety accompanying predictable or unpredictable changes in individuals or in the interpersonal relationships in the community—including individual physical changes such as birth, puberty, marriage, pregnancy, delivery, and death.

As one of the most important junctures of human life, the puberty ceremony has been celebrated by almost all races. This rite separates boys from their mothers' protection and initiates them as adult members of the men's society. Among the primitives as well as the ancient civilized peoples, the initiation ceremony was a serious and solemn rite with both social and educational functions which decided the course of the candidate's future life. Even in highly developed societies and higher religions, the initiation ceremony has still survived in various ways, after having been transformed and reinterpreted.[26]

[25] See Van Gennep, *Les rites de passage* (Paris, 1909).
[26] Cf. Eliade, *Birth and Rebirth* (Chicago, 1958).

According to Van Gennep, initiation rites are to be divided into three stages: separation, *marge* or transition, and integration. The most important is the second, in which the candidates are initiated into socio-religious mysteries concerning the tribe's myths, traditions, special knowledge, and techniques peculiar to adult society. Candidates also underwent such surgical operations as circumcision, subincision, and extraction of teeth or severe ordeals. These ordeals tested the competence of each candidate to fulfill the tasks of married life, labor, hunting, fishing, and fighting which the given society required of him as an adult member. This rite seems completely to separate childhood from adulthood by such means as the revelation of the tribal deities or ancestors, the granting of a new adult name, and the learning of a new language.

The fundamental principles of the initiation rite are common to almost every primitive or ancient society. However, the actual contents of the rite are different in each society. Even in the same society, there is some variation according to the candidate's social class or rank. In Japan, puberty rites have been widely performed among both the upper and lower classes from ancient to modern times. Since the Nara period, youths of the noble class have been ceremonially initiated in a rite definitely influenced by Chinese customs called *ui-kōburi* or *kakan* (first wearing of a crown). This rite included the giving of a new name, the conferring of a court rank, and the first ceremonial cohabitation with the betrothed (*soi-bushi*). The puberty rite among the lower classes is sometimes called *gen-buku*, *eboshi-gi* (wearing the *eboshi*), or *eboshi-iwai* (celebration for the wearing of the *eboshi*) under the influence of the samurai-class puberty rite. It also includes the change to the adult name peculiar to the candidate's own family or family group, ceremonial cohabitation with his fiancée (*hada-awase*), several ordeals such as austerities in the sacred mountain led by village *yamabushi* (mountain ascetics), or a feat of strength witnessed by the leaders of the men's or youths' society. For girls, dyeing the teeth or tattooing either on the face or on the back of the hand was a symbol of adulthood.[27]

As I shall discuss in detail in the next section, where the *dōzoku* or a particular kinship system is firmly organized, the head of the main family is responsible for the puberty rites of the boys and girls of the branch families.

[27] In the middle ages, the samurai (warrior) class youths underwent puberty rites together with ordeals and austerities under the name of *gen-buku* (assuming the *toga virilis*), in which a special type of headgear peculiar to the samurai class named *eboshi* was used instead of the crown. In both cases, the man who ceremonially put the crown or headgear on the youth's head is called the *ushiro-mi* (ward) or *eboshi-oya* (headgear parent). Especially in the samurai class, which took a serious view of human bonds, it was a widespread custom to ask the powerful and prosperous senior samurai or lord to become the headgear parent. Also in the middle ages, among the lower classes, dyeing the teeth took place ceremonially immediately after the first menstruation. However, in more recent times it came to be a symbol of the married woman, and it was performed immediately before the wedding ceremony. The tattooing on the face or the back of the hand can still be seen on women more than seventy years old among the Ainu as well as among the Okinawans and Amami Islanders. Cf. Kunio Yanagita, *Kon'in no hanashi* (*Lectures on Marriage Customs*) (Tokyo, 1948), *Yanagita Kunio shū* (*Complete Works of Kunio Yanagita*), XV (Tokyo, 1963); Yanagita, "Shakai to kodomo" ("Society and Children"), *Iye kandan* (*Lectures on the Japanese Family*) (Tokyo, 1946), in *Yanagita Kunio shū*, XV (1963); Tarō Nakayama, *Nihon wakamono-shi* (*History of Japanese Youth*) (Tokyo, 1930); Dai Nippon-rengō-seinen-kai (compiled), *Wakamono-seido no kenkyū* (*A Study of the Japanese Youth's Organization*) (Tokyo, 1936); Kazuo Obara, *Irezumi no kenkyū* (*A Study of the Customs of Tattooing*) (Tokyo, 1962).

The dōzoku consists of the main family and its consan-
guineally related branch families. On the other hand,
where the youths' lodge (*wakamono-yado*) or maidens'
lodge (*musume-yado*), based on the youths' association
(*wakamono-gumi*) or maidens' association (*musume-
gumi*), is firmly organized, the head of the association
and senior members have the responsibility for the initiation rite of the village boys and girls, at the age of approximately fifteen, to become association members
(*wakamono-iri*). In the third case, where the two systems
above mentioned are not institutionalized, the village
chief or seniors have the responsibility for the puberty
ceremony of their village boys or girls. Of course there
are variations in puberty rites among various village traditions and family systems as well as among magico-religious priests or village seniors. One of the most important
and widespread of these customs is that of the pseudo,
or social parent (*kari-oya*), who is formally asked to be a
social father of the candidate at the puberty rite, similar
to the *eboshi-oya* of the old samurai class. This custom is
not necessarily peculiar to the puberty rite, but there exist several kinds of social parents, usually connected with
the rites of passage. The *toriage-oya* (midwife-mother)
at the rite of birth and the *nakōdo-oya* (go-between parent) at the wedding ceremony are only a few examples.
However, the social father or parent called *oya-kata* or
oya-bun (literally, "boss") who enters into the contract
with the candidate at the puberty ceremony has a strong
regulating power on the future life of the candidate.[28]

[28] The Japanese word oya does not necessarily mean only a parent
by blood (which is called specifically umi-no-oya) but also may mean the
ancestors as well as their social or pseudo parent. The social oya has a
responsibility to the social children (ko-kata or ko-bun) for their per-

This system, together with the dōzoku system in the rural communities, seems to make clear that the social structure of the exclusive agrarian society puts more emphasis on the family group or community than on each individual family; the individual is recognized as a community member rather than as an independent personality. As many scholars have pointed out, the hierarchical principle permeates Japanese society, from political life to family and individual life. This political and particularistic social structure requires the use of the social parent. Since all folk religion is strongly influenced by this social requirement, it is noticeable that Japanese folk religion in particular has played an important role in maintaining this system. The complicated social-parent and child relationships came to be the basis for the recogni-

---

sonal activities as a member of the society, in striking contrast to the blood parent. In public life, the social oya has more power of compulsion and protection than does the blood parent. In other words, the person who has such power is usually asked to be the social oya and enters into contract with the candidates. The social children or ko-kata have to bear the responsibility of submission and service to their social oya in return for their protection and help. The relationship between social oya-kata and ko-kata is very similar to that between the head of the main family and the members of the branch families in the dōzoku system. Among the special societies of technicians, artisans, and even of merchants in cities or castle towns, the social parent-children system formed the basis of their social structure in pre-industrial Japan. And, we can find several survivals of this system even in the highly developed industrial cities of Tokyo, Osaka, Kyoto, and others. See Yanagita, "Oya-kata, ko-kata" ("Social Parent and Social Children"), Kazoku seido zenshū (Complete Lectures on the Japanese Family System), Vol. III (Tokyo, 1937); Tokuzō Ōmachi, "Jujutsu-teki oya-ko" ("Magical Parent and Children System"), Kōzu-shima no hana-shōgatsu (Flowering New Year in Kōzu Island) (Tokyo, 1943); Yanagita (ed.), Minzoku-gaku jiten (Dictionary of Japanese Folklore) (Tokyo, 1951), pp. 86–89; Taku Nakano, Shōka dōzoku-dan no kenkyū (A Study of the Dōzoku System among Merchants) (Tokyo, 1964).

tion of society as one family, and then led to the idea of the total society, or the state as one family.[29]

(*The Foundation of Japanese Folk Religion*

Japanese folk religion (or primitive Shinto) has its roots in the long tradition of an exclusive agrarian society. Yet, within that society are discernible two different systems of belief. The first of these may be called the *uji-gami* type (tutelary or guardian shrine system), which was based on the particular family or clan system. Each family had its own shrine as a central symbol of its solidarity, dedicated to the ancestral spirit who had been enshrined and worshipped by its ancestors. This type of belief system is characterized by particularism and exclusiveness from other families, so that its main function is to integrate all the members of the family into a patriarchal hierarchy. The maintenance of the good name of the hereditary family and the continuation of its ancestor's glorious work from generation to generation were the most important responsibilities, not only for the patriarch, but also for all the family members. Heavy emphasis on ancestor worship and filial piety (*kō*) in almost all Japanese groups has been closely connected with the ancient family system and *uji-gami* system. Indeed, the ulti-

[29] Even in a religious society—for example, in the *Tenri* sect—the founder is called *oya-sama* (My Lady Mother) and the headquarters the *oya-sato* (Mother's Home). It is also noticeable that the ethics of filial piety (*kō*) in Japan becomes a channel for loyalty (*chū*) through this particular social and value system, different from the Chinese ethics of filial piety and loyalty. Cf. R. N. Bellah, *Tokugawa Religion*, Chapter IV and Conclusion. See especially pp. 179-92.

mate destiny of individuals was conceived in terms of
their loss of individual identity and merger with a vague
community of ancestral spirits after death, although there
existed distinctions according to their social, political, and
magico-religious status.

The second system may be called the *hito-gami* type
(man-god system), which was based on the close relationship of an individual kami with a religious specialist
such as a shaman or a medicine man. More highly federated state systems, such as the village-states or small-scale
united kingdoms which appeared in ancient Japan, were
supposedly ruled by charismatic or shamanic leaders, such
as Pi-mi-ko of the Yamatai kingdom in the third century
A.D. This type of belief is characterized by the strong individuality both of the kami and of its transmitter, who
lived on for a long time in the memory of the believers.
With this type of kami, sincere reverence and obedience
were the only means by which one might gain the kami's
favor, which was not dependent on the believer's origin.
Charismatic personages and their descendants entered
into a special relationship with their *hito-gami* and made
a kind of *uji-gami* system independently, thus playing an
important role in the politics of ancient theocratic ages
by utilizing the divine power of these personages for
blessings or curses. However, this belief in *hito-gami*
seems not to have provided for any salvation or afterlife
for individuals, even though the charismatic personages
could be easily deified by their relationship with the *hito-
gami*.[30]

Under the rigidity of the ancient Japanese social structure and value system, which were characterized by the
primacy of political values, the emphasis on *on* and *on*

[30] See Hori, *Minkan-shinkō*.

hō-on increased. The term *on* means blessings or favors handed down, not only by invisible beings, but also by social and political superiors; the term *hō-on* means obligation of the recipient to return something for these blessings. As Tetsurō Watsuji has pointed out, the entire system of Japanese social relationships and values reflects family relationships, which are strictly controlled and regulated by the patriarch, according to the status of each member of the family. The emperor himself is responsible to his ancestors for his behavior. There was no room within such a value system to develop the concept of an almighty God, as in the traditions of Judaism, Christianity, and Islam. On the contrary, Japanese kami are not considered personalities that are any more independent than men but lowly figures dependent on their superiors in either the divine or the social hierarchy and in need of salvation and help. In this context, the superiors, including human beings and ancestors, were believed to be half kami or even low-ranking kami or buddhas. The beliefs in spirits of the dead and in the intimate connection between men and kami, being linked with ancestor worship and dependence on superiors, are, even today, widespread and important. In other words, the belief is that human beings can easily become deified as kami. The fact that the dead are commonly called *hotoke-sama* (buddha) among Buddhist families, and *reijin* (soul god) or *mikoto* (another name of kami) among Shinto families, is a typical example of this tendency.

To summarize, then, the characteristics of the *uji-gami* type in contrast to those of the *hito-gami* type are as follows. First, the *uji-gami* play symbolic roles of maintaining and integrating the political and economic autonomy of a particular family, clan, kinship group (*dōzoku*), or territorial society. Second, a strong exclusiveness of beliefs as well as of the quality of the kami is accordingly reflected by the exclusiveness of the community, of which the proverbial phrase "the jealousy of *uji-gami*" is a symbolic expression. Third, the divine functions of the *uji-gami* are undifferentiated, although they assume rather stereotyped forms in spite of the vagueness of the concept. Fourth, there is the concept of a contractual relationship between the *uji-gami* and its own clan, family, or kinship group members. Fifth, adherents of the *uji-gami* are strictly limited to the members of these groups or associated groups. Sixth, the authority or power of the *uji-gami* is directly reflected in the political, economic, social, and cultural circumstances of its adherents.

The characteristics of the *hito-gami* type are as follows. First, it establishes a super-family, super-clan, or wide circle of believers. Therefore, originally it played some symbolic roles of disintegration and reintegration rather than of simple integration. Second, the *hito-gami* type has an overt character in contrast to the covert quality of *uji-gami*—or comprehensive rather than exclusive. Third, the *hito-gami* has a strong personality and particular function or functions. Fourth, the focus of the relation between the kami and men is on faith rather than on genealogy or geography. Fifth, believers in the *hito-gami* are, therefore, not restricted to the fixed social family as its transmitter or attendants. The selected person or family is believed to be a divine descendant or divine servant—which leads to the *uji-gami* type religion. Sixth, the authority and power of the *hito-gami* are directly reflected in the magico-religious power of its transmitter, his techniques of ecstasy, his socio-political and economic situation, as well as contemporary opinion.

However, these two sharply contrasting types of beliefs —*uji-gami* and *hito-gami*—which form the basis of Japanese folk religion, do not survive in their pure forms, but have deeply interacted with each other. I shall leave more detailed discussions of this problem to the next chapter. There we shall see that the *uji-gami* type of beliefs is based exclusively on the consciousness of the in-group and its symbolical ancestor worship, while the *hito-gami* type of beliefs is based explicitly on shamanistic or charismatic personages and their activities, although both types are deeply rooted in the ancient animistic religion. Kunio Yanagita[31] and Genchi Katō[32] have studied the belief in the *hito-gami* type.

❲ Formation of Japanese Folk Religion

At what point were these two contrasting types of beliefs brought together? The so-called village Shinto shrines were not necessarily established only on the basis of the *uji-gami* type of beliefs. Actually, the *hito-gami* type is the more obvious in almost all village Shinto shrines, while the *uji-gami* type stays in the background. This is illustrated by the fact that more than 80 per cent of present Shinto shrines are dedicated to the deities of the *hito-gami* type. For example, many Shinto shrines are dedicated to the deities of Miwa, Kamo, Hitokotonushi,

[31] Yanagita, "Hito wo Kami ni matsuru fūshū" ("The Customs of Enrolling a Particular Human Being among the Kami"), *Imo no chikara* (*Magical Power of the Female*) (Tokyo, 1940), and *Yanagita Kunio shū*, Vol. IX.

[32] Genchi Katō, *Honpō seishi no kenkyū* (*A Study of the Custom of Dedicating a Shrine to a Living Person*) (Tokyo, 1931).

Hachiman, Sumiyoshi, Gion, Tsushima, Inari, and Kitano
(Tenjin)—all of which are typical deities of the *hito-
gami* type which throughout the history of Japanese religion since the time of the ancient records *Kojiki* and
Nihongi have been commonly called ara-*hito-gami* (fierce
man-god). At the same time, the rites and festivals have
been strongly influenced by elements originating specifically in the festivals of the *hito-gami*. Such *hito-gami*
elements are seen in the practice of carrying a portable
shrine through the streets in a colorful parade with dancing and singing and various kinds of magico-religious entertainment which attract many spectators at the shrine
precincts or on the streets. Again, the hereditary system
of Shinto priests may have developed from the *hito-gami*
type of religion. This may be contrasted with the *tōya*
system, in which the heads of individual families draw
lots for a one-year term of responsibility for the Shinto
services at the village tutelary shrine. The *tōya* system is
based on the genealogical or historical traditions which
may have originally emerged from the *uji-gami* type of
religion.

In northeastern Honshu, one finds erected at the en-
trance of every village a row of large stones carved with
the names of the deities and buddhas of the sacred mountains or great shrines and temples. At every farmer's
house, several kinds of charms or talismans which are
distributed by the great shrines and temples are attached
to the gate, front door, well, stable, and barn. In the precincts of the village shrine, several subordinate shrines
are dedicated to the powerful and miraculous deities from
outside the village. The psychological basis for invoking
kami from outside the village in order to ensure the protection of the village and security of the family seems to

me to be in attitudes originating in the exclusive societal structure. In the exclusive agrarian community, there is a feeling of solidarity between human beings and plants, which is accompanied by feelings of being limited and interdependent in a cyclical universe. A form of hospitality peculiar to agrarian peoples has emerged from this fundamental religious view, so that supernatural powers must usually come to the people from the outside, because the latter, like plants, are immobile, having settled permanently in a specific area.

These supernatural powers may work for either good or ill, which ambivalence has led to two contrasting attitudes. On the one hand, it led to a belief in benevolent deities, spirits, or ancestors who visit the community or the family periodically or on special occasions. On the other hand, it has led to a belief in malevolent deities, spirits, demons, or devils which come from outside the village to attack the community or family. In this ambiguous situation, the villagers depend upon power from without to oppose the threats which also enter the village from without. This ambiguity is manifested in various contradictory magico-religious rituals and customs. For example, on the one hand, there are festivals dedicated to the god of the plague, evil spirits, or haunt spirits of the dead. On the other hand, there is the enshrinement of various functional *hito-gami* from outside the village, in order to strengthen the productive power and protective strength of the community.

Several scholars have pointed out that this ambivalence should be considered a manifestation of the irrationality of religion itself. Rudolf Otto referred to this ambivalence in his book *The Idea of the Holy*. The universal human attitude toward superhuman beings or ultimate reality is mixed with awe and fear, or *mysterium tremendum* and *fascinosum* (*das Numinose* or numinous). From the phenomenological viewpoint, in the course of development from the archaic small-scale community to the unified empire system, through the formation of village-states brought about by the introduction of agriculture, there may have been penetration of strong political, economic, and technical influences from without. However, this strong external power was never able to destroy the exclusive type of *uji-gami*; rather, the *uji-gami* type of belief was subsumed under the powerful functional belief of the *hito-gami* type. This commingling formed the basis for the diverse religious attitudes of the Japanese people—in other words, for Japanese syncretism.

The process whereby Buddhism and religious Taoism or Yin-yang magic and techniques filtered down to the masses seems to have been made possible by a connection with beliefs of the *hito-gami* type. In Buddhism, this process is called the mixture of Shinto and Buddhism (*Shin-Butsu konkō*), twofold Shinto (*Ryōbu Shintō*) and the manifestation of the prime numenon (*Honji-suijaku*). When Buddhism penetrated into local communities, the priests had to compromise with local people and their community gods. As a result of these compromises, a special Buddhist temple, called a *Jingū-ji*, was built within the precincts of almost every Shinto shrine and dedicated to the Shinto kami of that shrine. The *Jingū-ji* were built so that Buddhist priests could serve the kami with Buddhist rituals by special permission of the kami. In reverse, the local or tutelary kami was enshrined in the precincts of each Buddhist temple and served by Buddhist priests and Buddhist formulas.[33] Under these circumstances, the Japanese kami of Shinto shrines have gradually tended to become functional and personal, which is clearly seen in the custom of offering the title of buddha or bodhisattva to the Shinto kami, especially and at first to the *hito-gami*. I might repeat that the religious forms of the *hito-gami* type had already preceded it. Therefore, not only was Buddhism successful in the modification of *hito-gami* into a functional and personal kami, but in turn buddhas and bodhisattvas seem to have been transformed into *hito-gami*.

In order to verify this hypothesis of *hito-gami* and *uji-gami*, I should like to discuss here the *kō* system (fraternity or religious association),[34] the basic form of which consists of the religious leader and the believers, or the organizer and the followers. Here is a good opportunity for magico-religious leaders of the *hito-gami* type to become active. I might say that there are also two types of

[33] Zennosuke Tsuji, "Honji Suijaku setsu no kigen ni tsuite" ("On the Origin and the Historical Processes of the Establishment of the Manifestation of the Prime Numenon"), *Nihon Bukkyō-shi no kenkyū* (*Studies on the History of Japanese Buddhism*) (Tokyo, 1931), pp. 49–194.

[34] The term *kō* originated in the Buddhist term for "lecture meeting." However, in the course of Japanese history, *kō* has gradually changed in meaning to indicate those present at a Buddhist lecture meeting and the members of a religious fraternity. Finally, in the Tokugawa period (1603–1868) the term *kō* lost its express religious significance and was sometimes used to mean a group organized for a common cause such as economic cooperation (*tanomoshi-kō*), mutual aid (*moyai-kō*), or even amusement (*yusan-kō*). Cf. Hajime Shuzui, "Buraku to kō" ("Community and the Religious Associations"), *Sanson seikatsu no kenkyū* (*Reports from the Field Researches on Japanese Mountain Villages*), edited by K. Yanagita (Tokyo, 1937), pp. 82–100; Tokutarō Sakurai, *Nihon minkan-shinkō ron* (*Studies of Japanese Folk Beliefs*) (Tokyo, 1958), pp. 127–80; Sakurai, *Kō-shūdan seiritsu-katei no kenkyū* (*A Study of the Process of Establishment of Religious Associations*) (Tokyo, 1962).

religious *kō:* the *uji-gami,* and the *hito-gami.* Some *kō* are organized by an in-group or sub in-group such as *dōzoku* or *maki* (a small-scale territorial society). This is similar to the *uji-gami* type of belief which is not led by any professional religious leader. We might classify in the first category: *Ta-no-kami-kō* (*kō* for the kami of the rice-field), *Yama-no-kami-kō* (*kō* for the kami of the mountain), *Hi-machi-kō* (*kō* for awaiting and worshipping the rising sun), *Nijūsanya-kō* (*kō* for awaiting and worshipping the rising moon on the twenty-third night of the lunar month), *Koyasu-kō* (*kō* for praying to *Koyasu Kannon* for easy delivery and protection of children), *Kōshi* or *Kinoene-kō* (*kō* for *Daikoku* deity, a guardian of the household and good fortune on the day of the elder rat), *Kōshin-kō* (*kō* for *Kōshin* deity on the day of the monkey, a complex worship having various functions).

The *hito-gami* type of *kō* may be seen either in the form of the *kō* association for enabling representatives to visit some famous distant shrine or temple (*Dai-san-kō*), or in the form of the *kō* association connected with the institutionalized religious bodies and large Shinto shrines, or in the form of the *kō* association for the purpose of climbing sacred mountains in order to practice austerities led by the village or local *yamabushi* or *shugen-ja.*[35]

[35] The *kō* for representative visits to the Ise shrine by members (Ise-kō), *kō* to the Akiba shrine in Aichi prefecture (Akiba-kō), or *kō* to the Kotohira shrine in Shikoku (Kompira-kō), and others are some examples of the first form. The Hōon-kō (*kō* for memorial services for the founder of the Shin sect, Shinran Shōnin, found among the Shin sect's believers), Daimoku-kō (*kō* for memorial services for the founder of the Nichiren sect, Nichiren Shōnin, among the believers of the Nichiren sect), Taisha-kō (association of believers in the Izumo Grand Shrine in Shimane prefecture) are some examples of the second form. The Ontake-kō (*kō* for climbing and practicing austerities in

If we examine these kō systems carefully, we can derive from them the historical types of religious figures which transmitted these forms of folk religion. These migrated from village to village and together they seem to hold the key to the formation of Japanese folk religion. They were all hijiri (originally, "holy man"), and, although they came from different religious traditions, were finally received by the villagers as identical in function.[36]

As I shall discuss in the next chapter, one of the major clues for resolving the problem of the formation of Japanese folk religion, from the viewpoint of the hito-gami

Mount Ontake in Nagano prefecture), Fuji-kō (kō for climbing and practicing austerities in Mount Fuji), Dewa-sanzan-kō (kō for climbing and practicing austerities in the three sacred mountains named Haguro, Gassan, and Yudono in Yamagata prefecture) are of the third form. This form of kō has become the present Sectarian Shinto. For example, the Fusō-kyō, Maruyama-kyō, and Jikkō-kyō originated in the Fuji-kō in the Tokugawa period, which was distributed throughout most of middle and eastern Honshu; Mitake-kyō came from the Ontake-kō in the Tokugawa period; and the Taisha-kyō was organized on the basis of the Taisha-kō. It is interesting to note here that even in the Hōon-kō of the Shin Buddhist believers there exist elements of the uji-gami type. At the Hōon-kō in each village a professional Shin priest necessarily attends to preach, but the Hōon-kō is never connected with neighboring Hōon-kō associations, maintaining exclusive independence based on the community or the parishioners' group of a particular village Shin temple.

[36] Shamanesses (miko), Shinto priests (onshi or oshi), mountain ascetics (yamabushi or gyōja), Yin-yang magicians (onmyō-ji and shōmon-ji), lower-class Nembutsu priests (Nembutsu-hijiri), semi-professional pilgrims (kaikoku-hijiri), migrating magicians and medicine-men (jussha or kitō-ja), as well as magico-religious artisans and technicians such as blacksmiths (imo-ji),woodworkers (kiji-ya), or reciters named sekkyō (literally, "preacher"), or sai-mon (literally, "address to the deities"), or uta-bikuni (literally, "singing nuns"), and so on. See Hori, Wagakuni minkan-shinkō-shi no kenkyū, II, and also, "On the Concept of Hijiri (Holy-man)," Numen, V, Fasc. 2–3 (Leiden, 1958), 128–60; 199–232.

complex, may be the widespread and highly active belief in goryō which appeared at the end of the Nara and the beginning of the Heian period. Originally, the goryō were the malevolent spirits of noble persons who died in political intrigues. They were associated with disasters, epidemics, and wars through divination or necromancy by magicians or shamanesses. Finally, malevolent spirits of the dead have been enshrined as kami, as is seen in the shrines Goryō-jinja and Kitano-jinja (or Kitano Tenjinsha) in Kyoto and other places. Originally, the belief in goryō was also influenced by the Chinese idea that if the spirits of the dead did not have memorial services performed by their descendants, they would become evil spirits or demons (kuei in Chinese) or be transformed into locusts or other noxious insects. The belief in goryō was also influenced by the Buddhist idea that every human being has Buddha nature within him and thus has the possibility of becoming a buddha. Later, the idea of goryō was gradually expanded through the reinterpretation that even an ordinary person could become a goryō or goryō-shin (goryō deity) by his own will power, ardent wish on the verge of death, or accidental death under unusual circumstances.

Although this belief should rightly be considered a kind of lowly superstition, it was successful in transforming Japanese Buddhism in two ways. In the first place, it stimulated popular Nembutsu practices and the mountain ascetics, which were later organized as the Jōdo school and the Shugen-dō respectively. In the second place, it caused Onmyō-dō to flourish among the nobility and the common people. I must leave for the following chapters the detailed explanation of belief in goryō and its important roles as well as of the diverse phenomena based on the belief in goryō.

In short, I might conclude that the belief in goryō forms the meeting point where various religions were handed down to the popular level and became mixed with folk religion. Belief in goryō was not merely a brief superstitious fad, but has also survived in folk beliefs, rituals, and customs as well as in folk arts, dancing, and music. Even the most refined classical dramas or plays are thought to have originated from the belief in goryō or the *hito-gami* complex.

(*Fragmentary Beliefs and Superstitions*

In concluding these preliminary remarks on Japanese folk religion, I must glance at some fragmentary beliefs as well as some superstitious phenomena in present-day Japan, because they have persisted at the very core of folk religion.

Generally speaking, these may be classified into five groups: beliefs and magic concerning omens; beliefs in divination; fragmentary customs concerning taboo; black magic; prayers or formulas with magical elements.[37] There are also some beliefs or rituals connected with legends and the beliefs in ghosts and goblins, some of which seem to have survived as transformed myths, fairy tales, or folk legends. These fragmentary popular beliefs (*zoku-shin* in

[37] Yanagita and Keigo Seki, *Nihon minzoku-gaku nyūmon* (Handbook of Japanese Folklore Studies) (Tokyo, 1947); Tokihiko Ōto, "Zoku-shin" ("Common Beliefs"), *Sanson seikatsu no kenkyū*, edited by Yanagita (Tokyo, 1937).

Japanese) become a social problem by the activities of common diviners, seers, healers, magicians or priests, who utilize them for their own interests. They are frequently called superstitious worship or heresy (*mei-shin* in Japanese), constituting actual evils for society.

From the viewpoint of the history of religion, it is difficult to define superstition as opposed to true faith. It has been a long time since one religion called another superstition or heresy. Among the various fragmental beliefs, there might exist the cultural experience or *Volkskunde* accumulated within the long history of the common people. Therefore, common beliefs or even superstitions must not be treated as non-scientific or irrational. The most important consideration is not necessarily that religious phenomena are scientific but that they consist of emotional associations which go beyond rationality. Thus irrationality is a special quality of any religion and does not belong solely to superstitions.

From this point of view, we historians of religion, together with cultural anthropologists, tend to avoid or hesitate to use the term "superstition" in order to preclude misunderstanding. We reserve the term "superstition" only for those beliefs and practices which are considered unreasonable by present scientific knowledge and at the same time actually inflict injury upon society.

The most significant superstitious phenomena in present-day Japan are probably the idea of possession by the spirits of foxes or dogs (*kitsune-tsuki* or *inu-gami-tsuki*) and related taboos as well as the tragic social alienation of the possessed person and his family members. These phenomena are seen in almost all Japanese rural communities, but the most cruel and injurious cases are

45

seen in western Honshu and Kyushu.[38] A superstition concerning the year of birth such as *hinoe-uma* (year of the elder horse) is another example of dangerous superstition. According to this superstition, a woman who is born in the year of the elder horse will be so powerful that her husband will die young. Many persons who disapprove of these extremely dangerous beliefs often believe in milder forms of superstition. For example, they may subscribe to the belief in lucky or unlucky years (*toshi-mawari*), the belief in compatibility of temperament (*ai-shō*), the divination of good or ill luck concerning the day or the direction, the divination concerning a house or tomb, or the written oracles published by various Shinto shrines and Buddhist temples, either consciously or unconsciously, positively or negatively.

These unsystematized popular beliefs play various roles in the lives of the people, such as enabling decision of behavior or temporal resolution of daily anxiety. From the viewpoint that no human creation or human enterprise is absolutely meaningless, the social meanings of such superstitious or popular beliefs should be reexamined because they regulate the conduct of a great number of persons. This does of course not imply the rediscovery of the value of popular beliefs. The problem is their socio-psychological significance for those who need such beliefs.

The regulating power of popular beliefs on the people's daily life in Japan was clearly described in the three volumes of *Nihon no zoku-shin* (*Japanese Superstitions*) compiled by the Department of Education. These volumes include many statistical tables from the results of

[38] See Takatoshi Ishizuka, *Nihon no tsukimono* (*The Phenomena of Possession in Japan*) (Tokyo, 1959).

field research throughout Japan based on questionnaires.[39] *Gendai no meishin* (*Superstitions in Contemporary Japan*), by Ensuke Konno,[40] a member of the Research Committee of Japanese Superstitions in the Department of Education (*Monbu-shō meishin chōsa-kai*), describes actual circumstances.

Superstitions or popular beliefs are like weeds in a wilderness. If the old superstitions are destroyed, new ones emerge after them. In the present scientific age, superstitions connected with science may come into existence. By the relationship between supply and demand, superstition would survive as a whole insofar as man cannot completely resolve the self-consciousness of human weakness, the difficulties of life in human society, the ultimate frustration of human life, and the vague but acute anxiety caused by international or economic-political crises.

Therefore, all religious leaders who have a sense of vocation to enlighten the common people, regardless of their religious affiliation, share an urgent responsibility. They should lead people from folk beliefs into a high level of religious experience, or from popular superstitions into right faith, as well as from magic to metaphysic, if we may borrow Max Weber's term.

❰ *Editors' Note*

[In addition to Ōbayashi's hypothesis (footnote 4), readers might consult J. M. Kitagawa, "The Prehistoric Background of Japanese Religion," *History of Religions*, II (No. 2, Winter 1963), which discusses the culture-complex hypothesis of Masao Oka.]

[39] Meishin Chōsa-kai (ed.), *Nihon no zoku-shin* (*Superstitions and Common Beliefs in Japan*) (Tokyo: I [1949], II [1952], III [1955]).

[40] Ensuke Konno, *Gendai no meishin* (*Superstitions in Contemporary Japan*) (Tokyo, 1961).

CHAPTER

II

Japanese Social Structure and Folk Religion

🙚🙚🙚 The purposes of this chapter are twofold: to discuss the relationship between the basic social structure and the religious organization in Japanese rural culture, and to explain the historical circumstances and processes which have led to present Japanese folk religion.

I believe that the essence of Japanese folk religion lies in the interaction of two belief systems: a little tradition, which is based on blood or close community ties; and a great tradition, introduced from without, which is adopted by individual or group choice. The belief patterns found everywhere in Japanese rural society are complex, multi-layered, and syncretistic. These patterns are based both on the existence of native religion centering in the worship of ancestors and on the various kinds of religion brought from outside by missionaries or believers who

49

belong to the great traditions or to the more advanced little traditions.

Little tradition here refers to the native or folk religions, including the advanced Shinto, which was shaped by ancient Japanese geographic and cultural circumstances; great tradition refers to Confucianism, religious Taoism, and Buddhism—highly developed religious and philosophical importations. These two systems became intertwined after centuries, and Japanese folk religion developed as an integral whole out of the interaction of many separate elements.[1]

I shall first discuss the so-called *dōzoku* group and *dōzoku* beliefs. *Dōzoku*, as it is called by Japanese sociologists, is thought to be the basic kinship system of Japanese rural society.[2] Next, I shall describe actual instances

[1] Robert Redfield, *The Primitive World and Its Transformations* (Ithaca, 1953); see also the same author's *The Folk Culture of Yucatan* (Chicago, 1941), and *Peasant Society and Culture* (Chicago, 1956).

[2] Kizaemon Aruga, *Nihon kazoku-seido to kosaku-seido* (A Study of the Japanese Family System and Tenant System) (Tokyo, 1943); Yanagita, *Zoku-sei goi* (Folk Vocabulary of the Family System and Kinship in Japan) (Tokyo, 1943); Ken'ichi Sugiura, "Dōzoku-shin" and Takayoshi Mogami, "Dôzoku no ketsugō" ("The Tie of the Dôzoku"), both in *Sanson seikatsu no kenkyū* (Report of Field Researches in Japanese Mountain Villages), edited by Yanagita (Tokyo, 1937); Tsuneichi Miyamoto, "Kazoku oyobi shinzoku" ("Family and Kin"), *Kaison seikatsu no kenkyū* (Report of Field Researches in Japanese Fishing Villages), edited by Yanagita (Tokyo, 1949); Seiichi Kitano, "Kō-shū sanson no dōzoku-soshiki to oya-kata ko-kata kankō" ("Dōzoku System and Pseudo-Parent-and-Son System in Yamanashi Prefecture in Japan") and Hiroshi Oikawa, "Dōzoku-soshiki to kon'in oyobi sōsō no girei" ("The Dōzoku System and Marriage and Funeral Rites and Ceremonies"), both in *Minzoku-gaku nenpō*, Vol. II (Tokyo, 1939); Michio Nagai, "Dōzoku: A Preliminary Study of the Japanese 'Extended Family' Group and Its Social and Economic Functions," *Interim Technical Report 7*, Research in Japanese Social Relations (Columbus: Ohio State

group focus
family
hoehle

- shaman able to break out
  of this cur ~~~~ acts
  outside formalized sy
- & able to transcend
  barrier of instit'n too

of folk religion in rural society and illustrate with a typical farming village in central Honshu to show that folk religion consists of many separate elements deriving from the little tradition, the advanced little tradition, the great traditions, and a mixture of the little and the great traditions. The third part of the chapter will discuss the possibility of cohesion between the little tradition and the great traditions combined into newly integrated folk religion. Religious "hospitality" seems to have developed around such beliefs and concepts as ancestral spirits, the spirits of the dead, and the other world, which have been at the center of in-group beliefs in Japanese rural society. When the two clearly unrelated belief systems—the former ancestral and particular, and the latter expansive and universal—are accepted and supported by the villagers, internal change in village community structure and village life can occur. The activities of a wandering preacher may open up a new religious world to the villagers through his miraculous demonstrations or his preaching to the rural audience of hitherto unknown messages while he is divinely possessed. A grasp of the role played by such wandering preachers in forming folk religion in Japan is profoundly important for our understanding of the culture and ethos of the Japanese people. The final section of the chapter pursues this role in relationship to the belief in goryō-shin (unfriendly spirits of the dead), Nem-

---

University, 1953); R. K. Beardsley, J. W. Hall, and R. E. Ward, *Village Japan* (Chicago, 1959); Harumi Befu, "Patrilineal Descent and Personal Kindred in Japan," *American Anthropologist*, LXV (1963), 1328 ff.; Teigo Yoshida, "Cultural Integration and Change in a Japanese Village," *American Anthropologist*, LXV, 102 ff.; David W. Plath, "Where the Family of Gods Is the Family: The Role of the Dead in Japanese Households," *American Anthropologist*, LXVI, No. 2 (1964), 300 ff.

butsu magic, Onmyō-dō (religious Taoism mixed with primitive shamanism), and Shugen-dō (Buddhist asceticism mixed with Shinto, Buddhism, Taoism, and popular shamanism). These last three came into conflict with the belief in goryō-shin and then penetrated into Japanese rural society to establish the dualistic structure of Japanese belief and society.

(Dōzoku and Its Belief System

Dōzoku is the smallest family unit in contemporary rural Japan and is, so far as we know, the smallest unit in which collective beliefs lie. The term dōzoku denotes a family grouping of a main family (hon-ke) and branch families (bun-ke) which are linked by patrilineal kinship.[3] The dōzoku group which one may find exemplified in several districts at the present time seems to have a historical connection with the clan system of antiquity and the kinship system of the medieval period. The dōzoku is thought to have been the basic unit of Japanese rural society. One of the oldest and most common Japanese terms for the dōzoku group is the word maki (literally "an enclosure"), which is a group having the same surname. Even today, the main family is called maki-gashira, which means "head of the maki."[4]

The dōzoku is the smallest economic, social, and cul-

[3] While the dōzoku group consists of the main family and its patrilineally related branch families, occasionally some branch families are not actually related but have been elevated from the status of servant family to that of a branch family by its head. See Aruga, Nihon kazoku-seido to kosaku-seido, pp. 98–100.

[4] Yanagita, Zoku-sei goi, pp. 14–15.

tural unit in the village. The religious unity of any given dōzoku group is shown by the fact that in principle each has its own particular shrine and its own cemetery. The members of the dōzoku group must take part in the annual festivals and the memorial services for ancestors un-

A*—A—A—A—A—A—A—A	(Main Family)
L--S₁—S₁—S₁—S₁—S₁—S₁	(Fictive Branch Family)
L--S₂—S₂—S₂—S₂	(Fictive Branch Family)
L--S₃—S₃	(Fictive Branch Family)
L—B—B—B—B—B—B—B	(First Branch Family)
L--S₄—S₄—S₄—S₄—S₄—S₄	(Fictive Branch Family)
—Ba—Ba—Ba—Ba—Ba	(Sub-branch Family)
L—S₄'—S₄'—S₄'	(Sub-fictive Branch Family)
L—C—C—C—C—C	(Second Branch Family)
L—Ca—Ca—Ca	(Sub-Branch Family)
L--S₅	(Fictive Branch Family)
L—D—D	(Third Branch Family)

Key:

Solid line = patrilineal descent.

Dotted line = non-consanguineally related branch family.

* Ancestor of the main family.

FIG. 1.—Dōzoku group descent pattern

der the leadership of the head of the main family. The main family, or its head, possesses political, economic, and spiritual authority, and has the responsibility of overseeing the daily life of all the branch families. In turn, members of the branch families are obliged to serve the main family spiritually and materially. The principle on which a patrilineal *dōzoku* group is based is illustrated in Figure 1.

The Saitō *dōzoku* group in Iwate prefecture[5] offers a typical example of an actual *dōzoku* system. It consists of

[5] Ariga, *Nihon kazoku-seido to kosaku-seido*, pp. 118–20, 636–39.

Main Family.....has 18 "fictive" branch families which consist of
   (*Hon-ke*)   three upper-class families (*Bekke-kaku Nago*), nine middle-class families (*Bun-ke Nago*), four lower-class families (*Yashiki Nago*), and two lowest-class families (*Saku Nago*).

First Patrilineal Branch Family.....has five "fictive" branch
   (*Saka-ya*)   families, two middle-class, and three lower-class.
       Patrilineal Sub-branch Family

Second Patrilineal Branch Family...has two "fictive" branch
   (*Naka-ya*)   families, one middle-class, and one lower-class.

Third Patrilineal Branch Family....has one lower-class
   (*Tahei*)   "fictive" branch family.
       Patrilineal Sub-branch Family

Fourth Patrilineal Branch Family
   (*Himeguri*)

Fifth Patrilineal Branch Family
   (*Shin-ya*)

* Saka-ya, Naka-ya, etc., are the names of the houses.

Fig. 2.—Structure of an actual *dōzoku* system: the saitō *dōzoku* group (Arasawamura, Ninoe-gun, Iwate prefecture).

thirty-four families: a main family, five patrilineal branch families, two patrilineal sub-branch families, and twenty-six non-consanguineally related ("fictive") branch families and their sub-branch families promoted from servant status. Its structure is shown in Figure 2.

The relationship between the main family and the branch families in the Saitō dōzoku group is reflected in mutual aid in daily life. This cooperation is especially apparent on such occasions as the building or thatching of a house, well sinking, and at the times of births, marriages, and deaths. There is also a custom that the members of branch families must periodically greet, or in some way help, the main family as the following calendar shows:

Thirtieth day of the twelfth month of the lunar year. —One person from each branch family goes to the main family to help make rice cakes (mochi), the most important and sacred food at the New Year and other festival days and ceremonies in Japan. About this time, the main family gives gifts to the branch families, who in turn offer their small, hand-made goods to the main family (seibo-rei).

First day of the first month.—The men of the branch families usually visit the main family to give greetings on the New Year; the host and hostess of the main family give them special food and sake in return. On the next day, the same greetings are performed by the women of the branch families.

Fifteenth of the first month.—Members of the branch families gather at the house of the main family to make rice cakes for the Little New Year (ko-shōgatsu). After dinner, there is a mock celebration of rice planting in the garden of the main family's house.

Nineteenth of the first month.—Sacred rice cakes for the New Year are ceremonially distributed. The members of the branch families take pieces of sacred cakes and dine together at the main family's house.

Thirteenth to sixteenth of the seventh month.—This is the time of the Bon festival (memorial services for the spirits of ancestors and all souls of the dead). Members of branch families clean the ancestors' tombs (usually stone monuments) in the main family's graveyard on the thirteenth day. Early in the morning of the fourteenth day, members of branch families gather at the main family's house in order to celebrate the Bon festival; they clean the house and prepare the ornaments and new altars for the coming spirits or souls from the other world. After this, all members of the dōzoku group go to the graveyard with offerings and worship at their ancestors' tombs. Breakfast and lunch are served by the host of the main family. On the afternoon of the sixteenth day, members of the branch families again gather with the main family to honor the ancestors' spirits as well as all the souls enshrined in the special altars and to say good-bye to those who are returning to the other world.

Centering in the New Year and the Bon festival, ceremonial gatherings or visitings at the main family's house take place on the third day of the third month (so-called Hina-matsuri or Doll festival), on the third day of the fourth month, on the fifth day of the fifth month (so-called Tango-no-Sekku or Boys' festival), on the fifteenth day of the eighth month (the Harvest Moon), on the twenty-ninth day of the ninth month (Twenty-ninth Day festival) and on the twentieth day of the tenth month (Twentieth Day festival).

These customs are not unique to this dōzoku group, but are universal in dōzoku groups in Japanese rural society. The ancestral tablets are often in the Buddhist altar of the main family's house, and therefore members of branch families usually gather with the main family to take part in the services. I suppose that underlying these customs are deep-rooted and ancient feelings of ancestor worship which are reflected in the New Year festival, in the ancestor worship at the equinoctial week in spring and autumn, and in the Bon festival.

The spiritual and religious center of the dōzoku group is symbolized by the kabu-kō or senzo-kō. Kabu is a synonym for maki and essentially means dōzoku. Thus, the kabu-kō is the religious association of the dōzoku group, and the senzo-kō is the association governing the ritual meeting for common ancestor worship. One of the significances of these kō is that the privilege of joining them is limited to members of the dōzoku group and never extended to members of families which are related only by marriage. Presumably it reflects the prototype of ancestor worship, basic to the social structure in Japan.[6]

Ancestor worship in senzo-kō or kabu-kō gradually deteriorated with the rise of the tutelary kami[7] or deities of these dōzoku which attained social prominence, and these newly emergent kami ultimately became the ordinary village kami (mura-uji-gami) of today.[8] The beliefs which

[6] Hori, Minkan shinkō, pp. 139–43.

[7] The Japanese kami is a very complicated concept. It should not be translated merely by the term "god" or "deity." For an explanation of kami, see D. C. Holtom, "The Meaning of Kami," Monumenta Nipponica, III (Tokyo, 1940), 1–27; III, No. 2, 32–53; and IV, No. 2, 25–68.

[8] Hori, Minkan shinkō, pp. 143–68.

evolved from the *dōzoku* groups are of basic importance in the structure of contemporary Japanese village society. These beliefs center in the idea that the spirit becomes deified thirty-three years after death, and becomes subject to ancestor worship along with the kami who have some connection with the ancestor of the *dōzoku* group.

There are a number of increasingly complex steps proceeding from the undifferentiated, vague concept of spirits to the gradual articulation and clarification of such deification and the divinity of spirits. In each Japanese farming community the growth and development of beliefs originally made for a self-sufficiency in spirits, a self-sufficiency that was found in economic and social as well as in religious aspects of life. In brief, a differentiation took place among *dōzoku* groups which were originally in a state of autonomy; the rise of a particular *dōzoku* group to economic preeminence was accompanied by the spread and gradual dominance of its own original beliefs, which in turn may have been modified by or infused with new elements but which never lost their essential identity with their particular *dōzoku* group. Moreover, the state of autonomy among the *dōzoku* groups was also disturbed from without; new religions such as Buddhist sects, Confucianism, religious Taoism, and advanced Shrine Shinto penetrated it. This external influence came in various forms: invasion and domination, an influx of new settlers, or missionaries. Thus, the original vague, local, spiritual concept became differentiated and individualized. The family kami or tutelary kami became the village kami or district kami and thus the kami of those of different surname and families. In this fashion it is believed that the multi-layered religious pattern characteristic of Japan was evolved.

This process is seen in the relation between the circles of believers and the social units: the village shrine and temple serve all the villagers, and the subdivided village shrines and temples serve only the villagers of the sub-division. The beliefs concerning these two have similar characteristics and functions; only the scope of each is different. The existence of such a manifold belief system is the universal form in Japanese rural society, and the beliefs of members of the village usually coincide with their particular position in the social, economic, and political structure.

This concept is seen most clearly in a small island village and isolated community. Hime-shima, for example, is an island in the Inland Sea near Kyushu (belonging to the Higashi-Kunisaki-gun in Ōita prefecture) where I did field research in 1947. This one administrative village, covering an area of about thirteen square kilometers, consists of nine subdivided village units (*aza*) with a total population of 4,090 in 839 families. The center of Hime-shima-mura, the western sector (*hon-son*), has five *aza* and contains 90 per cent of the population. In the eastern part of the island there are three small *aza*: Ōmi *buraku*, with fifty-three families; Kane *buraku*, with sixteen families; and Inazumi *buraku*, with twelve families.

The village Shinto shrine is Hachiman-jinja, situated in the middle of *hon-son*, the main village of the western part, and all the villagers of the island are obliged to serve it. This shrine was established under the influence of the Great Shrine of Usa-hachiman-jinja in northern Kyushu, just across the sea from Hime-shima. The parishioners are divided into six units (*ku*) consisting of the five *aza* of *hon-son* and the combined three *buraku* of the eastern part (Kane, Ōmi, and Inazumi).

These three eastern *buraku* have their particular sub-village shrine, Himekoso-jinja on the seashore in the eastern part of the island, which is attended primarily by the villagers of these three *buraku*. At the annual festival (on the third day of the third month of the lunar calendar), four youths from Ōmi *buraku* and two youths each from Kane and Inazumi *buraku* are chosen to carry the portable shrine (*mikoshi*) from the main shrine to the top of the nearby hill. This festival is held under the leadership of the heads of the Nagao families in Kane and the Ōmi families in Ōmi *buraku*.

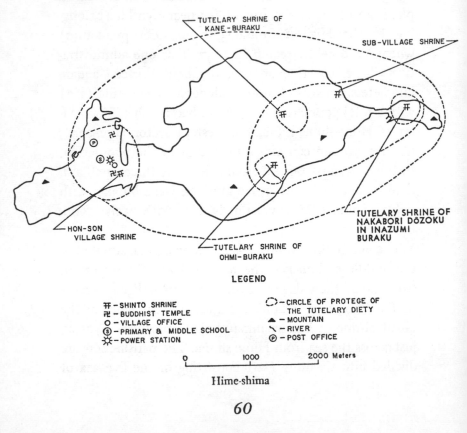

LEGEND

丮 – SHINTO SHRINE
卍 – BUDDHIST TEMPLE
O – VILLAGE OFFICE
Ⓢ – PRIMARY & MIDDLE SCHOOL
☼ – POWER STATION

◌ – CIRCLE OF PROTEGE OF
　　THE TUTELARY DIETY
▲ – MOUNTAIN
＼ – RIVER
Ⓟ – POST OFFICE

0　　　　1000　　　　2000 Meters

Hime-shima

60

The Ōmi families in Ōmi *buraku* are divided into two spiritually and materially cooperative groups and then into fifteen subfamily groups, each with a main family and some branch families. The main family usually has a Shinto altar as well as a Buddhist altar which enshrines the ancestral monumental tablets. This *buraku* has a particular shrine, called *Kōjin*, which is attended by the whole *buraku*. The first initiatory rites on the thirty-third day after birth take place at this shrine, suggesting that this was once a tutelary shrine. In addition, there is an Inari shrine (enshrining a kami of agriculture), an Ura-ebisu shrine (dedicated to a kami of fishery), and a Daishi-dō temple (enshrining Kōbō Daishi, the founder of the Buddhist Shingon sect).

On the eastern part of the island in Inazumi *buraku*, nine Nakabori families form one *dōzoku* group which consists of a main family, two sub-main families, and six branch families. The main family has an Izushima-myōjin shrine (enshrining a kami of water or of the sea); one of the sub-main families has an Inari shrine, the other, a Kōjin shrine. All members of this *dōzoku* group participate in the annual festivals in the second and eighth months of the lunar calendar and serve these kami. Thus, for example, Matasaku Nakabori, who is a member of the branch family, must join in the festivals of the Kōjin shrine (sub-main family's shrine), and Izushima-myōjin shrine (main family's shrine), the Himekoso-jinja (sub-village shrine), and the Hachiman-jinja (main village shrine).[9]

This structure may be understood as being intimately related to the political, economic, and cultural conditions of the islands; the power and influence of the western vil-

[9] *Ibid.*, pp. 107–18.

61

lage gradually expanded and spread over the isolated eastern *buraku*. In other words, the present religious structure can be viewed as a symbol of the enlargement of the
consciousness of the villagers, whose economic, political,
and cultural environment expanded, creating an association of *buraku* and the consciousness of an organized island community without a corresponding decrease of in-
group feeling and cooperation.

It is interesting to note survivals of the *dōzoku* and its
belief system in the *miya-za* system in the festivals of village shrines, the religious union of regional *kumi*, *kaito*,
and *kō*. The *miya-za* (also called the *tō-ya*) system is a
group of families having the privilege of caring for the
kami in the village shrine. There are three systems for
serving the village shrine: service permitted only to a
single family which was a main family of a former *dōzoku*
group; service permitted to several special families of the
combined *dōzoku* groups; and service permitted to all
residents of the village.[10] The *kumi* is the regional group
of families based on economic and religious union. *Kaito*
means "enclosure within a fence," and each *buraku* is a
block separated by a hedge or moat. One *kaito* usually has
one or two Buddhist temples, a Shinto shrine, and one
common burial ground. There are many cooperative associations for harmonious teamwork, religious practices,
annual festivals, funeral ceremonies, mutual aid, and so
on. *Kō* is the village religious association based on such
criteria as age, sex, situation of the family, and occupa-

10 Kazuo Higo, *Miyaza no kenkyū* (*A Study of the Duty House at
the Village Shrine*) (Tokyo, 1941); Tarō Wakamori, *Chūsei kyōdō-tai
no kenkyū* (*A Study of the Community System in Medieval Japan*)
(Tokyo, 1950); I. Hori, *Minkan shinkō*, pp. 169–86.

tion. *Kumi, kaito,* and *kō* apparently assumed some of the functions of the primitive *dōzoku* group.[11]

⟨ Folk Beliefs in Japanese Rural Society: The Case of Satoyamabe-mura

The relationship between folk beliefs and everyday life in an average rural community can be illustrated from my field research in Satoyamabe-mura, Nagano prefecture. This village consists of 682 families divided into thirteen ō-aza (large sub-village units) and thirty-three ko-aza (sub-village sections). The central Shinto shrine of this village, which all villagers have the duty and right to serve, is called Susuki-no-miya (literally, "Pampas-grass shrine"), in reference to the tradition of the origin of the local kami, who is supposed to have journeyed down the nearby river from a neighboring mountain on a pampas-grass leaf. The Susuki-no-miya now enshrines two kami: Takeminakata-no-kami, the ancestral kami of famous ancient feudal lords and the religiously powerful Suwa family who had presided over the neighboring district of Suwagun, and who were known as the Jin-shi (kami's family) until the end of the Ashikaga shogunate (A.D. 1338–1573); and Gozu-tennō, who was originally believed to be a kami of epidemics but later became known as a guardian against epidemics. The latter is a type of goryō-shin, the character and function of which will be described below.

In addition, there is a Buddhist-style miniature shrine and a Buddhist bodhisattva's statue (Batō-kannon, in

[11] Hori, *Minkan shinkō,* pp. 187–202.

Japanese; Hayagrîva, in Sanskrit) in the inner shrine. This is a remnant of the commingling of Shinto and Buddhism in the medieval period, and indicates that this shrine has been influenced by beliefs from the Zenkō-ji temple in Nagano, one of the most flourishing Buddhist temples, belonging to both the Tendai and Jōdo sects. There is also a small branch shrine which enshrines Prince Shōtoku, a crown prince of the sixth century who played a decisive role in the introduction of Buddhism into Japan. He is especially honored by the Buddhist Shin sect as well as by carpenters and other craftsmen.

Thus, at least four religious elements are found in this shrine: belief in an ancestral kami of a politically powerful and religious family (a developed little tradition); belief in *goryō-shin* (super-community, but belonging to a little tradition); belief in Zenkō-ji temple (great tradition); and belief in Prince Shōtoku (great and little traditions).

The main Buddhist temple in Satoyamabe-mura is Tosen-ji. It belongs to the Shingon sect and was originally built to serve the main Shinto shrine (Susuki-no-miya). A large number of families have religious celebrations at this temple during the annual Bon festival, at the anniversary rites for ancestors, and during funeral rites.

Beyond these two central religious affiliations, each family and each person in the village has relationships with many other religious belief systems, the most important of which center in the *iwai-den* or *iwai-jin*, which house the tutelary kami of the extended family. Twenty-eight kinds of Shinto and Buddhist deities are enshrined in ninety-one of these *iwai-den*. Among them the Inari shrine contains the largest number, comprising 46 per cent of the total. The following tabulation gives a partial list of the families, shrines, and festival days of Fujii *buraku*, and illustrates the village members' relationship to the *iwai-den*:

NAME OF FAMILY	NAME OF SHRINE	FESTIVAL DAYS
Yamato and two other families	Inari	Beginning of the second month
Futatsugi (A)*	Kompira	10th of the fourth month
Akagi and seven other families	Inari	Beginning of the second month
Futatsugi (B) and 13 other families	Genkō-Inari	25th of the fifth month, and 16th of the eighth month
Yamazaki	Shinmei	Obscure
Fujii (A)	Shinmei	15th of the ninth month
Kawakami and two other families	Taga	6th of the fourth month
Futatsugi (C) and two other families	Hachiman	1st of the third month
Futatsugi (D)	Hachiman	1st of the third month
Fujii (B) and four other families	Inari	Beginning of the second month

* A, B, C, D refer to Figure 1.

These relationships are based upon the old social structure of Japan and are still maintained by a consciousness of the relationships within the *dōzoku* kinship system (the same surname grouping system), and by the small, local, cultural-economic community. At festivals, representatives of the members gather in the shrine owner's house (usually the traditional *hon-ke*, main family) and worship at the shrine under the leadership of the head of the main family or of the owner.

Attention should also be given to the other religious phenomena in this village, such as the many stone shrines, stupas, phalli, monuments, memorial statues, charms, and taboo symbols. There are now about 144 small shrines and stone symbols, among which are forty-two Nembutsu stupas and Amida figures, twenty Kōshin stupas, a number of offering stupas for the Lotus Sutra (formally, *Saddharmapundarîka-sûtra* in Sanskrit), memorial stupas for pilgrimages, Batō-kannon statues (Buddhist guardian deity of horses), Nijūsan-ya stupas (for worship on the twenty-third night's moon after the new moon), statues of Dōso-jin (kami of the road and travel and of sex), statues of Kodama-gami (kami of silk and the silkworm), and others. Moreover, there are many religious associations (kō) in this village.

> Kōshin-kō.—*Kōshin belief is an amalgamation of Shinto, religious Taoism, and Buddhism. Kōshin is believed to have many and various functions in the village. He is, for instance, the agricultural kami, the protector against misfortune, the kami of soil, the kami of craftsmanship and so forth, and one buraku has two or three associations for service to this kami. In Fujii buraku there are four such Kōshin-kō, one association each being organized by the eight Hanaoka families, the fourteen Futatsugi families, the four Fujii families, and the fourteen consisting of Akagi, Nehagi, Sakashita, and Yamoto families. These associations often overlap with the iwai-den system or combine two or three iwai-den. The members of each association must meet six times yearly at the duty house (tōya) and, after a small festival, discuss the economic and cooperative matters of the community and the common problems of daily public life. Often the old persons talk about the folk traditions, legends, and history of*

the village. They feast together and, following the old customary Kōshin belief, sit up throughout the night.

Nembutsu-kō.—This is composed of the believers in Amida Butsu (Amitâbha Buddha). Their main function in the community is to serve the spirits of the dead and sometimes to help during funeral rites. This association often combines with the Kōshin-kō and is sometimes called Kōshin-nembutsu-kō.

Isc-kō.—Members are believers in the mythical ancestral goddess of the imperial family which has been enshrined at Ise shrine. Each member of this association must pay monthly dues. One or two delegates, who are decided upon by lot, worship at the Ise Shrine in Mie prefecture once a year. They distribute the charms and the calendars published by this shrine to each member. This association includes almost all members of the village. Almost the same function is performed by Akiba-kō.

Akiba-kō.—This is the association of believers in Akiba-sama, the protector against fire.

Nijūsan-ya-kō.—This association for the worship of the 23rd night's moon after the new moon is a volunteer group of women who meet once a lunar month at the village shrine or the duty house. They remain together throughout the night in order to worship the moon which appears at the next dawn. Nijūsanya-sama is believed to be the guardian of easy childbirth and good fortune.

Kannon-kō.—This is an association of believers in Batō-kannon, the Buddhist deity of the horse. The members are primarily horse drivers and owners of horses and cattle.

Other kō associations are Yama-no-kami-kō (an association of believers in the mountain deity) and Kinoene-kō (an association of believers in Daikoku, a kami of good luck and good harvest, the festival of which is held each Kinoene Day (Elder Rat Day).

In addition to these complicated religious observances, each family has its own Shinto and Buddhist altars in the living room which serve the spirits of the family ancestors and where the kami are prayed to for good health and good harvest. In the kitchen there are usually altars of Daikoku-sama and Ebisu-sama, both of which are generally believed to be kami of good harvest and good luck. Moreover, there are many Shinto, Onmyō-dō (way of Yin-yang), and Buddhist charms and amulets on the pillars and walls, distributed by wandering preachers from some of the larger shrines and temples. The villagers also believe there are many kami—of the well, the fireplace, the privy, the gate, and so forth—in each house.[12]

(Hito-gami (man-gods) and the Religious Beliefs and Traditions of Wandering Preachers

Japanese rural society has both a little tradition (based on the dōzoku type of ancestral spirit worship) and a great tradition (based on the subdivision of the buddhas' or bodhisattvas' spirits). The little tradition in Japanese folk

[12] Ibid., pp. 94–107. This type of myth is sometimes related to the belief in Mother-and-Sacred-Son, and to family myths in which an ancestor was believed to have been an attendant of a kami who descended and settled in a particular local territory. In such a case an individual may be under contract to become a priest, and his descendants will become a sacred family by this covenant.

religion had a dualistic system which evidently originated in the coalescence of aboriginal and later immigrant cultures. This coalescence is directly symbolized in Japanese mythology as the coordinate concept of the kami which were named the *ama-tsu-kami* (kami of heaven) and the *kuni-tsu-kami* (kami of the earth or territory). The former were usually believed to be the ancestors of the rulers; the latter, of the ruled.

The mythology in the *Kojiki* and the *Nihongi*, both of which were compiled by the oral transmitters of the imperial family's myths in the seventh century, abound in stories of the activities of the heavenly kami and the culture heroes who came from the other land (*Tokoyo* or eternal land) and from beyond the sea to establish and transmit new political and social orders, techniques, cultures, and beliefs. The existence of these myths seems to indicate that supernatural powers and superior culture usually came from the outside to the exclusive in-group society, and it reflects some of the contacts between the aborigines and immigrants in prehistoric times.

The idea of a supernatural power and superior culture coming from outside was probably related to general feelings of inferiority among the ancient villagers, who were aware of community exclusiveness and isolation. At the same time, they may have been conscious of cultural and religious distinctions between their own group and the out-groups, and felt a certain longing for the outsiders' cultures. Moreover, as we have already seen, in Japanese rural communities there are many indications of the existence of guardian spirits, ancestor spirits, kami of the rice field, and spirits of the dead who usually come and go between two worlds periodically or seasonally. This may account in part for the fact that the heavenly kami, mani-

69

fested and worshipped by the ruling and shamanistic families, were peacefully accepted in aboriginal society.

Heavenly kami and culture heroes usually appeared in the oracles of shamans or shamanesses, and were enshrined by the descendants of such shamans or shamanesses. Great shamanistic families became the ruling classes in the ancient theocratic period, and many national political decisions were controlled by shamans or shamanesses who belonged to the imperial or other powerful families. In Japanese mythology there are famous stories in which marriage occurs between a powerful kami and a great shamaness, and in which great shamanesses are possessed by the spirits of powerful *hito-gami*. For example, the kami of Mount Miwa, near Nara, one of the most powerful in ancient political history, became the ancestor of the famous shamanic Miwa and Kamo families through the conception of the noble virgin Tama-yori-hime. Her name literally means a "shamaness possessed by a spirit of a kami (*tama*, "spirit"; *yori*, "possessing"; and *hime*, an ancient honorific title for a noble woman). In another tradition, this kami was said to be the husband of Princess Yamato-totohi-momoso-hime, who was an aunt of the Emperor Sujin and a great royal shamaness, though her marriage with the kami was dissolved by her breaking of a taboo. This kind of myth is called the Miwa type, of which there are many varieties in Japanese classic literature as well as in folk tales and legends of many rural communities. This sort of tradition is also found among some of the local historic families and in some Shinto priests' families who are proud of their sacred lineages.[13]

Proto-Shinto is neither idolatrous religion nor nature worship, as it has often been characterized. In spite of the

[13] Hori, *Wagakuni minkan-shinkō-shi no kenkyū*, I, 308–65.

strong influence of Buddhism beginning in the sixth century, graphic representations of divine beings were not produced; rather, people believed in *hito-gami* (man-gods) and those who were disguised as deities. Sometimes a kami possessed persons, especially women, or even things in nature. In ancient times there were two kinds of personalities, spirits, or souls—one pertaining to the nobles and priests, the other to the common people. The possibility of deification after death was permitted only to the former. In addition, Confucianism, religious Taoism, and Buddhism infiltrated from China and Korea from the third to the middle of the sixth century. Confucianism brought a new family code and social ethic based on the ancient Chinese feudal system; religious Taoism introduced new magic and techniques, such as astrology, the calendar, and geomancy; and Buddhism proclaimed human equality and the equal possibility for all to become buddhas (saints of enlightenment). Consequently, the ancient religious forms were not only differentiated by internal political, economic, and cultural changes, but also fused with these great traditions.

The *hito-gami* system was transformed into the belief in *goryō-shin*, which first appeared in the documentary record at the end of the Nara period (latter part of the eighth century). Originally, it consisted of a belief in malevolent spirits of noble persons who had died in political intrigues. These spirits were enshrined in Shinto shrines as kami, and to them were devoted special festivals and memorial services which were mixtures of Shinto, religious Taoism (Onmyō-dō), and Buddhism, for the purpose of soothing their angry spirits. The first official services on record took place in Kyoto in A.D. 863 under the auspices of the emperor. During their gradual spread to the rural society, these beliefs stimulated an awareness in the common people of the extent of human possibilities. The theories of the great traditions exerted revolutionary influences upon Japanese spiritual life, including funeral customs and the belief in spirits of the dead. Each person, regardless of social status, began to be conscious of the possibility of his own deification. This awareness was furthered by the activities of the village shamans or shamanesses, who communicated by trance with various spirits, including those of commoners, in order to explain disasters in the land.

The period from the middle of the eighth century to the twelfth century might be termed the *goryō-shin* age. There are many examples of the prevalence of *goryō-shin* in the literature of the Heian period (A.D. 784–1185), such as the *Genji-monogatari* (*The Tale of Genji*) written by Lady Murasaki in about A.D. 1000, and *Makura-no-sōshi* (*Pillow Book*), written by Lady Sei-shōnagon, a famous essayist of the same period, as well as in the diaries of nobles and in official documents of the times. These documents indicate that the people were afraid of spirits of the dead, who preyed upon them. All social and personal crises—such as political changes, civil wars, epidemics, famines, droughts, earthquakes, thunderstorms, typhoons, difficult childbirths, diseases, and deaths—were believed to be the result of the vengeance of angry spirits of the dead. Sometimes, too, they were believed to be caused by the angry or jealous souls of living men and women. The angry spirits were revealed by shamanesses. These beliefs continue to survive in Japanese rural society today. For example, there must be special memorial services for a person who has met an untimely death, because it is believed that his spirit may become vengeful or malevolent and bring misfortune to an enemy or to the community.[14]

Three kinds of magic sprang up to oppose the goryō at the end of the ninth and the middle of the tenth centuries: the Nembutsu, the Shugen-dō, and the Onmyō-dō. Nembutsu belief and practices originated in the Pure Land school of Chinese Buddhism (*Ching-t'u*, founded in China by Hui-yüan, A.D. 334–416), but in the middle of the Heian period it was only a negative magic against goryō, aimed at sending the angry or dangerous spirit into Amida's Pure Land. Shugen-dō is a mixed school or sect of Shinto, religious Taoism, and Buddhism. The priest of this school practiced a positive magic which was opposed to that of the Nembutsu priests. Onmyō-dō is a mixture of Shinto and Taoist magic and art.

The literal meaning of Nembutsu is "prayer for Buddha or Buddhas," but in the history of Japanese religions Nembutsu refers to a prayer offered only to Amida-butsu (Amitâbha Buddha), who presides over the Western Pure Land (*Saihō jōdo*) as the savior of human souls and spirits of the dead. The practice of Nembutsu and the belief in Amida-butsu appeared in about the ninth century and flourished in the tenth and eleventh centuries; they were connected with the rising belief in goryō. Many magical Nembutsu dances and dramas still exist in rural villages. They have the function of driving off evil spirits of the dead which may become transformed into epidemic spirits, noxious insects, and so on. As popular Nembutsu beliefs and practices degenerated into magico-artistic entertainments and lost their religious character, there appeared in the twelfth century many Buddhist saints who purified and restored the orthodox Buddhist sects. Among

[14] *Ibid.*, II, 76–78; Hori, *Minkan shinkō*, pp. 176–280.

them, Hōnen (1133–1212) founded the Jōdo sect, introduced the theology of Chinese Pure Land Buddhism, and resystematized the belief in Amida-butsu and the practice of Nembutsu. Succeeding him, his disciple Shinran (1173–1262) founded the Shin sect, the largest and most flourishing Buddhist sect in contemporary Japan. Chishin (known as Ippen Shōnin—1239–1289) founded the Ji sect. Nembutsu, as a system of counter-magic against the belief in goryō, is a kind of animistic superstition and an obstacle to intellectual progress, but the fact that it proclaimed the value of humanity and of the human will should not be overlooked.

Despite these restorative movements, popular Nembutsu still survives in rural communities and has continued its social functions until recent times. Descendants of popular Nembutsu priests of the lower class usually survive as outcast minorities. For example, there are *Kane-uchi-buraku*, *Hachiya-buraku*, and *Hachitataki-mura* ("villages of those who say prayers to Amida-butsu" [*Namu-Amida-butsu*]). The founder of the Kabuki play is said to have been a famous Nembutsu magic dancer at the beginning of the Tokugawa period (1615–1867).[15]

If we can say that Nembutsu magic is a negative magic against the goryō, the magic of Shugen-dō is positive; the former attempts to ward off the goryō, whereas the latter aims at exorcism. Shugen-dō was formerly a kind of Buddhist asceticism. It consists of magical practices and spiritual and physical training, the object of which is to attain magical power against evil spirits. Since this is practiced in mountain areas, the ascetics are called *yamabushi* (literally, "the priests who lie down on the mountain"). It is said that Shugen-dō was founded by En-no-gyōja

15 Hori, *Wagakuni minkan-shinkō-shi no kenkyū*, II, 249–470.

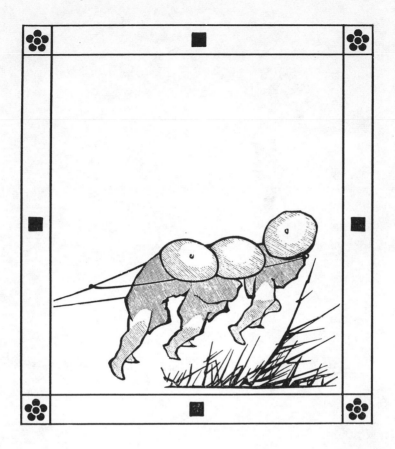

or En-no-Shōkaku (priest of the En family), who is said to have lived in the middle of the seventh century A.D. Although this is not an established fact, there is some reliable evidence to show that many shamans or magicians practiced and trained in the mountains in that period.

Many students of Japanese religious history have pointed out that Shugen-dō consisted of a variety of elements such as popular or primitive beliefs in mountains, the *dhûta* practices (*zuda-gyō* in Japanese) of Indian Buddhist asceticism, Chinese mythology and Taoistic beliefs, the theology and practices of the Japanese Tendai (*T'ien-t'ai* in Chinese) and Shingon (*Cheng-yen* in Chinese) Buddhist sects, and the magic and ritual of Shinto. After a period of decline, the Shugen-dō sect was apparently restored and reorganized by a Shingon monk, Shōbō (A.D. 832–909), who lived in the *goryō-shin* age and whose magicians were actively engaged in subduing the malevolent spirits of the dead. Shamanesses were usually employed as assistants. Subjected to suggestion by the *yamabushi's* magical spells and techniques, they fell into trances, became possessed by a spirit, and announced the will or grievances of the malevolent spirit.

Later, Shugen-dō became a sub-sect of both the Tendai and Shingon sects and practiced the mysteries of Esoteric Buddhism which came from the Indian Tantrism or Mantrayâna. Among the many sacred mountains which they occupied, Mount Kumano in Wakayama prefecture, Mount Haguro and Mount Yudono in Yamagata prefecture, and Mount Hiko in Fukuoka prefecture became the centers of these sects. In principle, Shugen-dō priests were trained to travel from mountain to mountain and from village to village. Especially, the *Shugen-ja* (Shungen-dō priests, the same as *yamabushi*) of Mount Kumano traveled and preached their religion from Hokkaido to the Ryukyus, thus significantly influencing the magic and belief systems of villagers in the medieval and modern periods. Sometimes the *yamabushi*, who had special uniforms and magical instruments, became not only village magicians but also Shinto priests. Most of the village Shinto shrines in the Tōhoku district (northeast Honshu) and Hokuriku district (mid-north Honshu) before the Meiji restoration (1868) had *yamabushi* as their professional priests. Although they belong officially to the Tendai and Shingon sects, the priests do not cut their hair and they marry according to the permissive theory; sometimes they marry female shamans. If a priest marries a shamaness they work together, a case of possession being diagnosed through the shamaness's trance and then given relief by the priest's exorcism.

In recent times, the *yamabushi* have governed several sacred mountains in northeast and southwest Japan and have continued to perform some social functions, such as conducting initiation ceremonies for village youths, praying for good harvests, exorcising evil spirits from a house or a village, and offering prayers for newly built houses or for sick persons. The magical techniques of the *yamabushi* and the mediumistic techniques of shamanesses were also transformed into various kinds of public entertainment, and some of the priests and shamanesses became the predecessors of professional reciters, ballad singers, c popular narrators, as did the popular Nembutsu priests and priestesses.[16]

[16] The *yamabushi* always carry and blow shell trumpets; in Japanese colloquial speech, "to blow a shell trumpet" means "to boast" or "to talk tall." This reveals a critical attitude on the part of the villagers, since the shell trumpet symbolizes the *yamabushi*, who often abused the hospitality accorded them. See *ibid.*, pp. 57–205.

Onmyō-dō was a popular belief which came to Japan from China through Korea in the seventh century A.D. It included some philosophical, astrological, animistic, and magical theories and practices. At a later date, the scholars and magicians of the Onmyō-dō sect became techno-religious officials at the imperial court. Astrology and the preparation of the official calendar came within their jurisdiction. They also practiced magical invocations for good harvests, good weather, purification, and good fortune: in addition, they engaged in such matters as divination, astrology, and fortune telling. Onmyō-dō became intermingled with Shinto and thus merged imperceptibly into the popular beliefs which spread over all of Japan.

The most famous Onmyō-dō priests' families—Abe and Kamo—also grew in prosperity from the ninth to eleventh centuries, the goryō-shin age. The magic of Onmyō-dō was rather negative, since the priest offered many kinds of food at crossroads or entrances to villages or cities in order to soothe the evil spirits or demons of plague or requested the villagers to purify themselves by bathing in the streams or sea or by abstaining from certain kinds of foods and by remaining at home on unlucky days. Sometimes, too, they employed shamanesses as assistants to communicate with the spirits of the dead or to hear the will of angry deities.

Descendants of the Onmyō-dō priests or magicians of the lower class also traveled from village to village to propagate their beliefs and to give relief to villagers. Some who belonged to large Shinto shrines and Buddhist temples periodically visited the villages or cities within their jurisdiction to distribute their shrine's or temple's charms, talismans, amulets, phylacteries, and professional agricultural calendars. Some of them settled in villages and survived as members of outcast minority groups. Remnants of this sect may be found today in the *Onmyōji-mura* (village of Onmyō-dō priests), or *Shomo(n)ji-mura*, *Innai-mura*, and *Sanjo-mura* (villages of the lower-class Onmyō-dō priests). Inhabitants of these communities still preserve some of their original social and religious functions. For example, they make seasonal visits to purify each house and oven by reciting magical words and songs, and to dance for a happy New Year, a good future harvest, and good luck at the beginning of the year. Sometimes these people became actors. In the medieval period, actors in the Nō and puppet plays usually belonged to this group. It is significant that there are many surviving elements of the worship of the spirits of the dead in the Nō plays, Jōruri recitals, narrative stories, and in other literature and art. Recalling the voice of spirits of the dead by local shamanesses is still considered an important memorial service for the dead in northeast Honshu and in other districts of Japan.[17]

From this brief sketch of the ethno-history of Japanese religious beliefs, some hypotheses may be set forth. The concept of *hito-gami* (man-god) and its practices are deeply imbedded in ancient Japanese folk religion, and, furthermore, the man-god groups have formed separate religious and political estates or classes in isolated and settled farming communities. Thus, there is a sharp distinction between the two complexes: the traditional rural Japanese in-group, and the man-god. The coexistence of these two religious and cultural patterns in the rural village was complicated by the historical social circumstances and by the passive and non-individualized mentality of the villagers, which centered in acceptance of

[17] *Ibid.*, pp. 471–596.

strangers, outsiders, wandering preachers—that is, *hito-gami* (man-gods).

On the other hand, the *hito-gami* type is traceable to the worship of the dead or the spirits of the dead, accompanied by the idea of the other world which was imagined to be in heaven or beyond the sea. This dual organization, which already existed in original Shinto, underwent a complicated process of socio-religious change with the acceptance of the great traditions from the Asian continent. The cohesion and mixture of the little tradition and the great traditions took place during the *goryō-shin* age, when the *hito-gami* complex and the great traditions reciprocally influenced each other, underwent varying changes, and were ultimately amalgamated.[18]

[18] *Ibid.*, pp. 751–66; see also Hori, *Minkan shinkō*, pp. 248–97.

CHAPTER
III

Nembutsu as Folk Religion

ǝ ǝ ǝ It is the purpose of this chapter to discuss Nembutsu belief and practices among the Japanese people from ancient times to the present day. We find in Nembutsu some of the main characteristics of popular Buddhism mixed with Japanese folk religion. Japanese Buddhism must be seen first of all as an integral part of the total dynamic movement which spread from India across Southeast Asia to the Far Eastern countries. There is a definite continuity in Buddhism which can be demonstrated not only historically but also phenomenologically. To be sure, the special social and cultural circumstances which it encountered on Japanese soil worked some remarkable transformations. Some scholars go so far as to say that Japanese Buddhism is not real Buddhism at all or is at best a deformed version.[1]

[1] Cf. Shōkō Watanabe, *Nihon no Bukkyō* (*Japanese Buddhism*) (Tokyo, 1958), especially pp. 64, 66–67. See also Eliot, *Japanese Buddhism*, pp. 179–96.

We shall speak here of the direction which Buddhism has taken in Japan and of the conditions which have made it unique among the many forms of Buddhism in the world. Two key phenomena serve to focus our discussion. They are the *samgha* (monastic order) and the *vinaya* (disciplinary system). These traditional Buddhist forms were transmitted by missionary efforts from India through China and Korea. They are important here because of their necessary relation to historical and sociological patterns. When these forms were first introduced into Japan, they were in conflict with the existing social patterns. The history of the inevitable modification which took place in Japanese Buddhism in the *samgha* and the *vinaya* may also be seen as a movement toward the popularization of the Buddhist religion.

The character of Japanese Buddhism may be traced to certain decisive events in the reign of Empress Suiko and Prince Regent Shōtoku. At the time of the official recognition of Buddhism in Japan in A.D. 593, the nation had been undergoing a great spiritual and cultural upheaval. China was rising to political and cultural eminence in the Far East under the Sui dynasty. Great numbers of immigrants were pouring into Japan from China and Korea, bringing scholarship, skills, and religion from the Asian mainland.[2] The ancient theocratic clan system was break-

[2] The great extent of this influence is indicated by an official record named *Shinsen-shōji roku* (*Newly Selected Records of Family Titles and Names*) which was compiled in A.D. 815 by imperial edict. Among 1,065 families around the capital and its neighboring areas, there were 326 powerful families of *banbetsu* class who were naturalized foreigners. All families were divided into three groups: *kōbetsu* (335 families), who were the cadet families of princely lines; *shinbetsu* (404 families), who were believed to be descended from the mythical gods or goddesses who founded the country; and the *banbetsu*.

ing down under the new forces that were assailing the nation, and the people were ready to look to an alien religion for their spiritual foundations.

Prince Shōtoku (574–621), statesman and religious thinker, played a significant role in shaping Japanese Buddhism. In fact, his influence extended far beyond the span of his own life. Under him Buddhism developed into a religion of the aristocracy with strong lay leadership. At the same time, Shōtoku's emphasis on the Lotus Sutra promoted a social consciousness that encompassed all classes. The Lotus Sutra's promise of salvation for all mankind was in sharp contrast with the pre-Buddhistic and shamanistic folk religion. The latter had two classes of deities, corresponding to the two social classes of ancient Japanese society, and offered life in the hereafter only to the ruling and shamanic families, which constituted the imperial, noble, and magico-religious class. The new Buddhist social concern was expressed in the building of temples which served as centers of philanthropic and cultural activities.[3]

Twenty-four years after Shōtoku's death, the Taika reformation (A.D. 645) put into effect some of his principles. The establishment of a unified empire meant that for the first time in the history of Japan one emperor completely ruled the whole nation. The political prin-

[3] One example was the building of Shiten'ō-ji Temple. This temple has had four centers of social services: a charity hospital, a charity dispensary, an orphanage, and an old people's home. These were the first public social services of a Buddhist temple in Japan. See *Jōgū Shōtoku-hōō teisetsu* (*Biography of Prince Shōtoku*), supposedly compiled in the seventh century immediately after the Taika reformation, published by Iwanami Bunko with annotations of Shinshō Hanayama and Saburō Iyenaga (Tokyo, 1941). Also see Hori, *Wagakuni minkan-shinkō-shi no kenkyū*, I, 157–61, 165–70.

ciples of the empire were modeled after those of the T'ang dynasty. This reformation was prepared secretly, and was executed by several Buddhist monks together with some government scholars. Both these groups had been previously dispatched by Prince Shōtoku to Sui and T'ang China for study.

The principles of the Taika reformation included the prohibition of private ownership of land, the foundation of the ancient clan system, and the distribution of farm-land to the peasants. At the beginning of this reformation a messenger was sent to the large temples near the capital to summon together Buddhist priests and nuns and to address them on behalf of the emperor. Thus Buddhism gained official recognition as a state religion.[4] The religious policy of the Taika government was to guard and promote Buddhism, and also to place under the sovereign's supervision a Buddhism completely subservient to state control.[5]

Thus, at the beginning, Japanese Buddhism was made a spiritual principle of the empire system, and also the spiritual foundation of the great family system of that time. Ancestor worship became one of its most significant functions. Buddhist magic, commingled with Shinto and Yin-yang magic, also flourished.

In the early days almost all Buddhist temples belonged either to the state or to some powerful family or clan. Formal Buddhism was maintained on the official and aristocratic level. Side by side with institutionalized forms of Buddhism, however, as early as the middle of the Nara period (eighth century) there arose movements among

[4] *Nihongi*, Vol. XXV; W. G. Aston, *Nihongi, Chronicles of Japan from the Earliest Times to A.D. 697* (London, 1896), II, 202.

[5] *Nihongi*, Vol. XXV; Aston, *Nihongi*, II, 202–3.

laymen centering in such charismatic figures as Gyōgi[6] and En-no-Shōkaku.[7] The aim of these movements was to distribute the Buddha's gospel and his salvation among the common people, or to save people by superhuman power acquired through unusual religious austerities. This they did wholly outside the orthodox Buddhist priesthood. They opposed the ecclesiastical systems of state and clan Buddhism, which were already beginning

[6] Gyōgi (A.D. 670?–749) was an outstanding leader of popular Buddhism in the Nara period. He endeavored to popularize Buddhism for the common people through easily understandable teachings and public services done in the Buddhist spirit. The last included the founding of charity hospitals, orphanages, and old people's homes; excavation of canals for navigation and irrigation; the building of irrigation ponds; bridge construction; harbor construction in the Inland Sea near Osaka and Kobe; free clinics; free lodging houses. All of these projects were managed by disciples who lived in small seminaries named *dōjō* near the projects. According to the authentic biography in *Shoku nihongi* (*The Second Official Historical Records*, succeeding the *Nihongi* and edited from A.D. 697 to 791), he was called a *bosatsu* (Buddhist saint, bodhisattva) by the masses even while he lived. He was *upâsaka* (*ubasoku* in Japanese, profane believer) for a long time. Then in 745 Emperor Shōmu, applauding his virtue and religious personality as well as his enterprises, elevated him to the rank of *Dai-sōjō* (Archbishop). His death in 749 at the age of eighty was greatly lamented by the nation as well as by the emperor. It is said that he built forty-nine *dōjō* (seminaries) around the metropolitan areas for the purposes mentioned above. See *Shoku nihongi*, XXII, in *Kokushi taikei* (Tokyo, 1935), II, 196. Also see Hori, *Wagakuni minkan-shinkō-shi no kenkyū*, I, 256–93.

[7] En-no-Shōkaku was a famous magician who lived in the middle of the seventh century. His family was believed to have had the priestly function of serving the god of Mount Katsuragi in Nara prefecture, whose name was Hitokoto-nushi (Deity of Divination by One Word). It is said that Shugen-dō in Japan was founded by him, but this is not yet an established historical fact. However, there is some reliable evidence to show that many shamans and magicians practiced and trained in the mountains, accepting the new-styled form of Buddhist Mantrayāna in that period.

87

to turn toward secularism, and concentrated instead on individual personal piety, and discipline in the common life. Thus the lay movement denied not only the *samgha* in its orthodox form but also the *vinaya*. Those who became priests were encouraged to marry and have families. This so-called household religion has persisted to the present over almost all Japan.

It should be evident from this discussion that Japanese Buddhism never had its own independent ecclesiastical order, as such other Buddhist countries as Ceylon, Burma, or the Indo-Chinese states, but has always flourished under the existing sociological and political structures.

Japanese Buddhism developed in three stages: the first was the Asuka and Nara periods (A.D. 593-793); the second was the Heian period (794-1185); and the third was the Kamakura period (1186-1333).

Roughly speaking, the Buddhism of the first stage was represented by the Hossō (*Fahsien* in Chinese), Kegon (*Avatansaka* in Sanskrit), and Ritsu (*Lü* in Chinese; *Vinaya* in Sanskrit) sects, and was characterized by direct transplantations from Chinese and Korean Buddhist sects. At the same time, it was actually influenced by the state religion, though these sects were mainly scholarly and philosophic, not essentially religious. The next stage, Heian Buddhism, shows a remarkable contrast to the Buddhist sects of Nara. Politically, the transfer of the capital from Nara to Kyoto brought about a new mood, one motive for the transfer having been to separate church and state. Religiously, two sects of Buddhism were predominant throughout the period—Tendai *T'ien-t'ai* in Chinese) and Shingon (*Chên-yen* in Chinese). Heian Buddhism was shaped by the transmission of the Chinese T'ien-t'ai and Chên-yen sects, though in

actual practice these sects became highly aristocratic and emphasized magical functions.

Kamakura Buddhism was represented by the Pure Land (Jōdo), Zen, and Nichiren sects, and was characterized by the indigenization and resystematization of former Buddhist sects and popular beliefs on the one hand, and on the other by the transplantation of Chinese Ch'an (Zen) Buddhism which had been mixed with the Taoistic philosophy and way of thinking.

The Pure Land (Jōdo) and the Nichiren sects became widespread among the common people, while Zen Buddhism became the spiritual foundation of the warriors (samurai) who had come into political power in the feudal age.[8]

[8] Monbu-shō (comp.); *Shūkyō nen-kan* (*Religious Year Book*) for the year 1956 (Tokyo), shows us as follows:

Sects	Number of Temples[a]	Number of Priests	Number of Adherents
Shin-shū (Jōdo)............	21,578	38,821	8,838,179
Sōtō-shū (Zen)............	15,021	15,224	1,574,311
Shingon-shū..............	12,381	21,060	7,720,236
Jōdo-shū (Jōdo)...........	8,233	9,130	8,303,785
Rinzai-shū (Zen)..........	5,854	5,951	3,007,405
Nichiren-shū..............	5,516	14,141	8,308,291
Tendai-shū...............	3,942	17,935	2,695,163
Ōbaku-shū (Zen)..........	523	520	148,861
Ji-shū (Jōdo).............	426	398	40,099
Yūzū-Nembutsu-shū (Jōdo).	357	312	101,099
Hossō-shū................	78	676	165,104
Kegon-shū................	53	503	57,620
Ritsu-shū................	24	56	10,300

· Some independent temples are omitted.

Taking an average for each sect of the total number of temples, priests, and adherents, we find that the Pure Land sects occupy the foremost position of all Buddhist influence with more than 30 per cent; second place is occupied by the Zen sects; third place by the Shingon sects; fourth place by the Nichiren sects; and fifth place by the Tendai sects. The Nara Buddhist sects barely maintain their existence, as shown by their figure of about 1 per cent of the total average.

These statistics do not necessarily indicate the real influence of Buddhism on the Japanese people, because some sects are conservative

([Emergence of Nembutsu Belief and Practices

The Heian period of Japanese religious history was characterized by five factors: (1) the introduction of Mantrayāna or Esoteric Buddhism from China by Saichō and Kūkai in A.D. 805 and 806 and its ready reception by the people; (2) the *hijiri* (holy men), who established common or folk Buddhism outside the orthodox ecclesiastical system, became pioneers of Kamakura Buddhism, and took over the movements of Gyōgi and En-no-Shōkaku of the Nara period; (3) the appearance of the belief in goryō, which, as I have described in Chapter II, originally consisted of a belief in the malevolent or angry spirits of noble or charismatic persons who died in political tragedies or intrigues; (4) the emergence of a consciousness of the Latter Law age (Mappō), which I shall discuss later in detail; and (5) the commingling of various religious elements such as primitive shamanism, Shinto, Yin-yang magic, and Mantrayâna Buddhism. If the aristocrats and intelligentsia had an articulate notion of the relationship of Shinto and Buddhism, the masses had little sense of discrimination in such matters. The man in

---

and retrogressive, while others are progressive and aggressive; some sects' adherents and believers are pious, positive, or fanatic, while others are indifferent, negative, or passive. However, even though they are the results of long-established conventions and feudalistic politics, these statistics show some historical reality. In other words, the major stream of Japanese Buddhism has been represented by the Kamakura sects of Buddhism, which account for 70 per cent of all Japanese Buddhist temples, priests, adherents, and believers.

the street accepted all kinds of beliefs derived not only from Buddhism and Shinto but also from religious Taoism, Confucian ethics, and the more primitive, native Japanese animistic folk religion. This syncretism gradually penetrated upward, even to the imperial court. Such events as political change, civil war, epidemic, famine, drought, earthquakes, thunderstorms, typhoons, as well as difficult delivery, diseases, and death were believed to be the working of the spirits or deities.

The first commingling of primitive shamanism with Yin-yang magic and Mantrayâna Buddhism appeared in the latter part of the Nara period and developed rapidly in the Heian. Three major streams emerged in the religious world as a result of the historical cohesion of these five factors:

Nembutsu.—the Buddhist Pure Land school (Jōdo-kyō) mixed with animistic and shamanistic elements.
Shugen-dō.—the Buddhist Mantrayâna school (Mik-kyō) mixed with Shinto animism and shamanism.
Onmyō-dō.—religious Taoism or the Yin-yang school mixed with Shinto animism and shamanism.

The term Nembutsu has philosophical and religious connotations in Buddhism. It is believed that the recitation of the sacred name Amitâbha or Amitâyus (Amida in Japanese: Namu-Amida-Butsu) enables human beings to reach the Western Paradise or Pure Land. This belief was originally founded by Hui-yüan in China about the fourth century, and the Amitâbha sutras[9] were intro-

---

[9] There are three sutras concerning the Amitâbha Buddha: the first is Sukhâvatyamritavyûha-sûtra (Fo-shwo-ö-mi-tho-kin in Chinese) translated into Chinese by Kumârajîva in A.D. 402; the second is the Buddhabhâshitâmitâyurbuddha-dhyâna (?)-sûtra (Fo-shwo-kwân-wu-liân-

duced into Japan by several Buddhist priests early in the Nara period. As early as A.D. 652, lectures about them were given at the imperial court. According to the historical documents,[10] there were then several priests who believed in Amida and practiced Nembutsu prayers for the purpose of their rebirth in *Sukhâvatî* (the Western Pure Land: *Saihō Jōdo* in Japanese) of Amitâbha Buddha.

The first Japanese sect to accept this belief officially was the Tendai. At first Saichō (Dengyō Daishi, A.D. 767–822), the Japanese founder of the Tendai sect, introduced practices of four kinds of *samâdhi* (*sammai* in Japanese: "meditation")[11] based on the teachings of the *Mo-hö-ki-kwân* (*Maka-shikan* in Japanese) written by Chih-kai, the founder of the Chinese T'ien-t'ai sect.[12] One of these four methods of *samâdhi* was called *Jōgyō-*

---

sheu-fo-kin in Chinese) which was translated into Chinese by Kâlayasas in A.D. 424; and the third is the so-called "*Larger Sukhâvati-vyûha-sûtra*" or "*Buddhabhâshita-mahâyânâmitâyur-vyûha-sûtra*." The original of this book was lost in A.D. 730. Nos. 200, 198, and 863 in Bunyū Nanjō, comp., *A Catalogue of the Chinese Translation of the Buddhist Tripitaka* (Oxford, 1883), hereinafter cited as *Nanjō Catalogue*.

10 See, for example, *Nihon ryōi-ki*, the first Buddhist legendary literature, compiled in the early ninth century (Tokyo, 1950), annotations by Yūkichi Takeda; *Nihon ōjō-gokuraku ki* (*Biographies of Persons Who Went to the Amida's Pure Land after Death*), written by Jakushin in A.D. 985–986; see *Dai Nippon Bukkyō zensho*, Vol. CVII (Tokyo, 1912–22).

11 The other two kinds of meditation besides *jōgyō* and *jōza-zammai* are called *hangyō-hanza-zammai* and *higyō-hiza-zammai*. In the former, the devotee alternately recites some sacred text, for example, the Lotus, and sits down to meditate on it; in the latter, he concentrates all his mental efforts on realizing the truth, but follows his inclination as to sitting or walking. Cf. Eliot, *Japanese Buddhism*, pp. 330–31; Hori, "On the Concept of Hijiri (Holy-man)," 214–15.

12 *Taishō daizō kyō*, Vol. 46-1, No. 1911; *Nanjō Catalogue*: No. 1538.

jōza-zammai.[13] It was based upon the *Pratyutpanna-buddhasammukhâvashita-samâdhi,*[14] which teaches meditation by means of repeated chantings of the sacred name of Amida (*Namu-Amida-Butsu*) and ninety days of attentive and ceaseless contemplation of Amida and his Pure Land. This method of meditation had been introduced into the T'ien-t'ai sect by Chih-kai from the Chinese Pure Land school founded by Hui-yüan (A.D. 334–416) at Mount Lu-shan.

Later, Ennin (Jikaku Daishi: A.D. 793–864), the successor of Saichō, brought back this method of *samâdhi* from the Mount Wu-tai-shan seminary in China and built his own seminary at Mount Hiei.[15] The *Jōgyō-jōza-zammai* and its Nembutsu practices gradually influenced the temples and priests of the Tendai sect.[16] In the middle of the

[13] *Jōgyō* means a practice done while incessantly moving around, and *jōza* means practice done while sitting immobile.

[14] This should be translated "Sutra on the *samâdhi* called *pratyutpanna* (etc.)," *Pân-keu-sân-mêi-kin* in Chinese. *Nanjō Catalogue:* No. 73, translated into Chinese by K'leu-kiâ-khân of the Eastern Han dynasty.

[15] This *samâdhi* method was also called *in-zei* Nembutsu after the repetition of Nembutsu in a singsong tone; or *fudan* Nembutsu after the incessant chanting of Nembutsu; or *yama-no-Nembutsu* (Nembutsu of the mountain) because this Nembutsu had originated at one of the seminaries of Enryaku-ji on Mount Hiei, near Kyoto. See Ennin, *Nittō guhō junrei-kō ki* (*Ennin's Diary: The Record of a Pilgrimage to China in Search of the Law*). An English translation has been published with annotations by Edwin O. Reischauer (New York, 1955). See also Reischauer, *Ennin's Travels in T'ang China* (New York, 1955); Hori, *Wagakuni minkan-shinkō-shi no kenkyū,* II, 253–54.

[16] It is said that in A.D. 865 this Nembutsu practice became one of the annual rites of the Tendai sect and was observed unceasingly from the dawn of the eleventh to midnight of the seventeenth of the eighth month of the lunar calendar, thus centering on the harvest moon. See Hori, *Wagakuni minkan-shinkō-shi no kenkyū,* II, Part II, "Shoji Jōgyō-dō

Heian period, the most popular daily practices of Tendai temples and priests were samâdhi based on the Lotus Sutra (Hokke-zammai) in the morning and the Nembutsu-zammai in the evening—that is, chanting the sacred title of the Lotus Sutra in the morning (Asa-Daimoku) and repeating the sacred name of Amida in the evening (Yū-Nembutsu).[17]

Although originally Nembutsu-samâdhi had as its object salvation in the future life, it gradually expanded its function to become a memorial service for spirits of the dead, with the expectation that Amida's helping hands would be extended to them. Thus, professional Nembutsu priests and Nembutsu prayers became connected with the funeral ceremony as well as with memorial services.[18]

As I have already pointed out in Chapter I, from the very beginning, one of the main social functions of Japanese Buddhism on the common level has been religious services for spirits of the dead as well as for divine favors in this world.[19] Even today there remain many statues of

no konryū to fudan-Nembutsu no seikō ("The Buildings of the Jōgyō-dō Seminaries at Buddhist Temples and the Popularizing of Continuous Nembutsu"), 255–56.

[17] Rozan-ji Engi in Dai Nippon Bukkyō zensho, Vol. CXVII (Tokyo, 1912–22); Hōnen Shōnin gyōjō ezu (The Diagram of the Biography of Hōnen Shōnin) in Jōdo-shū zensho, Vol. XVI (Tokyo, 1911–14). See also Hori, Wagakuni minkan-shinkō-shi no kenkyū, II, p. 256.

[18] Hori, Wagakuni minkan-shinkō-shi no kenkyū, II, pp. 255–56.

[19] Immediately after Prince Shōtoku's death, his survivors made two mandala called Tenju-koku mandara (Mandala of the land of heavenly life), where they believed that Prince Shōtoku had been reborn. On the back of the halo of the bronze statue of the Sakya-muni Buddha dedicated to Prince Shōtoku, which is now standing in the main hall of

buddhas or bodhisattvas, dating from as early as A.D. 606, with inscriptions for spirits of the dead. There are also buddha halls and handwritten copies of Buddhist sutras dedicated to the spirits of the dead and offered as prayers for the salvation of the dead in the afterlife.[20] From the seventh century to the end of the Nara period several Pure Lands are mentioned.[21] However, under the influence of the Tendai sect, in the mid-Heian period Amida's Western Pure Land occupied the predominant position among both the nobility and the masses, even though belief in the other Buddhas' Pure Lands also survived.

There are many examples from the sources of that time.[22] At the funeral procession for Emperor Daigo in

---

Hōryū-ji Temple, we find an inscription (presumably engraved in A.D. 621) stating that the survivors prayed that the spirit of Prince Shōtoku might go to the Buddha's Pure Land. See *Jōgū-Shōtoku-hōō teisetsu*. Takurei Hirako interpreted Tenju-koku as being identical to the Amida's Pure Land—that is, Muryōju-koku (Land of Everlasting Life), cited by Hanayama and Iyenaga in their commentary of *Jyōgū-Shōtoku-hōō teisetsu*, p. 82.

[20] Amida's Western Pure Land, Kannon or Avalokiteśvara's Southern Pure Land, Potalaka (Fudaraku in Japanese); Ashuku or Akṣobhya's Eastern Pure Land, Abhirati, Yakushi; Bhaisajyaguru's Eastern Pure Land, Vaidûryaprabha (Ruri-kō in Japanese); as well as the future Buddha Maitreya or Miroku's Tusita Heaven (Tosotsu-ten in Japanese) and the Vairocana's Padma-garbha-loka-dhâtu (Renge-zō-sekai in Japanese)—all of which were believed to be abodes of pious spirits of the dead. Before Hōryū-ji Temple was destroyed by fire in 1951, the famous wall paintings of the main hall showed the so-called Ten Pure Lands of the ten directions, presided over by the Ten Buddhas or Bodhisattvas. See *Jōgū Shōtoku-hōō teisetsu*, p. 82.

[21] Shinkō Mochizuki, *Bukkyō daijiten* (*Large Dictionary of Buddhism*) (Tokyo, 1933), III, 2699–702.

[22] *Ibid.* In A.D. 952 at the funeral services for the Emperor Sujaku (20th Day of the Eighth Month); in 1101 for the minister Fujiwara-

A.D. 930, professional Nembutsu priests, selected from among the Tendai priests, lined both sides of the street at eighty-six places where the funeral procession passed, repeating Nembutsu prayers for the deceased emperor's spirit and ringing special bells and gongs.[23]

When a sick person was near death, Nembutsu priests entered the sick room in place of the *shugen-ja* magicians or medicine men and offered their prayers to make his last moments easier. Then after death they prayed for the protection of the corpse, which might be in danger of disturbance by evil spirits, and for early rebirth of the spirit into Amida's Pure Land. During the period of mourning, which lasted for seven weeks, there was incessant repeating of the name of Amida as a memorial service. From the tenth and eleventh centuries there remain many written supplications for these memorial services on the forty-ninth day after death[24] offering up prayers to the Lotus Sutra and Amida for the salvation of the spirits of the dead.[25]

---

no-Morozane (described in *Denryaku* [*Diary of Fujiwara-no-Tadazane* (1078–1162)], twenty-two volumes of copies in Yōmei Bunko, presumably copied 1246–1268); in 1096 for Imperial Concubine Ikuhōmon-in (*Chūyū-ki* [*Diary of Fujiwara-no-Munetada: 1062–1141*], edited by *Shiryō taisei* [Tokyo, 1934–44]); in 1107 for the retired Emperor Horikawa. See Hori, *Wagakuni minkan-shinkō-shi no kenkyū*, II, pp. 450–51.

[23] *Rihōō-ki*, the diary of Prince Shigeaki (906–954), *Daigo-ji zōji-ki* (Tokyo, 1931), in the article of the Eleventh Day of the Ninth Month in A.D. 930.

[24] Hori, *Wagakuni minkan-shinkō-shi no kenkyū*, II, pp. 451–54.

[25] According to the famous *Written Opinion* (*Iken-fūji*) presented to Emperor Daigo by the Confucian scholar Kiyotsura Miyoshi in the tenth century, the memorial services on the forty-ninth day and on the first anniversary day were overvalued by the nobles and government officials as well as by the common people, leading to several bad results. Kiyotsura

❨ Awareness of the Arrival of the Latter Age of Buddha's Law (Mappō-tōrai) and a Pessimistic View of This Impure World (Onri-Edo)

In the Nara Period there was a sharp distinction between state Buddhism, which developed under the patronage and control of the government, and private or popular Buddhism. The attitude of the government toward private beliefs and practices was negative and suppressive. The popularization of Buddhism initiated by Gyōgi was frequently prohibited and suppressed, while En-no-Shō-kaku was said to have been exiled. Both these men, as I have pointed out, endeavored to distribute Buddha's gospel and Buddhistic mystical power to the common people. Many tried to become government priests by taking the state examination for licensure or to broaden their education by studying abroad. The *biku* (*bhiksu* in Sanskrit), or othodox Buddhist priest, was treated as a government official. Many state temples established by the government or by the imperial family included lands and peasants as an economic endowment. The bureau for re-

---

asked why it is necessary for the descendants to insure the rebirth of one's deceased father in Amida's Pure Land, even to the extent of incurring debts or of becoming bankrupt. We can realize from this how memorial services based on the worship of Amida and the Lotus Sutra flourished widely and presumably brought wealth to the Nembutsu practitioners. See Miyoshi-no-Kiyotsura (A.D. 847–918), *Iken jūnikajō* (*Written Opinion Consisting of Twelve Articles*) written in 914, published in *Gunsho ruijū*, Vol. XXVII (Tokyo, 1930).

ligious affairs in the government was called Sō-gō.[26] The headquarters for the state and large temples was called San-gō.[27] The government Buddhist priests acquired the religious and social status of their temple.[28]

Many state and clan temples were built for the sole benefit of their own supporting group, and gained political and economic independence. Their religious functions were never opened to the public. The interests of the priests in the state or clan temples, as well as those of the *gaku-sō* and *dai-shū* groups, likewise became more and more political and secularistic and less religious. The nobles of the Heian period were strongly superstitious. They feared revenge of the spirit of a dead enemy; they believed in necromancy and telepathy performed by female shamans and in divination based on astrology and the calendar as taught by professors of Yin-yang philosophy and magic (*Onmyō-hakase*).[29] Consequently, the reli-

---

[26] The *Sō-gō* consists of a *Sō-jō* (bishop), a *Sōzu* (sub-bishop) and a *Risshi* (head controller of disciplinary affairs). Afterward, these titles became only honorary ones given by the government to scholarly and outstanding Buddhist priests.

[27] The *San-gō* consists of three classes. The head of *San-gō* was called *Ji-shu* (head of the temple).

[28] Status could be improved by length of service after ordination as well as by study and merits. Among the government Buddhist priests, the so-called *gaku-sō* (literally, scholar monks) were many lower-class unordained priests who engaged in the practical affairs of managing the temples and buddha halls and serving the higher priests. One class, called the *dai-shū* or *shū-to* (literally, masses), sprang up in rivalry to the *gaku-sō* group. Afterward, this *dai-shū* or *shū-to* group seized power in certain temples and formed a great political and economic bloc against other politically powerful families. See Hori, "Wagakuni no gaku-sō kyōiku ni tsuite" ("On the Training of Scholarly Buddhist Monks in Japan"), *Nihon shūkyō-shi kenkyū* (Tokyo, 1963), II, 141–64.

[29] See Hori, *Wagakuni minkan-shinkō-shi no kenkyū*, II, 76–78.

100

gious functions of the gaku-sō were limited largely to scholarly discussions of the mysterious world of phantoms and to the performance of magic for rain, defeat of the enemy, recovery from illness, or easy childbirth.[30] The gaku-sō were honored by awards, donations, and promotions in ecclesiastical status extended to them by the emperor, nobles, or supporters.

Institutional Buddhism nominally opened its doors to the common people. Nevertheless, with the lapse of time, the princes, princesses, and children of noble families who went into the religious world generally occupied the higher ranks in the sects as well as in the temples. As a result, the state and the larger temples inevitably became more and more aristocratic, formalistic, and secularistic. Consequently, a person awakening to a real religious need, who wanted to live a life in pursuit of Buddhist truth and enlightenment as well as to distribute the Buddha's gospel to the common people, rejected the official Buddhist order. In other words, one had to retire again from the religious world. Consequently, and because of a widespread awareness of the arrival of the Latter Age of the Buddha's Law (Mappō), as well as because of the social disturbances and anxiety cropping up simultaneously with this consciousness, new religious movements and groups of hijiri (holy men) appeared.

The idea of Mappō, according to Anesaki,[31] was based on a group of predictions offering a pessimistic view of fate long fashionable among Buddhists. There were to be

30 *Ibid.*, 84–88.

31 Masaharu Anesaki, *History of Japanese Religion* (London, 1930, and Tokyo, 1963), pp. 131–33; See also Mitsusada Inouye, *Nihon Jōdo-kyō seiritsu-shi no kenkyū* (*A Study of the History of the Formation of Japanese Pure Land Sects*) (Tokyo, 1956).

three periods of deterioration in Buddhism after Sakya-muni's death. The first thousand years (or five hundred years, according to another tradition) constituted the period of the Perfect Law (in Japanese Shō-bō), in which monastic discipline would be perfectly observed. The second thousand years constituted the age of the Copied Law (in Japanese Zō-bō), in which true faith would decline but piety would be evidenced in the founding of numerous temples. Finally, the third period, that of the Latter Law (in Japanese, Mappō), to last another ten thousand years, would be an age of complete degeneration, full of vice and strife. This apocalyptic legend was almost universal in Buddhist countries. Since Chinese and Japanese Buddhists usually dated the Buddha's death as 949 B.C., they believed, either in apprehension or in hope, that the last period was to start in the year A.D. 1052.

It was Saichō who first awakened to the critical situation of Buddhism and society. He is credited with the book Mappō tōmyō ki (Light in the Latter Law Age),[32] though it is somewhat doubtful that it is really his work. The message of this book deeply influenced thoughtful persons, not only among the ecclesiastical monks,[33] but also among the intelligentsia and even the masses. The author gave warning of the arrival of the Age of the Lat-

[32] Saichō, Mappō tōmyō ki (*Light in the Latter Law Age*), in Nihon daizō-kyō (Tokyo, 1919–21), Vol. XL, Tendai Section No. 12.

[33] For example, see Genkū, *Wago tōroku*, a collection of Genkū's preachings, in Taishō daizō kyō (Tokyo, 1931), LXXXIII, No. 2611, 171–238; Yōsai (Eisai), *Kōzen gokoku ron* (*The Rise of Zen Buddhism as Guardian of the State*), in Taishō daizō kyō, LXXX, No. 2543, 6; Nichiren, *Shishin gohon shō* (*Four Kinds of Faith and Five Classes of Practitioners*), in Taishō daizō kyō, LXXXIV, No. 2696, 287; Shinran, *Kyōgyōshinshō* (*Doctrine, Practice, Faith, and Realization*), in Taishō daizō kyō, LXXXIII, No. 2646, 633.

ter Law in the near future and insisted on the necessity of accommodating the truths revealed in the Lotus Sutra to the character and needs of this degenerate age.

Thus the new *hijiri* movement stressed the essential importance of individual faith and unworldliness. This movement was from magico-religious and secular restriction to the spiritual freedom of individuals. It suddenly appeared in the latter part of the tenth and the early part of the eleventh centuries. Kōya, Jakushin, Genshin (known as Eshin-sōzu), and Ryōnin may be pointed out as representative *hijiri* among the Amidists. Zōga,[34] Shō-

[34] Zōga-hijiri was a famous scholar of the Tendai sect. However, he hated the secularism of the Tendai monasteries and escaped from Mount Hiei under pretense of madness, and at last settled in seclusion on Mount Tōno-mine. He never went down the mountain to Kyoto even when the emperor invited him. One day a concubine invited him so that she might receive the Buddhist initiation from him. He declined several times with thanks. The concubine, however, never gave up, having great respect for him. At last he made an exception and reluctantly consented. He went to her palace in Kyoto. However, he did not give her the commandments of Buddhism, but was eccentric in his conduct, indulged in remarks to induce her to leave him alone, and hurried home. Having completely abandoned all interest in this world, he died sitting in Buddhist contemplation and praying the Lotus Sutra. Many priests and laymen admired him for his personality and behavior, and contracted warm friendships with him. Among them were Shōkū, Genshin, and Jakushin. See *Hokke gen ki* (*Mysterious Legends Concerning Belief in the Lotus Sutra*), in *Zoku gunsho ruijū* (Tokyo, 1930), Vol. VIII, Upper Part, Chapter III; *Zoku ōjō den* (*Biographies of Persons Who Went to Amida's Pure Land after Death* [succeeding the *Nihon ōjō gokuraku ki*]), in *Gunsho ruijū* (Tokyo, 1930), Vol. V; *Konjaku monogatari* (*Legends Old and New*), in *Kokushi taikei* (Tokyo, 1931), Vol. XVII, Chaps. XII–XXXIII; *Uji shūi monogatari*, a collection of Japanese legends, in *Kokushi taikei*, Vol. XVIII, Chap. XII; *Washū Tōnominedera Zōga Shōnin gyōjō ki* (*Biography of Zōga Shōnin in Mount Tōnomine Temple*), in *Zoku gunsho ruijū*, Vol. VIII, Lower Part; see also Hori, "On the Concept of Hijiri (Holy-man)," pp. 205–6.

kū,[35] and others were *hijiri* from the Lotus Sutra school, though some different attitudes should be recognized between the two groups. Those of the Lotus Sutra school

[35] According to the biographies and legends concerning Shōkū, he acquired faith in Buddhism in his early days. However, it was not until he was thirty-six years of age that he joined the Buddhist priesthood. Then he stayed on Mount Kirishima and Mount Seburi in Kyushu, where he assiduously practiced the austerities of the Lotus Sutra, received mysterious power, and attained enlightenment. He finally came to Mount Shosha in present Hyōgo prefecture and built a Buddhist temple on the top of the mountain. His personality and deeds were extremely unusual, and there are many anecdotes about him. He composed a poem entitled "Kantei go" ("Words about the Secluded Retreat"):

> I, a hermit at a secluded retreat, am
> Poor and also humble;
> I am not ambitious for wealth and distinction,
> But love my own life;
> Though the four walls are crude,
> The Eight Winds cannot trespass on them;
> Though one gourd for wine is empty,
> The *samâdhi* is full to the brim spontaneously;
> I do not know anyone,
> There is neither slander nor praise;
> No one knows me,
> There is neither hatred nor affection;
> When I lie down with my head resting on my arm,
> Delight and happiness exist in it;
> For what purpose should I wish again for
> Unstable luxury which is like a floating cloud!

Many priests and laymen loved him for his virtues and visited him in order to receive his teaching and salvation. Among them were the retired Emperor Kazan, Fujiwara-no-Michinaga, Genshin, Jakushin, and others. A famous poem composed by Izumi-shikibu dedicated to Shōkū is:

> I who might pass from darkness to darkness
> To the Moon which is now coming out from behind the mountain,
> Oh! my Moon, please throw your light on me from afar!

See *Shōkū Shōnin den* (*Biography of Shōkū*) written in A.D. 1010, in *Gunsho ruijū*, Vol. V; *Shosha-zan Shōnin den* (*Biography of the Saint of Mount Shosha*), in *Chōya-gunsai*, which was said to have been writ-

were characterized by strict seclusion from both the secular and the ecclesiastical worlds, while the *Amida-hijiri* were characterized by a desire to proclaim Amida's gospel among the masses. The Lotus school *hijiri* was individualistic or self-perfectionistic; the *Amida-hijiri*, evangelistic.

There were two important reactions to the consciousness of crisis induced by the *Mappō* teaching. Helpless anxiety and despair largely overwhelmed orthodox Buddhist priests and the sophisticated upper class.[36] The forerunners of the new movements endeavored to find ways of self-enlightenment to cope with this hopeless and depraved age as a given reality, and strove for the salvation of the common people in their everyday life.[37]

---

ten by the retired Emperor Kazan, in *Kokushi taikei,* Vol. XXIX, Upper Part; *Hokke gen ki,* Chap. II, 45; *Konjaku monogatari,* Chaps. XII–XXIV. See also Hori, "On the Concept of Hijiri (Holy-man)," pp. 206–7.

[36] For example, Jichin (1155–1225), *Gukanshō,* a historical view of Japan, Vol. VII, in *Kokushi taikei,* Vol. XIV, pp. 609–16; Kōen (d. 1169), *Fusō ryakki* (*Chronicles of Japanese History*), Vol. XXIX, in *Kokushi taikei,* Vol. XII, p. 796; Fujiwara-no-Sanesuke (957–1046), *Shōyūki* (1023), in *Shiryō taisei* (Tokyo, 1934–35), 3 vols.; Fujiwara-no-Sukefusa (1007–1057), *Shun-ki* (1052), in *Shiryō taisei.*

[37] These leaders included Genkū (known as Hōnen Shōnin; 1133–1212) and Shinran (1173–1262), both followers of the Amidist group and its organizers; Eisai (1141–1215) and Dōgen (1200–1253), the transmitters of Zen Buddhism from China; and Nichiren (1221–1281), the successor of the Lotus school *hijiri* and the founder of the Nichiren sect. These all appeared in the twelfth and thirteenth centuries under the direct influence of the new movement and a consciousness of the arrival of the Latter Age. (See note 33, above.)

⟮ Emergence of the Nembutsu-hijiri or Amida-hijiri

The character of the *hijiri* was originally private and arbitrary, and always exhibited a negative attitude toward society, especially toward authority or social status. However, because the religious needs of the common people were not necessarily confined within the limits of the present world, the *hijiri*, with an anti-secularistic character and supra-mundane behavior and attitude, gained high esteem among those who were dissatisfied with official Buddhism. The personalities and conduct of a small group of early *hijiri* infused a fresh spirit into the religious world. Though their behavior seems somewhat eccentric at first glance, they never departed in the least from their unshakable faith in strict practices.

The pioneer of the *Nembutsu-hijiri* or *Amida-hijiri* was Kōya (popularly known as Kūya). Kōya had been an *upâsaka*, and belonged to the Tendai sect. According to the biographies written by his friends and followers, Yoshishige-no-Yasutane (Jakushin) and Minamoto-no-Tamenori, Kōya hid himself among the citizens of Kyoto, urging them to practice the Nembutsu. It is said that he was a son of the emperor, but he never revealed his identity. One day he descended from Mount Hiei, the location of the central headquarters of the Tendai sect where he had studied. He had found the mountain annoying and noisy but Kyoto quiet and peaceful and more conducive to his work. He was therefore called *Ichi-no-hijiri* ("*hijiri* in the city"). He continued to pray unceasingly

106

to Amida; thus he was also called *Amida-no-hijiri*. One of Kōya's biographers wrote that before he appeared there were few who had specifically practiced the *Nembutsu-zammai* in any of the temples or communities; further-more, the common people had avoided it. However, once Kōya appeared, praying the Nembutsu himself and strongly urging the people to pray to Amida, the whole nation was soon worshipping Amida. He also traveled through several provinces to distribute Amida's merciful gospel as well as to perform social welfare work. He died at the present Rokuhara-mitsu-ji temple in Kyoto in A.D. 972.[38]

In 984, twelve years after Kōya's death, Genshin was devoting himself to writing the famous work *Ōjō-yōshū* (*A Selection of Sacred Words Concerning Going to Amida's Western Pure Land.*)[39] Following the Nem-butsu-zammai founded by Ennin in the Tendai sect, Genshin lived in seclusion at Yogawa on the inner Mount Hiei—he despised honor and reputation in this world; there he made up his mind to practice the life of a *hijiri*. His work, his personality, and his scholarship exerted as far-reaching an influence on the nobles and intelligentsia as Kōya had on the common people. He started the *Mukae-kō* service, in which was performed a drama of the coming down of Amida, accompanied by many Buddhist

[38] Minamoto-no-Tamenori, *Kōya rui* (*A Tribute to the Memory of Saint Kōya* [written immediately after Kōya's death]), in *Gunsho ruijū*, Vol. VIII, Lower Part; Yoshishige-no-Yasutane (Jakushin, d. 997), *Nihon ōjō gokuraku ki*, in *Gunsho ruijū*, Vol. V.

[39] *Ōjō yōshū* consists of ten chapters, the first two being most famous because of the description of hell and paradise and which has been com-pared to Dante's *Divine Comedy* by some Japanese religious thinkers. It was published by Shinshō Hanayama with annotations (Tokyo, 1942). See also *Taishō daizō kyō*, Vol. LXXXIV, No. 2682.

saints and angels, to welcome the spirits of believers. It was enacted in the Pure Land Hall (*Gokuraku-dō* or *Amida-dō*), which is itself a symbolic model of Amida's paradise. Genshin also founded a religious association named *Nijūgo-zammai-kesshū*, the aim of which was to enable members to be reborn without fail into Amida's Pure Land as a result of the concentrated merit of Nembutsu said by like-minded persons.[40] In the preface to *Ōjō-yōshū*, he wrote that teachings and practices aimed at rebirth in Amida's paradise were best for the corrupt world of the Latter Age. Everyone—priest and layman, high and low—must be converted to faith in Amida's paradise; however, the Buddha's teachings were divided into apparent doctrines (in Japanese, *kengyō*) and secret doctrines (in Japanese, *mikkyō*), consisting of various theories and austerities. Although for the wise and diligent man it would not be difficult to understand and practice these several doctrines, the stupid and obstinate man, like Genshin, could be saved in the Latter Age only by invoking the name of Amida Buddha.[41]

These efforts of Genshin, together with Kōya's endeavors and Jakushin's movement to promote the virtues of Nembutsu among the common people as well as among the scholars and intelligentsia, had a deep influence on the Japanese people. As a result, there was an increase in the number of *hijiri* who practiced Nembutsu in the mountains around Mount Hiei as well as of lay *hijiri* (*zoku-hijiri*) in cities and rural communities.[42]

40 *Nijūgo zammai kishō*, written by Genshin in 986 and 988. See Hori, *Wagakuni minkan-shinkō-shi no kenkyū*, II, 284–88.

41 Preface to *Ōjō yōshū*, Iwanami Bunko edition, p. 19.

42 The legend of Kyōshin-hijiri or Kyōshin-shami was one of the models of such *zoku-hijiri* of the Nembutsu which had a far-reaching

Yoshishige-no-Yasutane, who called himself Jakushin after he took holy orders in Buddhism, lived at the same time as Kōya and Genshin. He was also known as *Naiki-no-hijiri* because he had formerly been a court official in the department of the secretariat (*Naiki*). After his conversion he began *Kangaku-e* meetings. Their aim was to allow students and professors of the state university in Kyoto and awakened scholarly Tendai priests to assemble once a month to discuss the theories of the Lotus Sutra in the daytime, to pray the Nembutsu in the evening, and to express their religious feelings in Chinese and Japanese poetry. In A.D. 985–986 he wrote *Nihon Ōjō-gokuraku-ki* (*Compiled Biographies of Persons Who Went to Ami-*

---

influence on Nembutsu practitioners in later ages. Kyōshin supported his wife and son by manual labor in a small farming village in present Hyōgo prefecture. He was converted to the Nembutsu belief and repeated the name of Amida incessantly day and night. Villagers nicknamed him Amida-maru (man of Amida). He died in a small hut repeating "Namu-Amida-Butsu." After he died, his corpse was fed to dogs, as he had willed. Several priests learned through dreams that the soul of Kyōshin had been welcomed into Amida's Pure Land. It was said that Shinran usually talked about the personality and behavior of Kyōshin as his model. Chishin visited the place of Kyōshin's death several times and wanted to die there. Afterward, the Noguchi Dai Nembutsu (Great Nembutsu Service at Noguchi) was dedicated to the memory of Kyōshin by Tan-amidabutsu, one of the Chishin's disciples, and it is practiced even today. See *Nihon ōjō gokuraku ki*; *ōjō jūin* (*Ten Causes for Rebirth in Amida's Land*) by Yōkan (1103), in *Taishō daizō kyō*, LXXXIV, No. 2683; *Goshūi ōjō den*, one of the biographies of persons who went to Amida's Land after death, by Miyoshi-no-Tameyasu (1049–1139), in *Gunsho ruijū*, Vol. VIII, Upper Part. *Genkō shaku sho*, biographies of Buddhist monks and the history of Japanese Buddhism, by Shiren (1287–1346) [1322], in *Kokushi taikei*, Vol. XXXI, Chap. IX; *Ippen hijiri e* (*Diagram of the Biography of Ippen Hijiri*), Chaps. IX and XI, in *Zoku gunsho ruijū*, Vol. IX, and in *Dai Nippon bukkyō zensho*, Vol. LXIX; *Gaija-shō*, a book of a convert to the true teachings of Shinran, by Kakunyo (1270–1351), in *Shinshū seiten zensho* (Tokyo, 1907).

da's Pure Land after Death). He recorded his intention in the preface:

> I had already prayed to Amida in my youth; however, after I was forty years old, my belief in the Nembutsu became more and more ardent. Therefore I chant the name of Amida with my mouth, and meditate on Amida and his Pure Land in my mind. These practices I have never forgotten in any moment of my daily life, not even for an instant. Wherever there are temples and halls in which the statues of Amida are enshrined, or where there are mandala of the Pure Land, I have worshipped without exception. I have formed a pious connection with all those who have an intention to be reborn in Amida's Pure Land—whether laymen or priests, men or women, without exception.[43]

Jakushin's legendary life was full of eccentricities. For example, he wandered about the country strongly urging people to embrace Nembutsu as well as to attend Buddhist masses. He always loved animals—even fat horses and bulls. When he saw temples, Buddha halls, pagodas, or stupas on his route, he never failed to get off his horse and worship at them piously. One day, the biographer says, he was invited to visit the home of one of his disciples, but he did not come until sunset. The host, wondering why he did not arrive, went to search for him. The disciple found him in a graveyard along the road. He was worshipping at each tomb, shedding tears and offering Nembutsu for the spirit of each of the dead.[44]

43 Preface to Nihon ōjō gokuraku ki, in Gunsho ruijū, V, 394.

44 Zoku honchō ōjō den (Succeeding Biographies of Persons Who Went to Amida's Land after Death), by Ōe-no-Masafusa (1041–1111), in Gunsho ruijū, Vol. V; Konjaku monogatari, Vol. XIX; see Hori, "On the Concept of Hijiri," p. 204.

❲ *The Belief in Goryō*

The belief in spirits of the dead which flourished in the Heian period seems to have had some connection with the ancient *hito-gami* type of belief already discussed in some detail in the previous chapters. Perhaps in the ancient theocratic ages it was permitted only for the spirits of persons of special political or magico-religious families to reappear in this world as powerful *hito-gami* (man gods). However, the ancient social order collapsed under the strong influence of Chinese and Korean immigrants and the Chinese civilization brought by them. Individual self-consciousness emerged under the influence of Buddhism, which taught both the equality of human beings regardless of social status and the innate existence of Buddha-ness (*Busshō* in Japanese) in every individual. As a result, the primitive concept of the human soul as well as the belief in *hito-gami* were gradually transformed in content and character. It may also be presumed that the consciousness of the shamans and priests who first revealed the *hito-gami* and served them was transformed in various ways.

By the end of the Nara period and throughout the Heian period superstitious and animistic beliefs were prevalent among the nobility as well as among the masses, and the magico-religious needs of the times made welcome the Mantrayâna magic brought by Saichō and Kūkai in a new and powerful form. As a result, the Tendai and the other sects were gradually "mantrayanized" by Saichō's successors, such as Ennin and Enchin (Chisō

Daishi: A.D. 814–891). The most significant of these superstitious and animistic beliefs was the belief in goryō. Found at the basis of popular beliefs in the early Heian period, this belief possibly originated in the ancient belief in *hito-gami* of the shamanic and charismatic folk religion, and under the influence of Buddhism and Yin-yang or religious Taoism was transformed into belief in individual evil spirits of the dead.

Though this belief may be only a survival or transformation of old folk religion, it seems to me that the flourishing belief in goryō at that time should be considered important in the history of Japanese religion, because many heterogeneous elements of foreign religions commingled around this belief, each taking a share in religious activities against the malevolent spirits of the dead. Usually the Tendai or Shingon Mantrayâna ascetics (*shugen-ja*) and shamanesses or their substitutes played the main roles. Shamanesses would announce the names and declare the will of the spirits of the dead in time of famine, epidemic, drought, flood, the falling of a thunderbolt, personal illness, evil dreams, and difficult childbirth. In order to soothe such revengeful and angry evil spirits, there was a reburial of their remains, a posthumous award of honorific name and court rank, and Shinto, Yin-yang, and Buddhist services. We must note that this belief provoked serious reflection on the part of those who achieved victory as well as consolation for the defeated, whose future vindication was assured.

By A.D. 863 there had already come into existence five major goryō-shin deities: the spirits of two disenthroned crown princes, the real mother of one of these princes, and two ministers who had suffered martyrdom. At this time epidemics were frequent, and many people died.

Public opinion attributed this to the anger of the goryō. Consequently, the Goryō-e festival was held under the auspices of the emperor at the imperial garden. This festival included music and dances, sumō wrestling, horse racing, archery, as well as Shinto, Buddhist, and Yin-yang services to soothe these angry spirits.[45] Afterward, two Shinto shrines—Upper and Lower Goryō-jinja—dedicated to the eight goryō-shin deities were erected in Kyoto.

After Sugawara-no-Michizane (845–903)[46] had died at his place of exile in Kyushu, a rumor arose to the effect that his angry spirit might retaliate against his enemies. The crown prince died suddenly in 923; in 930, the imperial palace was struck by lightning, and several of the court officials who had overthrown Sugawara died of shock; the emperor was indisposed, and soon died. Then in 942 a shamaness possessed by the deceased Sugawara's spirit announced that these disasters had been willed by him. In 955 an inspired young child of a Shinto priest also announced the same divine message and proclaimed that the spirit of Sugawara had become the deity of disasters and a chief deity of the thunder demons. The imperial court, surprised by these divine messages and the public rumor, enrolled his angry spirit among the deities and dedicated to him a shrine, named the Kitano-jinja, in Kyoto.[47]

---

[45] *Sandai jitsu-roku* (*Official record of the reigns of three emperors* [Seiwa, Yōzei and Kōkō, from A.D. 858 to 887]), Chap. VII, in *Kokushi taikei*, Vol. IV.

[46] Sugawara-no-Michizane was a famous scholar and politician of that time. Emperor Uda promoted him to a responsible post in order to set him against the powerful Fujiwara family. After the emperor retired, his rivals slandered him before the new young Emperor Daigo and condemned him to exile in Kyushu.

[47] See Hori, *Wagakuni minkan-shinkō-shi no kenkyū*, I, 414–18.

The appearance of Sugawara's goryō marked the climax of this belief, and ushered in the so-called Goryō age. We can realize from the diaries, essays, and novels written by the nobles and intellectuals at that time how the people were in constant fear and anxiety over rampages of goryō. As Lady Seishōnagon, the author of the famous essay *Makura no sōshi*, had wisely pointed out, these trends in the religious world were the result of abuses in an age which never manifested sound-minded belief. The magical Buddhist priests and upâsaka-magicians, as well as the shamans and Yin-yang priests, actively promoted this trend in collusion with each other and also possessed the confidence of the troubled persons by means of their magic. They threatened the nobles' minds freely, leading them by the nose, for they could also give them relief from their troubles.

The appearance of the Way of Yin-yang (*Onmyō-dō*), under the leadership of the Kamo and Abe families, is surely explained by this milieu. Old forms of magic still remained, but in an extremely passive state. The Kamo and Abe professors divined the causes of disasters and interpreted portents by astrology and the sacred book *Yiking (The Book of Changes)*. At their suggestion, nobles practiced purification ceremonies, abstinence, confinement to their houses on unlucky days, movement in lucky directions, and so on.[48] Nevertheless, after everything is considered, it may be said that the magic of the Mantrayâna priests and ascetics was more up-to-date and mysterious, more positive and aggressive, than either folk Shinto or Yin-yang magic. The Buddhist magicians held the public confidence, for by their magic and prayers the evil spirits

[48] See Bernard Frank, *Kata-imi et kata-tagae, Étude sur les interdits de direction à l'époque Heian* (Tokyo, 1958).

of the dead announced by shamans and Yin-yang diviners could not only be exorcised and driven away but also saved and sent off to Amida's Pure Land.

As the belief in goryō became more and more widespread, the possibility of becoming a goryō or a deified spirit was gradually extended to even the common people. The will of an individual, especially in the last moments of life, was believed to be most effective toward his becoming a goryō and taking revenge on his enemies. The belief in a future life gave a sense of freedom from danger and of calm resignation to fate. It was through the attractiveness of this hope that shugen-ja and Nembutsu practitioners achieved great prominence.[49]

(*The Rise of the Nembutsu Practices against the Goryō*

On the popular level, belief in goryō seemed to effect a sudden rise in Nembutsu practices and prayers at the same time as the rise of the shugen-ja in the mountains. The cohesion of Nembutsu practice with practices based on the Lotus Sutra centering in the Tendai sect necessarily brought about the cohesion of Nembutsu practitioners with shugen-ja ascetics. Both together revolutionized the popular Japanese concept of the soul. It was then that the Nembutsu came to be one of the most powerful forms of protection against goryō, being able to send the spirits of the dead and evil spirits into Amida's merciful hands. The professional Nembutsu practitioners also gradually came to embrace some of the shugen-ja asceti-

[49] Hori, *Wagakuni minkan-shinkō-shi no kenkyū*, II, 457–70.

cism. The fact that Nembutsu practitioners and mountain ascetics were both called *hijiri* (holy men) by the common people should, I believe, be attributed to this common characteristic.

As the movement of the early *Nembutsu-hijiri* group led by Kōya, Genshin, and Jakushin became more and more popular and widespread, esoteric characteristics such as mystery, symbolism, asceticism, and the merit of numerous repeated prayers were introduced into Nembutsu practice.[50] These devotions, all based on the Amida sutras,[51] have as their object firm faith in salvation in the future life by means of such religious sentiments as were evoked by the masked procession of angels and bodhisattvas of the Pure Land, sweet music and dances, and the mimic play of the coming down of Amida to welcome the spirits of his believers. The *Amida-dō* halls dedicated to Amida Butsu inspired people by creating an image of Amida's Paradise.[52]

[50] For example, we can find such mysterious and symbolic elements in the *Mukae-kō* or *Geisetsu-e* service of Genshin, as well as in the *Shijū-hachi-kō* for the repetition of "Namu-Amida-Butsu" and the recitation of the Forty-eight Vows of Amida described in the *Larger Sukhâvati Sûtra*, the *Ōjō-kō* for rebirth in the Pure Land after death, the *Amida-kō* for praying to Amida; see *Larger Sukhâvati Sûtra* or *Buddhabhâshita-mahâ-yânâmitâyur-vyûha-sûtra, Nanjō Catalogue*: No. 863. (See note 9, above.)

[51] Hori, *Wagakuni minkan-shinkō-shi no kenkyū*, II, 304–7.

[52] For this purpose they were constructed and decorated in accordance with the descriptions in the sutras concerning Amida Butsu. They were usually called "Halls for the Coming Down of Amida" (*Geisetsu-dō*), "Illuminated Halls" (*Hikari-dô*), "Golden-colored Halls" (*Konjiki-dō*), or "Paradise Halls" (*Gokuraku-dō*). Many paintings and scrolls represented the circumstances of the Pure Land and the figure of Amida and his accompanying angels and bodhisattvas appearing from the Western Heaven to welcome believers. The former were called *Jōdo-mandara* or *Jōdo-hensō-zu*; the latter, *Raigō-zu*. When a person fell into a critical

The Nembutsu ascetics engaged in fasting, flaying the skin of the palm of the hand or the side of the feet, touching a flame directly to the palm, writing the Buddhist scriptures with one's own blood as ink, and self-amputation of fingers and toes in order to offer austerity to Amida as well as to testify to firm belief. Sometimes they sought death at their own hands by drowning, burning, or hanging, so that they might go directly to Amida's Pure Land by virtue of unusually strong will power. Some announced their intention in advance. Many persons gathered at the appointed place to witness the event, weeping and worshipping with adoration. They often experienced the illusion of seeing the five-colored clouds which came down from the Western Heaven or heard the melodious music which announced the descent of Amida to welcome the suicide Nembutsu ascetic.[53]

The chanting of Nembutsu in extended repetitions was also typical. For instance, Yōkan (or Eikan) was said to have practiced repeating the name of Amida ten thousand times a day in his youth. In the prime of life, he said it sixty thousand times a day without missing a single day.[54] One nun named Anraku repeated the Namu-Amida-Butsu prayer fifty thousand times on each ordinary day and one hundred thousand times on each festi-

---

condition, the Nembutsu priest let him take hold of the five colored strings attached to the hands of a golden statue of Amida in order to assure him directly of the welcome and salvation of the Buddha. This custom, called ito-hiki, flourished in the Heian period. Fujiwara-no-Michinaga died holding the five colored strings tightly and repeating the name of Amida. See ibid., II, 304–17.

53 Ibid., II, 307–10.

54 Shūi ōjō den; Genkō shakusho; Hori, Wagakuni minkan-shinkō-shi no kenkyū, II, p. 309.

val day.[55] Chōi of Kurama-dera temple counted the number of recitations of the Nembutsu with red beans from March, 1127, to August, 1141. His total number of repetitions during these thirteen years and five months reached 1,427.33 bushels (287 *koku* 6 *tō*). He also strongly urged the repeating of Nembutsu by worshippers and pilgrims, and counted their numbers by the fruits of the linden tree (Bodhendrum, the Tree of Enlightenment, which is sacred to Buddhists). The total count was said to be 17,653.053 bushels (3,557 *koku*).[56] Gansai, who lived near Asuka-dera temple in Nara prefecture, also counted the number of Nembutsu for fifteen years or more, and his total was 3,474 bushels (700 *koku*).[57] Again, Kyōshin repeated the Nembutsu prayer one hundred thousand times a day, and a million times a fortnight.[58]

On the other hand, it should be mentioned that there are several examples of brutal or impious persons who went to Amida's Western Paradise by virtue of only one saying of the name of the Buddha with a faithful mind at the moment of death.[59] Many legends tell us that even

[55] *Shūi ōjō den;* Hori, *Wagakuni minkan-shinkō-shi no kenkyū*, II, p. 309.

[56] *Genkō shakusho*, Chap. XII; Hori, *Wagakuni minkan-shinkō-shi no kenkyū*, II, p. 309.

[57] *Genkō shakusho*, Chap. XVII; Hori, *Wagakuni minkan-shinkō-shi no kenkyū*, II, p. 309.

[58] *Sange ōjō den*, one of the biographies of persons who went to Amida's Land after death, by Zenren (about 1139), in *Gunsho ruijū*, Vol. VIII; Hori, *Wagakuni minkan-shinkō-shi no kenkyū*, II, p. 309.

[59] Even brutal robbers or murderers could go to Amida's Paradise through only one utterance of "Namu-Amida-Butsu." See *Hosshin-shū*, a collection of legends of converts to the faith of Amida, by Kamo-no-

some professional Nembutsu priests who strived for numerous repetitions of the Buddha's name fell into evil after death because their attention had strayed just at the moment of death.[60] This idea, I am sure, indicates that the state of one's mind at the moment of death is paramount in determining one's destiny in the future life, just as the possibility of deification or of becoming a goryō was believed to have depended primarily upon a determined mind in the last moment of life. The common belief, and the foundation of the belief in goryō, was that nothing was impossible to a determined mind at the moment of death.

Even though the merit of quantity as over quality in Nembutsu practices has been discussed for a long time by scholars of the Pure Land sects,[61] this was not only a theological problem among professional priests but also a

Chōmei (1154–1216), in *Dai Nippon Bukkyō zensho*, Vol. CXLVII; *Nihon ōjō gokuraku ki; Konjaku monogatari;* and other legendary literature. Cf. Hori, *Wagakuni minkan-shinkō-shi no kenkyū*, II, pp. 310–11; 316–37 notes.

[60] Hori, *Wagakuni minkan-shinkō-shi no kenkyū*, II, pp. 310–11.

[61] The doctrine of "Once Calling" (*ichinen-gi*) and the doctrine of "Many Calling" (*tanen-gi*) were points of dispute among Genkū's disciples. Kōsai was a representative of the "Once Calling" school, while Ryūkan was of the "Many Calling" school. The former doctrine was based on the metaphysical concept of the identity of our soul with Buddha's as taught in Tendai and Avatansaka philosophies. Being adapted to the inclination of easygoing believers, it found a number of advocates and grew in influence but led to neglect of moral discipline. Others brought scrupulous formalism into the religion of piety and insisted on the necessity of "many" (i.e., constant) thoughts of Buddha. This doctrine also found some followers and was identified with the prevalent mechanical repetition of Buddha's name, especially in company with many fellow believers. See Anesaki, *History of Japanese Religion*, pp. 179–80.

common problem among people of the workaday world. Especially the emphasis on the possibility of salvation in the afterlife for even a dissolute, uneducated, or pagan person by only one chant of Nembutsu, if he had a firm and pious belief at the very moment of his death, opened the door of the Pure Land to all human beings. On the other hand, this doctrine was attended by many evils.

The Pure Land school and Nembutsu practices originated in the Tendai sect, but were promoted and developed by early *hijiri* groups. They were later gradually transmitted through various sects such as Hossō, Sanron, Kegon, Ritsu, and Shingon. However, until Genkū founded the Jōdo sect after the teachings of Shan-tao in T'ang China, this movement was confined to an affiliated branch or to individual belief and practice within each sect.[62]

Concurrently with this movement, Nembutsu practices against the goryō were spreading among the masses. Famines, epidemics, civil wars, and fires were widely feared disasters among the people of the capital, Kyoto. Accord-

---

[62] The Nembutsu branch in the Tendai sect was founded by Ryōnin (1072–1132) in 1124 and afterward became the independent Yūzū-Nembutsu-shū sect. Integrating the Tendai and Kegon theologies with the teachings of the Chinese Pure Land school, Ryōnin systematized his own doctrine. He said that one person's faith and repetition of Amida's name included all other persons' merits, and all other persons' merits were transferable to one's own merits, so that all human beings could gain the benefit of rebirth into the Western Pure Land after death. This doctrine was based on the teachings of the Pure Land school, the "One-and-All" idea of the *Avatansaka-sûtra* and the "Salvation-for-All" idea of the Lotus Sutra. See *Goshūi ōjō den*, Chap. II; *Genkō shakusho*, Chap. XI; *Yūzū enmon-shō* (*Outlines of the Yūzū-Nembutsu Theology*) by Yūkan (1703), in *Dai Nippon Bukkyō zensho*, LXIV; see also Hori, *Wagakuni minkan-shinkō-shi no kenkyū*, II, pp. 291–94.

ing to documents and diaries[63] from the middle to the end of the Heian period, when famine and plague attacked Kyoto, the streets and river banks were covered with bodies of victims and there was no room to walk. As belief in goryō became more and more popular, disaster demons or deities, such as the god of plague, the demon of colds, the demon of thunderstorms, as well as the noxious insects causing famine, were gradually considered to be variations of the goryō. There were frequent demonstrations by popular Nembutsu practitioners or *hijiri*. They performed Nembutsu rituals as preventives against goryō who had become gods of plague or noxious insects on the one hand, and on the other they offered Nembutsu prayers for innocent victims who were believed to have a fair chance to become new goryō.[64]

[63] *Shoku Nihon kōki*, official records of the reign of Emperor Ninmyō from A.D. 833 to 850, in "The Article of A.D. 842," *Kokushi taikei*, Vol. III; Entry for A.D. 994 in *Honchō seiki* (*Uncompleted historical records from A.D. 935 to 1153*) compiled by Fujiwara-no-Michinori, in *Kokushi taikei*, Vol. IX; Entry for A.D. 1001 in *Nihon Kiryaku*, a historical record from Emperor Jimmu to Emperor Goichijō (compiled by an unknown author), in *Kokushi taikei*, Vols. X and XI, and *Gon-ki*, Fujiwara-no-Yukinari's diary: present written copies preserve the diaries from 991 to 1011 in complete form, in *Shiryō taisei* series; Entry for A.D. 1105 in *Chūyū-ki*, the diary of Fujiwara-no-Munetada; 1062–1141, in 7 vols., in *Shiryō taisei*; see Hori, *Wagakuni minkan-shinkō-shi no kenkyū*, II, pp. 459–61.

[64] Sometimes Nembutsu-hijiri advanced in the midst of battlefields to offer Nembutsu to the spirits of those who had fallen as well as to give dying soldiers assurance of salvation by Amida Butsu, urging them to pray the Nembutsu. According to a letter sent by Ta-a, who lived in Kamamura, at the defeat of the Hōjō forces at Kamakura in 1333, the battlefield resounded with repeated Nembutsu cries and prayers uttered by the soldiers of both sides under the influence of Nembutsu-hijiri of the Ji sect. Ta-a was a chief abbot of Yugyō-ji Temple in Fujisawa near Kamakura, which is still one of the headquarters of the Ji sect in the Jōdo school

Fear of spirits of the dead brought many ancient shamanistic ritual forms and customs into the popular Nembutsu practices. For example, dancing was reintroduced as a particular Nembutsu ritual form as a preventive against gods of plague. Musical instruments also appeared in the rituals. This became one of the most significant characteristics of popular Nembutsu practice, though some Buddhist scholars have explained that this custom might have come from a conventional phrase at the end of many Buddhist sutras: "All attendants, rejoicing and

---

founded by Chishin. This curious name—Ta-a—is an abbreviation of Ta-amidabutsu. The custom of this kind of ordained name—that is, "so-and-so-amidabutsu" was called Ami-gō or A-gō and was originated by Chōgen, one of the disciples of Genkū. He traveled about provinces soliciting contributions for the reconstruction of the Tōdai-ji Temple, which had been destroyed in the war. He also urged and favored Nembutsu practices among the masses. He struck on this idea which would force his followers to repeat Nembutsu: he called himself Namuamidabutsu. Then he began to give his disciples and followers the religious name of Amidabutsu, prefixing one word to it, such as Ta-amidabutsu, Kan-amidabutsu, Jō-amidabutsu. Later, these names were shortened to Ta-ami, Kan-ami, Jo-ami, or Ta-a Kan-a, Jō-a. Thereafter, these were called Ami-gō or A-gō, which were their title names as Amidabutsu. This idea rapidly came into fashion. There were already several priests named "so-and-so-amidabutsu," such as Ben-a and Nan-a, among the leading disciples of Genkū. Afterward, Chishin also accepted this idea and gave the name of Amidabutsu to his disciples. According to historical and ethnographical documents, we can find many such A-gō, not only among the Jōdo school's professional priests and popular Nembutsu-hijiri in villages, but also among retired village laymen, out-caste peoples, public entertainers, artists, and actors, as well as Yin-yang magicians and medical doctors. Even today there are several families whose names originated from this custom, such as Hon'ami, Tan'ami, Kōami. The name of Kanze, one of the master families of the Kanze school of the Nō play, also came from the names of their two great ancestors, Kan-ami and Ze-ami. The ancestor of the Tokugawas was said to be Toku-ami, who had been a priest of the Ji sect.

dancing at the teachings of Buddha, saluted him and went away." However, the form of dancing accompanied by music and songs sung in a circle around the central altar or symbol is thought to be a particular form of the ritual of ancient Shintoistic *Chin-ka-sai* or *Hana-shizume-no-matsuri* in such shrines as Ōmiwa, Sai, and Ima-miya —all of which were dedicated to deities of plague or great *hito-gami*.[65] It was believed that this ritual kept the blossoms from falling, and that the gods of plague would roam about and spread the epidemic with the falling of the blossoms. Hence, this ritual form originated in many of the shrines' own magic festivals connected with the gods of plague. Further, the *Michiae-no-matsuri* took place under the leadership of Shinto and Yin-yang priests, who entertained the gods of plague with dancing, singing, and music. They also offered several kinds of food on the public highways in order to check the advance of the gods of plague from the outside.[66]

These ancient and primitive ritual forms should not be thought unrelated to the customs surrounding ancient funeral rites.[67] Subsequently, these ritual forms were

[65] *Ryō no gige* (*Interpretation of Codes of Laws*), Chap. VI: "Kishun" ("Later Spring") in the chapter, "Jingi Ryō," which describes the annual Shinto festivals held in the imperial court or under the auspices of the Department of Shinto Affairs (*Jingi-ryō*), which was published in the *Kokushi taikei*, Vol. XXII. See Hori, *Wagakuni minkan-shinkō-shi no kenkyū*, I, 696–99.

[66] *Ryō no gige*, Chap. II; *Engishiki* (*Code of the Engi Era* [a code of laws and minute legal regulations of 927]), Chap. III: "Rinji-sai" ("Occasional Shinto Festivals Held under the Auspices of the Imperial Court and Government"), in *Kokushi taikei*, Vol. XXVI; see also Hori, *Wagakuni minkan-shinkō-shi no kenkyū*, I, 696–99.

[67] In the ancient Chinese ethnograpical documents such as *Wei-chih*, written in the third century A.D., the funeral customs in ancient Japan were described as follows: "When someone died, all family members

probably associated with the Buddhist ritual of walking in a circle around a central altar, sprinkling paper flowers, and chanting the sutras in order to exalt the Buddha's virtue (*sange-gyōdō* in Japanese). The new form of Nembutsu dancing (*Nembutsu-odori* or *odori-Nembutsu*)[68] came to flourish among the masses. *Odori-Nembutsu* was believed to have been created by Kōya, though there is no documentary evidence for this. However, Chishin, the founder of the Ji sect, introduced the popular *odori-Nembutsu* forms into his sect for the purpose of attaining religious ecstasy, bringing all his attention and energy to bear on the *odori-Nembutsu* prayer. He believed in the legend that *odori-Nembutsu* had been created by Kōya-hijiri.[69] In the early Kamakura period such magical Nembutsu arts became differentiated and transformed into various polite forms of music, singing, dancing, as well as sym-

---

observe mourning for about two weeks. During this period, the chief mourner cries and weeps, while the others sing and dance, eat and drink in the house of mourning. After this, the body is buried." According to the *Kojiki*, when Ama-no-Wakahito died suddenly by the Heavenly Arrow, the survivors and relatives gathered at the mortuary and held the *eragi* (crying, weeping, singing, and dancing). Moreover, in the *Nihongi*, when the creative goddess Izanami gave birth to the Fire kami, she was burned and died. She was, therefore, buried at the village of Arima in Kumano, in the province of Ki (Wakayama prefecture). The inhabitants worship this goddess by offerings of flowers. They also worship her with drums, flutes, flags, singing, and dancing. See Hori, *Minkan shinkō*, pp. 216–17.

[68] At first, Nembutsu-odori and odori-Nembutsu may have had the same meaning. Later, however, odori-Nembutsu meant professional dancing originally under the leadership of Nembutsu-hijiri. Nembutsu-odori meant dancing, dramas, music and so on, derived from odori-Nembutsu, but which had lost religious elements.

[69] *Ippen-hijiri-e*, Vol. IV; see Hori, *Wagakuni minkan-shinkō-shi no kenkyū*, II, 350–52.

bolic pantomimes and dramatic plays. According to the *Genkō-shaku-sho* (*Biographies of Buddhist Priests and History of Japanese Buddhism*) written by Shiren in 1321, many Nembutsu priests and priestesses of the lower class attended banquets to perform their Nembutsu singing and dancing, and thereby, together with the blind musicians and dancing girls, entertained the guests.[70]

❲ *Religious Reformation—*
Establishment of Pure Land Sects

The founders of the orthodox Pure Land sects rejected the animistic and magical Nembutsu which was flourishing among the masses, and insisted on a return to original forms, according to the teachings of the sutras and the theologies systematized by Chinese priests of these sects.

Genkū, known as Hōnen Shōnin, after having searched in the *Tripitaka* to find the best way to salvation in the latter age, discovered and was converted to the works of Shan-tao of the Chinese Pure Land school as well as to the works of Genshin and Yōgan (1032?–1111).[71] Genkū abandoned and criticized the way for the wise (*Shōdō-mon*) of severe training, intricate ritualism, methodic contemplation, and belief in salvation by one's own

[70] "Dancing girls" is used for convenience. At that time they were called *shirabyōshi* or *keisei*, which means professional female dancers in white robes or medieval courtesans.

[71] Yōgan (or Eikan; 1032–1111) was abbot of the Zenrin-ji monastery of Kyoto and wrote a work called *Ōjō-jūin* (*The Ten Conditions for Attaining Rebirth in Paradise*). Among the conditions he emphasized not only the protection of Amida but also meditation and good works. See Eliot, *Japanese Buddhism*, p. 253.

power (*jiriki*) and in the Buddhist and Shinto pantheons (*zō-gyō*). He taught that the way to the Pure Land is necessarily through simple faith in Amida's grace, called the easy way of salvation. This is in contrast to the difficult way of perfection. The easy way is also called salvation by another's power (*tariki*). Genkū inevitably alienated himself from the complicated teachings and practices of the prevailing forms of Buddhism, and finally came to declare his independence and to achieve thereby a religious reformation.[72]

His major work establishing the independence of his Jōdo-shū sect is the *Senjaku-hongan-Nembutsu-shū* (*On the Nembutsu of the Original Vow*),[73] written in 1198 (or 1204). But the most intense statement of his belief and teaching is to be seen in his last handwritten essay, *Ichimai kishō-mon* (*One Sheet of Paper Expressing Genkū's Final Enlightenment*):[74]

What I teach is neither a sort of meditation such as has been spoken of by many priests both in China and in our own country nor is it an invocation such as is possible only to those who have grasped by thought its real meaning. No, all that is needed to secure birth in the Paradise of perfect bliss is merely to repeat the words Namu-Amida-Butsu without a doubt that one will certainly be saved. Such details as the three states of mind and the fourfold practice[75] are all included in

[72] See Anesaki, *History of Japanese Religion*, pp. 170–71.

[73] See in *Taishō daizō kyō*, Vol. LXXXIII, No. 2608.

[74] See in *Jōdo-shū zensho*, Vol. X (Tokyo, 1911–14). Translation in Eliot, *Japanese Buddhism*, p. 267.

[75] The three states of mind are: (1) a most sincere heart; (2) a deep-believing heart; and (3) a longing heart which offers in the hope

the repetition of the words Namu-Amida-Butsu with
perfect faith. Had I any other profound doctrine besides
this, I should miss the mercy of the two Holy Ones[76]
and have no share in the vow of Amida. But those who
believe in the power of calling on the Buddha's name,
though they may have thoroughly studied all the doc-
trines which Shaka taught in the course of his whole
life, should behave like a simple man of the people who
cannot read a word or like an ignorant nun, and with-
out giving themselves airs of wisdom should simply fer-
vently call on the name of the Buddha.

Here we can see clearly Genkū's intentions: rationalization and simplification of religious theory and form; con-
centration of religious piety in pure and simple faith; the
rejection of overspeculation and ritualism; emphasis on
salvation for the lowest level of the people.

He organized his sect along lines quite different from
the other Buddhist sects. This was due to the religious
heritage of the early *hijiri* groups, which had been anti-
secular and *upâsaka*-istic. Genkū never built one temple
of his own. He believed and declared that any place where
people practiced Nembutsu—any small farmer's or fish-

---

of attaining paradise any merits it may have acquired. The point is that
ōjō or birth in paradise can be obtained merely by personal merit and
without faith in Amida, but that any merit one may have obtained
should not be devoted to any other object. The four-fold practice, as
prescribed by Zendō, is (1) to treat images and other sacred objects with
profound reverence; (2) to practice the repetition of the Nembutsu only;
(3) to practice it continuously and, if any sin has been committed, at
once to purify the heart by uttering it; and (4) to observe the above
three rules continuously throughout one's life. See Eliot, *Japanese Buddhism*, p. 267, and note 2.

[76] Two Holy Ones are Sakyamuni and Amida Buddha.

erman's hut where a few persons gathered to pray and repeat the name of Amida—was his temple or seminary.

Genkū's principle had strong influence on reformative movements of Buddhism, as well as on Shinto, in the Kamakura period. Among his followers, Shinran advanced Genkū's theory several steps, though he had been a pious pupil of Genkū and intended sincerely to succeed him and distribute his gospel. Shinran said that his sole reason for repeating the Nembutsu lay in the teaching of the good man (Genkū) who made him understand that it is the only condition of salvation.[77]

According to Shinran, human nature is originally so sinful and hopeless and the situation of time and society so absolutely confused that no one could attain spiritual enlightenment and peace by his own power, but must throw himself on the Other's mysterious power. Therefore, the original vow of Amida, expressing the desire to save without exception even the lowest and most wicked person, should be the one and only foundation for salvation of individuals in the latter age. His famous ironical expression—"Even a good man will be received in Buddha's Land; how much more a bad man!"—played upon a saying of the regular Amidists—"Even a bad man will be received in Buddha's Land; how much more a good man!" Neither virtue nor wisdom, but faith was his fundamental tenet, and faith itself has nothing to do with our own intention or attainment but is solely the Buddha's free gift.[78] Calling Buddha's name in pious devotion and absolute trust in Amida are the way to salvation, but

[77] *Tannishō*, written by a disciple of Shinran, Yui-en (around 1288), Section II, following the translation in Eliot, *Japanese Buddhism*, p. 270.

[78] *Tannishō*, following the translation in Anesaki, *History of Japanese Religion*, pp. 182–83.

there is no value whatsoever in theorizing about the actual process of invocation.

Shinran carried the idea of Genkū to the extreme of simplicity in his doctrine of once calling (*ichinen-gi*), though Kōsai and others among Genkū's disciples also advocated it.[79] Shinran was far from rejecting repetition of the Nembutsu, but he held that the essential thing was to say the prayer with full faith and confidence in the Buddha, and that one such believing utterance is sufficient to secure birth in Amida's land. All subsequent repetitions are to be regarded simply as expressions of joy and gratitude. Shinran strictly denied the formal temple-and-priest system of his time, following his teacher Genkū's principle as well as the tradition of the Amidist movement. He never lived in a temple but in huts or small hermitages, mainly in the East Province far from Kyoto, and preached his doctrine among the country people. He married, reared a family, and in every way lived like a normal citizen or farmer. He wrote many books, of which his major work, *Kyōgyōshinshō* (*Teaching, Practice, Faith, and Attainment*),[80] became the foundation of the Jōdo-shin sect. He also composed the *Wasan* (*Colloquial Hymns*) in the Japanese alphabet (*kana*). He seems to have favored the use of *kana* script and the national language as being more intelligible to the uneducated. Shinran severely criticized ritualism, magic, divination, and the worship of the old pantheon. The worship offered to Amida did not consist of prayers for health or temporal welfare or any petitions. After a

[79] See note 61, above.

[80] *Kyōgyōshinshō* was the major work of Shinran on which the Jōdo-shin sect was founded. The formal title is *Ken-jōdo-shinjitsu-kyō-gyō-shōmon-rui*, in *Taishō daizō kyō*, Vol. LXXXIII, No. 2646.

man has once obtained faith in Amida, he commits all to his power, and his worship consists of nothing but thanksgiving.[81]

Chishin later organized the Ji sect, which advocated pilgrimages for itinerant priests from village to village and from temple to shrine in order to disseminate Amida's gospel to the masses as well as to offer Nembutsu practices to the deities and the buddhas or bodhisattvas. Likewise, he never built his own temples, declaring that the edifices of Buddhist priests should be nothing but their bodily remains. Chishin's own religious activities were carried out by means of such pilgrimages, and he himself died as an itinerant. His principal headquarters was named Yugyō-ji (literally, "temple for itinerant priests"). By an unwritten law of this temple, the abbot was to go on a pilgrimage throughout Japan and die during the course of his pilgrimage. If he died in a temple, he must breathe his last breath in the garden wearing his pilgrim's costume.[82]

[81] Shinran composed many wasan among which were *Sanjō-wasan* consisting of three parts: *Jōdo-wasan*, composed of 118 wasan; *Kōsō-wasan*, a collection of hymns of the seven great masters of the Pure Land school: Nāgarjuna, Vasubandhu in India; Tan-Luan, Tao-ch'o, Shan-tao in China; Genshin and Genkū in Japan, composed of 117 wasan; finally *Shōzōmatsu-wasan* (*Wasan of Perfect, Copied, and Latter Law Ages*) describing the changes which will come upon the Perfect Law in the lapse of centuries, which included 108 wasan. See in *Taishō daizō kyō*, LXXXIII, No. 2650–52. See also E. J. Jurji (comp.), *The Great Religions of the Modern World* (Princeton, 1946), p. 134; Zennosuke Tsuji, *Nihon Bukkyō-shi* (*The History of Japanese Buddhism*), Medieval Period, No. 1 (Tokyo, 1948), pp. 368–69, 396–98, 401; Hori, *Wagakuni minkan-shinkō-shi no kenkyū*, II, 327–36.

[82] *Ippen-hijiri-e*; cf. Hori, *Wagakuni minkan-shinkō-shi no kenkyū*, II, 337–52.

⟨ Differentiation and Survival of Popular Nembutsu

As has been pointed out, the three founders of the Japanese Pure Land sects strongly denied animistic and magical Nembutsu beliefs and practices. However, in spite of the efforts of these outstanding religious leaders, the feelings of the masses concerning the Nembutsu seem not to have changed greatly. The Nembutsu was still considered a religious practice for going to Amida's Pure Land after death on the one hand, and on the other was requested as magic for celebrating or sending evil spirits into Amida's merciful hands. Nembutsu practitioners were sometimes treated on the same level as magicians performing against malevolent spirits of the dead.

Even Genkū himself, who is now considered the pioneering reformer of Japanese Buddhism, was welcomed as a magical Nembutsu practitioner by contemporary nobles. His most powerful patron, Fujiwara-no-Kanezane, the chief adviser of the emperor and a person who well understood his intentions, frequently invited Genkū for prayer and exorcism on behalf of sick persons. Kanezane also sometimes discussed the Amidist way of salvation with Genkū. Genkū is said to have dedicated to Kanezane his life work, *Senjaku-shū*.[83]

The later *Nembutsu-hijiri* became minority groups,

[83] Gyokuyō, a diary of Fujiwara-no-Kanezane; 1149–1207, in 1189, 1191, 1197 and 1200; Shinkō Mochizuki, *Jōdo-kyō no kenkyū* (A Study of the Pure Land School) (Tokyo, 1944), pp. 628–31; Tsuji, *Nihon Bukkyō-shi*, Medieval Period, I, 303–5; see also Hori, *Wagakuni minkanshinkō-shi no kenkyū*, II, 322–23, 457–58.

such as: *Sammai-hijiri* (*hijiri* who serve the graveyard), *Ji-shū* (*Roku-ji-Nembutsu-shū: Nembutsu* practitioners of six times a day), *Kane-uchi-hijiri* (*hijiri* who beat a gong or bell), *Hachi-ya* or *Hachi-tataki* (*hijiri* who beat a bowl or gong), *Chasen* (*hijiri* who make tea whisks), *Sasara* (*hijiri* who make bamboo whisks as musical instruments), *Nebutcho* (originally perhaps *Nembutsu-shū*), *Nama-dango* (originally from *Namu-Amida-Butsu*), *Jan-bon* (originally from the sound of the gong). These groups settled down in or around farming and fishing villages and near cemeteries as well as in large temples and shrines. Until recent times, they performed the same magical and religious functions as the lower-class priests or beggars—funeral services, memorial services, and magical techniques—exemplifying a change from *sacré pur* to *sacré impur*, following Durkheim's terms.[84] Some of them, having dropped their Nembutsu functions, were degraded to the status of the lowest-class people who engaged in home manufacture of the *chasen* (tea whisk), *sasara* (bamboo whisk), or other bamboo wares such as baskets, spatulas, ladles, or sandals—techniques believed to have been transmitted from the Kōya-*hijiri*. Some served as sentries on festival days, as detectives, or in miscellaneous capacities at funeral rites. Others made visitations from door to door to give blessings, recited traditional songs or sentences, and danced at the end and beginning of the New Year and the Bon festivals.[85] Some groups, composing and transmitting *Nembutsu-odori* (Nembutsu

[84] Émile Durkheim, *Les formes élémentaires de la vie religieuse* (Paris, 1912).

[85] See Hori, *Wagakuni minkan-shinkō-shi no kenkyū*, II, 380–84 (*Hachi-ya*); pp. 385–87 (*Chasen*); pp. 398–90 (*Sasara*); pp. 390–95 (*Kane-uchi*); pp. 432–40 (*Hachi-tataki*).

dancing) and dramas, became professional actors or puppet performers.[86]

Odori-Nembutsu still survives throughout Japan clus-
tered around several centers,[87] and many annual festivals

[86] For example, in the northern Kyushu villages there were several
famous semi-professional folk Nembutsu players and actors. The Nembutsu dramas played by them were called Ashiya-Nembutsu, Ueki-Nem-
butsu, Jichū-Nembutsu, Jika-Nembutsu, and so on, depending on the
name of their place of origin. (See *ibid.*, II, 382, 423.) The Kabuki play
is said to have been founded by a famous female Nembutsu dancer named
Okuni in the present Shimane prefecture (Izumo) and a male actor
named Fuwa Sanza. See Tatsuyuki Takano, *Nihon engeki-shi* (*History of
Japanese Drama*), 2 vols. (Tokyo, 1947 and 1948); Kiyonori Konaka-
mura, *Nihon kabu ongaku ryaku-shi* (*Short History of Japanese Drama
and Music*) (Tokyo, rev. ed., 1899).

Uta-Nembutsu (literally, singing Nembutsu) was supposed to have
originated in the Inzei-Nembutsu mentioned above, together with the
Odori-Nembutsu prayer. This was performed by special Nembutsu
priestesses or, originally, Nembutsu shamanesses called uta-bikuni (singing nuns), who distributed Amida's gospel to the masses in the form
of melodious religious songs and hymns. Afterward, some of them became
secular ballad singers, while others gradually were degraded to the status
of itinerant beggars or prostitutes. Hori, *Wagakuni minkan-shinkō-shi no
kenkyū*, II, 698–703.

[87] For example, in Kyoto there are the Jika-Nembutsu-odori, the Tōrō-
odori, the Hanazono-odori, the Daimoku-odori, and the Nembutsu-odori,
all of which were performed at the Bon festival in the seventh month
of the lunar calendar and in the wake of the ancient Odori-Nembutsu.
In Nara there is the Kyōki-Nembutsu-odori (literally, the fanatic Nembutsu-odori); in Shikoku Island, the Namoude-odori (originally Namu-
Amida-odori); in Ibaraki and Chiba prefecture, the Tendō-Nembutsu-
odori; in Tokyo and Saitama prefecture, the Kasai-Nembutsu-odori
(Nembutsu-odori originated from Kasai), or Hōsai-Nembutsu-odori
(Nembutsu-odori created by Hōsai-bō); in Fukushima prefecture, the
Jingara-Nembutsu-odori (jingara, from the sound of a gong or bell) or
Yūten-Nembutsu-odori (Nembutsu-odori created by Yūten Shōnin); and
in Kyoto prefecture the Rokusai-Nembutsu-odori (literally, the Nem-
butsu-odori on the six festive days of the month). It is said that the
Kashima-odori, widespread in southern Kantō and eastern Shizuoka

have developed from it. Among them, the most popular is the *Mushi-okuri-Nembutsu* ("Nembutsu for sending off noxious insects"). The villagers usually perform the million Nembutsu prayers (*Hyakuman-ben Nembutsu*) to the accompaniment of drums, gongs, and flutes under the leadership of a *Nembutsu-hijiri* or of pious village elders. This practice was sometimes held in order to pray for rain or to ward off the demons of plague and colds.[88] The Bon festival is held especially for the seasonal return of the ancestral spirits and of all spirits of the dead. Among the many spirits are believed to be souls of those who died leaving no relative behind as well as hungry or angry souls. Following this belief, two special altars are prepared in the Bon festival: one for ancestors, and the other for souls with none to provide spiritual benefits. It is called *Gaki-dana* ("altar for hungry spirits"). Farmers in ancient times thought of this, not only as a crisis period in which the agricultural processes were suspended, but also as a time of crisis for the farmers themselves, who had a consciousness of and belief in their own coexistence with rice plants. The *odori-Nembutsu* was specifically requested and performed during this season. *Bon-odori* (*Bon* festival dances), one of the most popular and widespread annual functions in Japan, may have been transmitted from the *odori-Nembutsu*, which originally were learned from the *Nembutsu-hijiri*. Even today in some areas the *Bon-odori* is performed for the spirits of those who had died in the past year as well as

provinces, also originated from the Odori-Nembutsu intended to ward off the *goryō* or gods of plague. (See Hori, *Wagakuni minkan-shinkō-shi no kenkyū,* II, 422–40.)

[88] Hori, *Wagakuni minkan-shinkō-shi no kenkyū,* II, pp. 410–21; 422–31.

for those whose death was untimely. This is done under the leadership of the *Nembutsu-hijiri* or the temple priests. Thus, we can see the many survivals of ancient primitive belief in *goryō* which lie behind the rites of the Bon festival.[89]

Among the most predominant schools of Buddhism, Tendai, Shingon, and Zen have been accepted by the upper classes and intelligentsia, while the *Shugen-dō*, *Nembutsu* (Pure Land schools), and *Nichiren* sects have flourished among the common people. The *Shugen-dō* sect and the Pure Land schools, especially, had deep roots among farmers and fishermen as well as among the out-castes. Thus, the *hijiri*, differentiating and degenerating in various directions, became the most popular religious leaders in the rural communities from the Heian period to modern times. Of course, their merits and their shortcomings may be balanced against each other in Japanese spiritual and cultural history. Nevertheless, their influence on the Japanese common people is so strong and so deep that we cannot discuss Japanese folk beliefs and popular religion without considering the activities of *hijiri* in the long history of Japanese religion.

[89] *Ibid.*, II, 457–70.

CHAPTER
IV

Mountains and Their Importance for the Idea of the Other World

ɞɞɞJapan has a highly complicated mountain worship which has developed along diverse lines and become widespread. Edward Morse, a pioneer of Japanese archeology and natural history, wrote that he was much impressed upon observing that almost every high mountain has its own shrine and that some of them are piously worshipped by thousands of people who climb there in summer after many miles of arduous travel.[1]

Mountain worship is intricately involved with Japanese history. On the one hand, there still survive some elements of ancient naturalistic beliefs. On the other, the syncretistic Shugen-dō sects were institutionalized under the strong influence of Mantrayâna Buddhism of the

[1] Edward Morse, *Japan Day by Day* (Boston, 1917), I, 95.

Tendai (T'ien-t'ai in Chinese) and Shingon (Esoteric Buddhism, Chên-yen in Chinese) schools in the Middle Ages. Before the Meiji Restoration almost every Shinto shrine had its own Buddhist temple, called *jingū-ji* or *bettō-ji*, where services were conducted according to Buddhist custom by Buddhist priests, frequently by those of Mantrayanistic Tendai and Shingon schools. According to Mizoguchi's study,[2] more than 90 per cent of the village shrines in mid-northern and northeastern Japan were served by Shugen-dō priests, including mountain ascetics —*shugen-ja* ("exorciser"), *yamabushi* (literally, "priest who lies down on the mountain"), or *hōin* (honorary title for a Buddhist exorciser, meaning literally "seal of the law"). These priests were also in charge of sacred mountains and hills near villages and guided parishioners to such centers of the order as Mount Kimpu (Yoshino), Mount Omine, and Mount Kumano in Kinki province (middle Honshu); Mont Hiko in Kyushu; Mount Ishizuchi in Shikoku; Mount Taisen in western Honshu; Mount Haku in mid-northern Honshu; and the group of Haguro, Gassan, and Yudono in northern Honshu. From these religious centers priests went once or twice a year to their parishioners' villages and visited from house to house to distribute charms, amulets, or talismans, to hold purification ceremonies, or to offer prayers for peace and prosperity. Accordingly, both the settled village *yamabushi* and the itinerant *yamabushi* exerted deep and lasting influence upon the spiritual life of the common people. Under these circumstances, while Japanese Shinto

[2] Komazō Mizoguchi, "Tōhoku, Hokuriku-chihō ni okeru Shugen Chakusai" ("On the Coloration or Influence of Shugen-dō in Northeastern and Mid-northern Honshu"), in *Shūkyō kenkyū*, IV, No. 4, 192–98.

was influenced by Shugen-dō, Shugen-dō itself borrowed many elements from ancient shamanism, Yin-Yang and Taoistic magic, Confucian ethics, and—above all—from Mantrayâna Buddhism. In other words, Shugen-dō has incorporated within itself many of the significant characteristics of Japanese religion.

Parenthetically, it might be added in this connection that in 1868 the Japanese government adopted the policy of dissolving the historic pattern of Shinto-Buddhist amalgamation and elevated Shinto as the de facto state religion. In this situation Shugen-dō, which had had precarious relationships with both Shinto and Buddhism, suffered a great deal. Many of the Shugen-dō priests were returned to secular life. Some of them chose to become priests of the Shingon or Tendai school of Buddhism, while others became engaged in secular professions. Only since the end of World War II has Shugen-dō been allowed to enjoy independent status as a minor religious group. Nevertheless, the historic importance of Shugen-dō in the religious life of the Japanese people cannot be overlooked.

(*Sacred Mountains and Cosmology*

Mountains have been the object of worship among many peoples. Their height, their vastness, and the strangeness of their terrain often inspire in the human mind an attitude of reverence and adoration.[3] Mountains in their very nature have some measure of holiness, in the sense in

[3] See, for example, J. A. MacCulloch, "Mountains, Mountain Gods," in J. Hastings (ed.), *Encyclopaedia of Religion and Ethics* (New York, 1930), VIII, 863.

which Rudolf Otto defined the term "holy," or "numinous," with the elements of *mysterium tremendum* and *fascinosum*.[4]

There is much significant evidence of mountain worship and mountain gods among ancient civilized peoples. The five sacred mountains (Wu-chen or Wu-yoh) in China; Kanchinjunga in Tibet; Sumeru or Meru in ancient India; Albûrz or Hara Berezaiti in ancient Persia; Sinai, Nebo, Hor, and Zion from the Old Testament; and Olympus in Greece—these are only a few examples. Also, we find numerous examples of sacred mountains among non-literate peoples in Oceania, Arctic Asia, Africa, and North and South America. In each case, the mountains were believed to be the center of the world, the cosmic mountain, the pillar supporting and linking heaven and earth, or the residence of a god or gods. They were the sites of religious services in which sacrifices and prayers were offered and divine revelations and oracles received. There ascetics practiced their religious austerities in order to acquire magical, superhuman power or to attain enlightenment. Taking on metaphysical significance, some of the sacred mountains were believed to possess such divine qualities as eternity, power, or stability, as in the case of Mount Sumeru, representing the stability of Buddha's body.[5] In Hindu and, more particularly, Buddhist traditions,[6] Mount Sumeru or Meru is thought to be the

4 Rudolf Otto, *Idea of the Holy*, trans. J. W. Harvey (rev. ed.; London, 1946), pp. 5–40.

5 See *Fo-su-khin-tsān-kin* (Sanskrit, *Buddhakarita-kârya-sûtra*; *Nanjō Catalogue*, No. 1351), I, i, 49.

6 Concerning the typical Buddhist cosmology centering on Sumeru, see *Jambu-dvîpa*, *Dîrghâgama-sûtra* (*Nanjō Catalogue*, No. 545), Vol. XVIII; "Numbers and Quantities," *Lo-shi-ö-phi-thān-lun* (Sanskrit,

cosmic mountain at the center of the world and the abode of the gods. It is the chief of mountains, the Golden Mountain which is eighty-four thousand miles high, whose upper part is divided into thirty-three heavens. At the very top of this cosmic mountain is the palace of Sakra Devânam Indra, the supreme god of the Vedic pantheon, who governs the whole cosmos. Seven concentric rings of large mountains surround it, with intervening seas. Between these and the outermost ring are the four worlds, including Jambudvîpa in the south, the world where we are now living. The sun, moon, and planets are believed to revolve around Mount Sumeru.

Cosmological significance of mountains is also recognized in Babylonian and Assyrian traditions, according to which seven-storied temple towers (ziggurats) were built symbolizing the seven heavens.[7] The famous temple tower of Borobudur in Java also has the form of a ziggurat, even though it was built between the seventh and the ninth centuries A.D. under the strong influence of Indian Buddhism. It consists of nine levels which pilgrims ascend step by step, worshipping at each statue of Buddha and chanting the sutras. When they reach the top level of the tower, they are believed to be able to pass from the profane world to the sacred world, from the human world full of ignorance and suffering to the Buddha's world of enlightenment and salvation.[8]

---

probably *Lôkasthiti* (?)-*abhidharma-śâstra* (Nanjō Catalogue, No. 1277), Vol. II; *Abhidharma-kösa-śâstra* (Nanjō Catalogue, No. 1267), Vol. XI. See Willibald Kirfel, *Der Kosmographie der Inder* (Berlin, 1920).

[7] See Theodor Dombart, *Der Sakraltum* (Munich, 1920), Part I: "Zikkurat"; A. Parrot, *Ziggurate als Tour de Babel* (Paris, 1949).

[8] Mircea Eliade, *Myth of the Eternal Return*, trans. E. R. Trask (New York, 1954), pp. 15, 18.

Cosmic mountains are also utilized in shamanism, especially in central Asia and Mongolia, where, for example, the shamans of the Altaic Tatar tribes believe that their supreme god, Bai Ulgen, presides over the whole world at his palace on the top of a golden mountain that emerges from the earth and stands at the center of heaven. These shamans believe that they must ascend this mountain, successively conquering each stage of the seven heavens (three, seven, or nine stages, according to the traditions of various tribes) in order to give offerings to Bai Ulgen, and then descend to the earth to transmit his oracles to the people.[9] There are also several instances, as Mircea Eliade has pointed out, in which the future shamans in northern Asia have had strange but characteristic experiences during their *maladies et rêves initiatiques*.[10] The souls of the novices are thought to ascend to heaven through a high and precipitous mountain, or through a symbolic birch tree with seven to nine notches manifesting the number of heavens they must pass through in order to receive the divine gift of shamanizing as the reward for long and excruciating ordeals.[11]

[9] Cf. Uno Harva (Holmberg), *Die Religiösen Vorstellungen der altaischen Völker* (FF Communication No. 125 [Helsinki, 1938]); Mircea Eliade, *Shamanism* (New York, 1964), pp. 181 ff.

[10] Eliade, *Shamanism*, pp. 33–66.

[11] The number of heavens mentioned above is supposed to be influenced by Lamaism and Buddhism from the south, or by Mithraism or Zoroastrianism from the southwest. See Eliade, *Shamanism*, pp. 257–87, 495–507. See also N. D. Mironov and S. Shirokogoroff, "Sṛāmana-Shaman," *Journal of the North-China Branch of the Royal Asiatic Society,* XXV (1924), 110–30; cf. Mircea Eliade, "Recent Works on Shamanism," *History of Religions,* I (1961), 297–308.

❨ *Religious Ceremonies in Mountains*

In many parts of the world, religious ceremonies in mountains are performed not only by institutionalized religions but also by folk religious groups in various popular festivals. May Day and Midsummer Day in Europe are examples of festivals connected with mountains.[12] In parts of Europe, the old pre-Christian festival of Midsummer Eve was taken over by Christianity and renamed St. John's Eve. Especially in northern European villages, a special tree was cut from a mountain to guard against fire or lightning, and the people gathered herbs and bathed in streams to avoid sickness. Bonfires or midsummer fires were kindled on mountaintops or hilltops at night to purify both men and cattle in the smoke of the fire. Among certain American Indians, the first fruits of the harvest were taken to a mountaintop and offered to the mountain gods.[13] A similar custom has also been reported in some tribes of Africa.[14] In Mexico, the mountain was an important site of religious festivals,[15] and where there were no mountains, the people constructed a mound exclusively for the purpose of celebrating a festival. In ancient China, kings regularly performed rituals facing

[12] Funk and Wagnalls, *Standard Dictionary of Folklore, Mythology, and Legend*, ed. Maria Leech (New York, 1949), II, 695–96, 723.

[13] MacCulloch, "Mountains, Mountain Gods," p. 866.

[14] *Ibid.*

[15] F. S. Dellenbaugh, *North Americans of Yesterday* (New York, 1901), pp. 195, 206; MacCulloch, "Mountains, Mountain Gods," p. 867; cf. Bancroft, *Native Races of the Pacific*, III, 123; IV, 756 ff.

a particular mountain or built two special mounds called heaven altar (*t'ien-tan*) and earth altar (*ti-tan*).[16] In India, many tribes held festivals upon or oriented toward sacred mountains and hills; especially interesting among these religious observances held on mountaintops is the rite held for the benefit of the dead (*śrâddha*).[17]

Parenthetically, it might be added that during the forty-nine days following death a person is said be wandering between this world and the next. The purpose of the *śrâddha* is to conduct the soul of the dead safely and easily to the next world. Such a rite is usually performed in the mountains. Should the relatives of the deceased fail to perform this rite, the soul of the dead is destined to wander about in this world, causing calamities and misfortune to the living. This rite was taken over by Buddhism and became the formal service for the souls of the dead; it is held every seventh day up to the forty-ninth day after death. The annual festival for the ancestors' spirits connected with the *śrâddha* is called *piṇḍapitṛyjña* in India; this custom is observed in Japan under the name of *bon*.

It is also interesting to note that in Japan the word for mountain pass is *tōge* (from *tamuke*, "to offer"; travelers always had to offer something to the god of the pass as a prayer for safe journey). This custom is not unique to Japan but can be seen also in Korea, Mongolia, and Tibet. There are many instances where large mounds have accumulated from the offerings of small stones. The stone mounds of the hilltop, mountaintop, and mountain pass

16 *Li-chi* (*The Book of Rites*), III, ii, 14–16; iii, 6; etc.; cf. J. J. M. De Groot, *Religion in China* (New York, 1912).

17 "Ancestor-worship (India)," in Hastings, *Encyclopaedia of Religion and Ethics*, I, 452–54.

in Korea and Japan and the *obo* in Mongolia and Manchuria are typical examples.[18]

❰ Three Categories of Japanese Mountain Worship

At the expense of oversimplification, mountain beliefs in Japan can be classified into three categories. The first is connected with conically shaped dormant volcanoes. In this respect, Mount Fuji is well known.[19] In addition there are other famous mountains, such as Chōkai in northeastern Honshu, Taisen in western Honshu, and Kaimon in the southernmost part of Kyushu—all of which rise near the seashore. Sailors and fishermen have traditionally believed that the deity who controls navigation resides at the summit of these mountains, which to them seemed to be the link between heaven and earth. Similarly, many conically shaped mountains in the Ryukyu and Amami archipelagoes are called *a-mori* or *a-furi* ("descent from heaven"), and the peaks of the mountains were venerated by these islanders. Even today there are some Shinto shrines, such as Miwa-jinja in Nara prefecture and Hiragiki-jinja at Mount Kaimon, that regard the mountains as the object of worship. Therefore, in these shrines there is no *shinden* ("inner sanctuary"). In Japan it was common practice for people to erect

[18] Yanagita and Hori, *Jūsan-zuka kō* (*Study of the Thirteen Mounds*) (Tokyo, 1948), pp. 194–216.

[19] Since the *Manyō-shū* we can find many poems and other literary works, as well as works of art, that represent Mount Fuji as a divine or sacred mountain.

iwasaka ("sacred enclosures made of stones") on mountaintops for religious purposes.[20]

The eruption of a volcano has been interpreted in many ancient documents as a divine creative act. For example, when the people viewed the major eruption of Mount Fuji in A.D. 865 at night, they thought they saw a magnificent divine palace newly built on the mountaintop in the midst of the flames and smoke.[21] Similarly, in A.D. 840 a volcanic eruption on Kōzu Island of the Izu Archipelago so impressed the people that they believed they saw, in addition to the divine palace, gods running across the water holding torches to assist in the divine re-creation of the island.[22]

The second category of beliefs is concerned with mountains as watersheds or sources of streams. Because agriculture formed the foundation of ancient Japan, there are many Shinto shrines dedicated to the gods of surrounding mountains who brought the rains and protected the water source.[23] In the Heian period (A.D. 794–1185) in the Kinki area around Kyoto, Osaka, and Nara, for example, there were fifty-three such shrines (and in the plain of the ancient metropolitan area of Nara alone, twenty-nine). Thus the mountain was integrally related

[20] See Yanagita, *Kainan shōki (Some Folkloristic Sketches on the Southern Islands of Japan)* (Tokyo, 1925); *Imo no Chikara*; Hori, *Yūkō shisō (Idea of the Migrating Kami, Heroes, and Priests)* (Tokyo, 1944).

[21] *Sandai jitsuroku*, in *Kokushi taikei*, Vols. IV, XIII.

[22] *Shoku Nihon kōki*, in *Kokushi taikei*, Vols. III, IX.

[23] See "Kiu shin-sai" ("Praying for Rain at Official Shinto Shrines"), *Engishiki*, in *Kokushi taikei*, Vol. XXIV (new ed.; Tokyo, 1964), in which eleven shrines in Yamashiro (present Kyoto prefecture), twenty-nine in Yamato (present Nara prefecture), three in Kawachi and Izumi (present Osaka prefecture), and nine in Settsu (now a part of Hyōgo prefecture) were institutionalized and authorized.

to agriculture in the eyes of the ancient Japanese. In fact, the god of the mountain (*yama-no-kami*) and the god of the rice field (*ta-no-kami*) were interchangeable. Even today many Japanese farmers believe that the mountain god comes down in early spring to guard the rice field and returns to the mountain in the fall. The villagers observe the rituals of welcoming and sending off the deity.[24]

The third category of beliefs is concerned with the relationship between the mountain and the souls of the dead, which beliefs have played an important role in the development of ancestor worship in Japan. There are two basic but contradictory beliefs in this connection. The belief that mountains are the abode of the dead reflects the ancient custom of actual burial on the mountain, while the belief that mountains are merely the meeting ground between this world and the next is predicated upon the tradition that heaven or the other world exists some place beyond the mountains.

These beliefs are illustrated in a poem written by Princess Oku lamenting the death of her brother, Prince Ōtsu (d. A.D. 686):

> *I, living in this world,*
> *From tomorrow look on*
> *Mt. Futakami as my brother*
> *(For today he was buried there.)*[25]

[24] Cf. Kōtarō Hayakawa, *Nō to matsuri* (*Agriculture and the Festivals and Rites*) (Tokyo, 1942); Ichirō Kurata, *Nō to minzoku-gaku* (*Agriculture and Folklore Studies*) (Tokyo, 1944); Yanagita, *Bunrui nōson goi* (*Classified Folk Vocabularies of Farming-Village Life*) (2 vols.; Nagano, 1937; rev. ed.; Tokyo, 1945–46).

[25] *Manyō-shū*, Vol. II, No. 165 (in the "Iwanami Bunko" series [Tokyo, 1927], p. 64).

Here the mountain where Prince Ōtsu was buried became the means of recalling his memory. Of ninety-four such poems of bereavement (*ban-ka*—"dirge," "funeral song," or "lament") in the *Manyō-shū* (the oldest official anthology of Japanese poems, compiled in the eighth century A.D.), there are fifty-one instances in which the soul of the dead is believed to rest on a mountain, a rock, or a mountain valley; twenty-three instances in which it is believed to rest in the sky or the clouds; several instances in which it is believed to rest in islands, the sea, or the wilderness. But there are only three instances in which the soul of the dead is believed to rest in the underworld; this belief was influenced by the Buddhist concept of the netherworld or the Chinese concept of *huang-chüan* ("underworld"). To be sure, these Manyō poems dealt only with the life of the nobility, but nevertheless they indicate the beliefs that were widely held among all the people in the seventh and eighth centuries concerning the future life.[26] It is significant that among these poems the names of Mount Hatsuse and Mount Yoshino appear often, since both of these later became sacred mountains of Buddhism, especially to the traditions of Mantrayâna and Shugen-dō.

In this connection we might also observe the close interrelationship between the mountain and the *kofun* ("burial mound"). Many tombs, especially those of the emperors, were erected on natural hills, but sometimes large mounds were artificially created on the plain for the purpose of burying the dead. Even in Heian times, when

[26] Hori, "Manyō-shū ni arawareta sōsei to takai-kan, reikon-kan ni tsuite" ("On the Funeral Customs, Conceptions of the Other World and the Soul of the Dead Which Appeared in the *Manyō-shū*"), *Nihon shūkyō-shi kenkyū*, II, 49–93.

kofun were no longer in use, the emperor's mausoleum was still called *yama* ("mountain"), and the official in charge of erecting the mausoleum was called *yama-tsukuri-no-tsukasa* ("official who erects the mountain").[27] These ideas have been handed down to our time, so that in rural Japan the term *yama* is often used in connection with funerary rites.[28] A similar belief is found in the Amami and Ryukyu archipelagoes, where the corpse is sometimes exposed in the bush, which significantly is called *goshō-yama* ("mountain of future birth").[29]

Almost all sacred mountains in Japan have two sites of religious services, the *yama-miya* ("shrine on the top of

[27] Cf. Kotosugu Tanikawa (1709–76), *Wakun no shiori* (*Dictionary of Japanese Words and Their Origin and History*) (Tokyo, 1887), Part I; Fujiwara-no-Michinaga (966–1027), *Midō-kanpaku ki*, Michinaga's diary in *Dai Nihon kokiroku* (Tokyo, 1938), "The 25th Day of the Sixth Month of the Eighth Year of Kankō" (1007); Fujiwara-no-Yukinari (d. 1027), *Gon ki*, Yukinari's diary in *Shiryō taisei*, Vols. XXXV–XXXVI (Tokyo, 1938–39), "The Eighth Day of the Seventh Month of A.D. 1007."

[28] The coffin itself is called *yama-oke* ("mountain box"). Digging the grave for burial is called *yama-shigoto* ("mountain work"). Choosing the site of burial within a graveyard is called *yama-gime* ("choosing [or selecting] the mountain"). And when the funeral procession begins, the leader calls out: "Yama-yuki! Yama-yuki!" ("We go to the mountain!") See Yanagita, *Bunrui sōsō shūzoku goi* (*Classified Folk Vocabularies of Funeral Ceremonies and Customs*) (Tokyo, 1937), pp. 117–19, 132–35, 145, 161, etc.; Hori, *Minkan shinkō*, pp. 216–17.

[29] The relatives and friends of the dead person would come to this place and offer food and a bottle of sake, singing and dancing around the corpse for from three to seven days. This custom reminds us of the ancient records of "Wo-jen chuan" in *Wei-chih* as well as of the legends of the *Kojiki* and *Nihongi*. See Fuyū Ifa, "Nantō komin no sōgi" ("Funeral Ceremonies and Customs in the Southern Islands of Japan"), *Minzoku*, II, No. 6, 131 ff.

the mountain") and the *sato-miya* ("shrine at the foot
of the mountain"). This system of having two shrines,
according to Kunio Yanagita, is the prototype of the ancestor worship of Japan.[30] Yanagita further states that the
earthly deities of ancient Japan were held to be the ancestral deities who ascend the mountain in order to observe
the activities of their descendants. They were believed to
come down from the mountains at the time of harvest
and the new year to receive the homage of their descendants. From this viewpoint, it is noteworthy that in the
Norito (ancient Japanese Shinto ritual prayers) of the
ō-*harae* ("great exorcism" or "purification") in the *Engishiki*[31] we can see clearly the ancient Japanese concept of
heavenly and earthly deities. For example,

> *When he [chief priest of the Nakatomi] thus pro-*
>   *nounces them [solemn ritual words]*
> *The heavenly deities (Ama-tsu-kami) will push open*
>   *the heavenly rock door,*
> *And pushing with an awesome pushing through the*
>   *myriad layers of heavenly clouds,*
> *Will hear and receive [these words].*

> *Then the earthly deities (Kuni-tsu-kami) will climb up*
> *To the summits of the high mountains and to the*
>   *Summits of the low mountains,*
> *And pushing aside the mists of the high mountains*

[30] The most significant example of this dual system is the festival
that celebrates the *yama-miya* and *uji-gami* simultaneously, an annual
event performed jointly by the members of hereditary priestly families
of the shrine of Ise—the Arakida and Watarai families—a tradition that
has continued for more than a thousand years. See Yanagita, *Yama-miya
kō* (*A Study of the Mountain Shrine*) (Tokyo, 1947).

[31] "Norito" ("Ritual Prayers"), *Engishiki*.

And the mists of the low mountains,
Will hear and receive [these words].[32]

The above discussion may indicate how important the mountain was to the religious life of the Japanese people, both as the connecting link between this world and the life to come and as the link between the profane and the sacred dimensions of life. It is readily understandable, therefore, that Mantrayanistic ascetics in Japan, as much as the shamans of central and northern Asia, practiced austerities within the mountains to obtain supernatural powers or to communicate with supernatural beings.[33] Related to this is the notion of *shide-no-yama* ("mountain leading to the other world"), which under Buddhist influence came to be portrayed as a state of loneliness and painfulness characterized by the existence of demons who torture the souls of the dead.[34] Another belief which

[32] Donald Philippi, Norito: A New Translation of the Ancient Japanese Ritual Prayers (Tokyo, 1959), p. 47. Philippi translated the term *ihori* as "mists"; however, Yanagita interpreted this as "hermitage" or "ritual hut."

[33] Even today in some places in Japan, puberty rites are conducted by *yamabushi* within the mountains. See Hori, Wagakuni minkan-shinkō-shi no kenkyū, II, Part II: "Sangaku Bukkyō no tenkai to Shugen-ja yamabushi no yugyō-teki kinō to keitai" ("Development of Mountain Buddhism and the Social Functions of Shugen-dō Priests"), pp. 58–248.

[34] In the Jigoku-byōbu (Scroll of Hell), for instance, a woman is depicted as barely able to walk because she is constantly beaten by demons. On this scroll the retired Emperor Nijō (reigned 1158–65) wrote a poem:

> One passes over the *shide-no-yama* alone,
> Without any relative or acquaintance,
> Accompanied only by his former life's sins,
> Tortured and crying all the while.

See the Shin zoku kokin waka-shū, an anthology of poems compiled by Masayo Fujiwara in A.D. 1439, in Kokka taikan (Tokyo, 1903), Vol. VIII.

came to be widely held in Japan was the cuckoo bird as the messenger between this world and the next.[35] These notions—the mountains leading to the other world and the cuckoo bird as the messenger—so often cited in Japanese classical literature, were not merely literary fancies but were important ingredients of the religious life of the Japanese, who took mountains very seriously.

The relationship between the soul of the dead and the mountain is also seen in the *bon* festival, which is usually held from the thirteenth to the sixteenth of the seventh month of the lunar calendar (July or August). In some places, big fires (*bon-bi*)[36] are kindled on the tops of mountains or hills to welcome the spirits of the dead ancestors, who are thought to return to their places of birth and receive offerings from their descendants.[37] There are

[35] The famous poet, Ise-no-Tayū (ca. 987–1036), composed a poem upon hearing the song of the cuckoo, in which she lamented her departed son who had died the year before:

> Please tell me all of
> How my beloved son fares
> In the Other World,
> Oh! cuckoo
> Because you must have passed over
> The *shide-no-yama* from the Other World.

See "Aishō" ("Dirge" or "Lament"), *Shūi waka-shū*, an anthology of poems supposedly compiled by the retired Emperor Kazan or Kintō Fujiwara about 996, Vol. XX, in *Iwanami Bunko* (Tokyo, 1938), Nos. 1774–75.

[36] The "bonfire" known to the European and American readers is different historically and etymologically from Japanese *bon-bi* (translated here as *bon* fire).

[37] One of the best-known *bon* fires is the *dai-monji-yaki* in Kyoto in which thousands of torches are kindled in the shape of the character *dai* (*ta* in Chinese) on the midslope of a peak of the East Mountain chain of Kyoto. In some places, boys and girls make a big fire or brandish a

also two widespread customs in rural areas which mark the beginning of the *bon* festival. The first is *bon-michi-tsukuri* ("making of the *bon* road"), according to which weeds from the top of a mountain or hill are cleared away in order to make way for the spirits of the ancestors. The other custom is *bon-bana-mukae* ("flower-gathering for the *bon* festival"), according to which special kinds of flowers, called *bon* flowers (such as the broad bell flower, the *Petrinia scabiosafolia*, the bush clover, the gold-banded lily, and the wild pink), are picked from the tops of mountains or hills. The people believe that the spirits of the dead ancestors enter into these *bon* flowers in order to visit their homes.[38] In many areas of Japan, catching certain kinds of dragonflies is strictly prohibited during the *bon* festivals because it is thought that they actually incarnate the spirits of the dead.[39]

On several sacred mountains—such as Mount Kōya, a center of the Shingon sect; Mount Asama in Mie prefecture; Mount Risshaku-ji in Yamagata prefecture; and Mount Osore in Aomori prefecture—parts of the remains of the deceased are buried.[40] In these mountains, certain

---

kindled straw rope separately on nearby hilltops, crying: "Grandpa! Grandma! See this fire, and come visit us!" See Yanagita, *Bunrui saiji shūzoku goi* (*Classified Folk Vocabularies on the Annual Festivals and Customs*) (Tokyo, 1939), pp. 517 ff.

[38] If there is no mountain or hill near the village, the villagers must go to the *bon-ichi* ("the market for *bon*") at a nearby town to buy the *bon* flowers. See Hiromasa Ikegami, "Bon-bana kō" ("A Study of the Bon Flowers"), *Shūkyō kenkyū*, XIV, No. 1 (1937), 107 ff.

[39] These dragonflies are sometimes called *shōryō-yamma* ("dragonfly of the spirits of the dead"). See Yanagita, *Bunrui saiji shūzoku goi*, p. 450.

[40] On the feast days for Bodhisattva Jizō (Sanskrit, Kshitigarbha, a Buddhist savior from hell), on those for other buddhas or bodhisattvas, and on the spring and autumn equinoxes, many persons ascend these

areas around the temple are designated as representing *jigoku* ("hell") and *gokuraku* ("pure land" or "paradise"); worshippers are expected to go through the former before entering the latter. In this manner the historic Buddhist notion of perpendicular cosmology, consisting of the three levels of heaven, earth, and underworld, has been reinterpreted to fit into the indigenous religious view of the Japanese. Furthermore, from the Middle Ages on, almost all the important mountains of Japan have been occupied by Buddhist priests and the *shugen-ja* ("mountain ascetics") of Shugen-dō. Inevitably, theologies of mountain religion developed in the two Mantrayanistic sects of Tendai and Shingon based on the twofold principle of the Esoteric mandala—that is, "realm of the indestructibles" or "diamond" (in Sanskrit, *vajra-dhâtu*; in Japanese, *kongō-kai*)—and "womb store" (in Sanskrit, *garbha-kukshi*; in Japanese, *taizō*). Significantly, these theologies were greatly influenced by the pre-Buddhist Japanese beliefs concerning mountains, as evidenced by the *dhûta* austerities, which are usually practiced on the mountain, as well as by shamanistic cosmology and practices.

I shall illustrate some of the important motifs of mountain beliefs in the following sections.

---

mountains to hold memorial services for the spirits of their dead relatives. Many wooden stupas dedicated to the spirits of the dead are erected on these mountaintops. There worshippers invoke buddhas or bodhisattvas for the easy passage of the dead into Buddha's Pure Land. See Hori, *Wagakuni minkan-shinkō-shi no kenkyū*, I, 229; Hori, *Nihon shūkyō-shi kenkyū* (Tokyo, 1962), I, 173–75.

([Sacred Mountain and Sacred Water

In the history of Japanese mountain religion there are a number of sacred mountains. Foremost among them is Mount Yoshino, around which many myths and legends have arisen. According to the ancient legends, the first emperor, Jimmu, had crossed over Mount Yoshino during his campaign from Kyushu to Yamato, the present Nara prefecture. We are told that Jimmu had encountered mountain tribes in this region. One night while Jimmu was sleeping by the Nifu River in this area, he was given magico-religious power by the sun goddess (Amaterasu), and with the aid of the cross sword and a gigantic crow he was able to pacify these mountain tribes.[41]

More pertinent for our purpose is the historical account of the Emperor Temmu (A.D. 622–686), who at one time retired to Mount Yoshino and underwent austere Buddhist training on the mountain. At that time he composed the following poem.

> On the peak of Mimiga of fair Yoshinu[42]
> The snow is falling constantly,
> The rain is falling ceaselessly;
> Constantly as falls the snow,
> Ceaselessly as beats the rain,
> Ever thinking I have come,

[41] *Kojiki* (*Records of Ancient Matters*), trans. Chamberlain (Tokyo, 1906), pp. 157–74; Aston, *Nihongi*, I, 112–30.

[42] Mount Yoshino was called Yoshinu in the Manyō-shū period.

Missing not one turning
Of that mountain-path![48]

During the civil war which ensued, Temmu, much as the legendary Emperor Jimmu had done before him, prayed to Amaterasu for victory and received a favorable oracle in his dream. This event also took place at Mount Yoshino.[44] It is apparent that the legend of Emperor Jimmu and the account of Emperor Temmu follow the same pattern, and, significantly, Mount Yoshino appears prominently in both accounts. Furthermore, it was at Mount Yoshino that Emperor Temmu, after the civil war, demanded and received oaths of loyalty from the imperial princes, thus recognizing the special sacredness of this mountain.[45]

[43] The Emperor Temmu, then known as Crown Prince Ōama, was involved in succession rivalry with another prince following the death of Emperor Tenchi in 671, and left the imperial palace in Ōmi (near present Ōtsu) for Mount Yoshino. In 672 he defeated the Ōmi dynasty and founded his Asuka dynasty in Nara prefecture. See The Manyōshū, One Thousand Poems Selected and Translated from the Japanese (hereinafter cited as The Manyōshū) (Tokyo, 1940), p. 17.

[44] Nihongi, II, 301–20.

[45] Nihongi, pp. 341–42; Temmu: 8th year (A.D. 679): "5th month, 5th day: The Emperor proceeded to the palace of Yoshino. 6th day: The Emperor addressed the Empress-consort, the Imperial Prince Kusakabe, The Imperial Prince, Ohotsu, the Imperial Prince Takechi, the Imperial Prince Kawashima, the Imperial Prince Osakabe, and the Imperial Prince Shiki, saying, 'We wish today to unite with you in making a vow in the Court, so that after a thousand years there may be no trouble. What think ye?' The Imperial Princes answered together, saying, 'The reasonableness of this is manifest.' Accordingly, His Highness the Imperial Prince Kusakabe stood forward first and made oath, saying, 'Ye gods of Heaven and Earth, and ye Emperors, bear witness! We, elder and younger brothers, young or of mature age, more than ten Princes in all, born each of different mothers, without respect of birth from

It is also interesting to note that Empress Jitō, who succeeded Temmu in 687, was greatly impressed by the beauty and numinous atmosphere of Mount Yoshino and paid thirty-two visits to it in the course of her life.[46] We must bear in mind once again that this mountain was

---

the same or different mothers, together comply with the Emperor's behest, and will give each other mutual support and avoid contention. If, from this time forward, any of us should not keep this vow, may he himself perish and may his line become extinct! There will be no forgetfulness or failure.'

"The (other) five Imperial Princes took oath together in the above terms in order one after another, and thereupon the Emperor said, 'Ye, my sons, though each born of different mothers, are now in affection as if born of one mother.' Accordingly, loosening out his collar, he took the six Imperial Princes to his bosom, and made oath, saying, 'If we contravene this oath, may our body perish instantly!' The Empress-consort's oath was like that of the Emperor.

"7th day: The Emperor's car returned to the palace. 10th day: The six Imperial Princes together paid their respects to the Emperor before the Great Hall."

[46] The following poem in the *Manyō-shū*, Vol. I, No. 36 (English translation from *The Manyōshū*, p. 20), was composed by Kakinomoto-no-Hitomaro on the occasion of one of her visits to Mount Yoshino:

> Though, in the Land where rules our Sovereign,
> The Provinces are many,
> She loves, in Yoshinu, the field of Akitsu,
> Encircled by clear streams and towering mountains,
> Where cherry-flowers fall,
> And there she has reared herself
> A mighty-pillar'd palace.
>
> Here the courtiers row their barges
> Side by side across the morning waters
> And race upon the evening stream,
> Endless as this river flows,
> Lofty as those mountains,
> Will it stand for aye,
> And never tire my eyes,
> This palace by the stream!

noted not only for its beauty but also for its sacredness, so that a number of shrines came to be built there in honor of the mountain deities.[47] Some scholars assert that the frequent visits by Jitō and later royalty were motivated by their search for the sacred water with which the heavenly deities might best be served and worshipped and in which they, as the heads of the imperial court, might bathe and purify the court and the nation.[48] This seems to be a sound interpretation of the magico-religious function of sacred mountains implied in these visits. In fact, the sacred mountains in Japan without exception have sacred waters which proceed from them.[49] Among them,

[47] It should not be considered mere rhetorical flourish that in the *Kaifūsō* (a Chinese-style anthology compiled about the same time as the *Manyō-shū*), Mount Yoshino was frequently praised with the Chinese Taoistic expressions as the "abode of holy wizards" or the "palace of divine genii." See *Manyō-shū*, Vol. VIII, No. 1133.

[48] Yasaburō Ikeda and Kenkichi Yamamoto, *Manyō Hyakka* (*One Hundred Poems from the Manyō-shū* (Tokyo, 1963), pp. 175, 276.

[49] These sacred waters are usually called *harae-gawa* ("rivers of purification") or *mitarashi-gawa* (literally, "rivers of divine girdle"; nowadays they write the characters of *mitarashi* as "holy washing of one's hands"). An early poem which celebrates mountains is important for our purposes. The following poem from the *Manyō-shū*, "In Praise of Mount Tachi," was composed in 747 by Ōtomo-no-Yakamochi:

> In the land of Koshi
> Famous among the distant regions,
> Many are the mountains
> And countless rivers run,
> But on Mount Tachi of Niikawa
> Because of its divinity,
> Snow lies throughout summer,
> Unlike the mists that form and lift
> Each morning and evening
> Over the limpid shallows

Mount Tachi and Mount Futagami became the centers of Shugen-dō in the medieval period, and many Shinto shrines and Shugen-dō temples were built near them.[50]

The streams invariably girdling the sacred mountains of Japan may be explained as symbolic of the boundaries

---

Of the engirdling Katakai,
The Mountain will not leave our memory.

Envoys

The snows on Mount Tachi
Refresh me all through summer,
Thanks to its divinity!

Unfailing as the limpid water
On Katakai's shallows,
Will I come and gaze upon the mountain.

Manyō-shū, Vol. XVII, Nos. 4000–4002; English translation from *The Manyōshū*, pp. 182–83.

[50] *Manyō-shū*, Vol. XVII, No. 3985, records another poem composed in 747 by Yakamochi entitled "In Praise of Mount Futagami."

Mount Futagami, round which flow
The waters of Imizu,
When I come out and gaze upon it
In the rich and blossomed spring,
Or in the glorious leaf of autumn
How sublime it soars
Because of its divinity,
And how beautiful it stands,
With its shapely peaks.

Ceaselessly as the white waves break
As morning calm,
And increasing as the flood-tide swells
At evening lull,
About the rocky cape of Shibutani,
The godlike skirting ridge,
All who gaze upon it
Give admiration to this mountain
From old times to this day!

English translation from *The Manyōshū*, pp. 144–45.

between the profane and sacred worlds, the human and divine worlds, this world and the other world. Therefore, whoever wants to possess the divine power of the mountains or to communicate with the mountain deities must undergo some initiatory mysteries by these sacred waters. Six empresses reigned in Japan from A.D. 593 to 770, a period in which the *Kojiki* and *Nihongi* were compiled and in which Buddhism was introduced. These empresses frequently visited the sacred mountains, sacred waters, and sacred hot springs. We have no documents to explain the purposes of these frequent imperial visits; however, legends of the ancient shamanistic Queen Pi-mi-ko of the Yamatai Kingdom have remained in the memories of the Japanese people and have been enhanced by the activities of shamanistic Buddhists throughout the ages.

([*The Mountain as the Divine Mother*

One of the significant characteristics of mountain religion in Japan is the belief that the mountain itself has a mystical power to cause the birth or rebirth of human beings and animals. More often than not, in ancient Japanese myths mountain deities are portrayed as female. For example, it was a female deity, Ō-hirume (the Great August Sun Goddess, which is another name for Amaterasu-Ō-mikami, the ancestral deity of the imperial family) who is believed to have brought down, presumably from the sacred mountain, the "soul box" of the new emperor at the time of his enthronement. According to this belief, the imperial charisma is embodied in the imperial soul, which has to be given to the new emperor when he ascends the throne.[51] In the popular belief of rural areas, the mountain deity is believed to be a goddess who once a year gives birth to twelve children. She is therefore called Mrs. Twelve (Jūni-sama), and her twelve children symbolize the twelve months of the year.[52]

These beliefs in mountain deities probably originated in ancient Japan among the hunting tribes who believed in the existence of the Divine Mother of the Mountain. We are again indebted to Yanagita[53] for depicting three major types of these mountain beliefs.

[51] In the Heian period, a symbolic drama was performed at this rite in which the priestess brought a mysterious box in her hand and wore a special wig made of creepers from the sacred mountain recess named Miyama-katsura. See the "Songs of the Chinkon Ritual" cited in the *Nenjū-gyōji-hishō* (*Memorandum of Annual Rites*), which is a manuscript of unknown authorship written in the latter years of the Heian period in the twelfth century (*Kojitsu Sōsho* [Tokyo, 1931]). See also Hori, "Mysterious Visitors from the Harvest to the New Year," in Dorson, *Studies in Japanese Folklore*, pp. 96–97, and n. 37.

[52] Also, she is believed to assure easy child delivery. In many districts, if a woman is having a difficult delivery, her husband or a relative will usually lead a horse in the direction of the mountain in order to receive the mountain deity. Sometimes a scroll depicting the mountain deity or some magical symbol such as a rice spoon or pillow is hung at a pregnant woman's bedside. The rice spoon is a symbol of the phallus and is held in the right hand of the mountain deity. See Ichirō Kurata, "Yama-no-kami" ("Mountain God"), in Yanagita, *Sanson seikatsu no kenkyū*, pp. 414 ff.; Yanagita, *San'iku shūzoku goi* (*Folk Vocabularies of the Customs of Childbirth and Nursing*) (Tokyo, 1936), pp. 38 ff.; Yaichirō Yamaguchi, "Nanzan niwa Yama-no-kami" ("Mountain God for Difficult Delivery"), *Minkan denshō*, X, No. 2, 14 ff.

[53] Yanagita, "Yamatachi to yamabushi" ("Hunters and the Yamabushi"), in *Sanson seikatsu no kenkyū* pp. 538–47; *Yama no jinsei* (*Life in the Mountain*) (Tokyo, 1926); "Kami wo tasuketa hanashi" ("Legends of Persons Who Helped Deities"), *Yanagita Kunio chosaku-shū* (2d ed.; Tokyo, 1950), Vol. X; Kizen Sasaki, "Banji, Banzaburō no hanashi" ("Legend of Banji and Banzaburō [two hunting brothers]"), *Tōō ibun*

According to the first—the Kōya type—the mountain goddess and her son play dominant roles in guiding the people and granting them permission to build houses or temples and in guarding the mountain. The name "Kōya" is taken from the mountain where Kūkai, the ninth-century patriarch of the Shingon sect, established his monastic center. According to the legend, he met a young hunter who was accompanied by two dogs, and through him Kūkai met the hunter's mother, Nibu-tsu-hime, the goddess of the mountain, and secured her permission to build monasteries at Kōya.[54] This legend, which undoubtedly was influenced by those of hunting tribes, came to be widely circulated in various parts of Japan, especially among the hunters in northeast Honshu.

According to the second—the *Nikkō* type—the goddess of the mountain rewards certain hunters for their meritorious deeds with the right of hunting within her domain. The goddess of Mount Nikkō (in Tochigi prefecture) was at one time attacked by the deity of nearby Mount Akagi, whereupon the goddess of Mount Nikkō asked the help of a young hunter, Banzaburō, who was known for his skill in archery. Banzaburō shot out the eyes of the deity of Mount Akagi, who was disguised as a

---

(*Legends of Northeast Honshu*) (Tokyo, 1926), pp. 15–65; Buntarō Takahashi, *Akita Matagi shiryō* (*Folklore of Hunters in Akita Prefecture Named Matagi*) (Attic Museum Note, No. 12 [Tokyo, 1937]); Takahashi, *Futara-jinja bunka-bu: Nikkō kari-kotoba ki* (*Hunting Traditions in Mount Nikkō*) (Tokyo, 1960).

54 Consequently, Kūkai built a shrine in honor of the mountain goddess and her son Kariba-myōjin (literally, "Deity of the Hunting Field") as the guardians of Shingon Buddhism, and more particularly of the Kongō-bu-ji temple on Mount Kōya. The meaning of the name of the mountain goddess Nibu-tsu-hime will be discussed later. See Yanagita, "Yamatachi to yamabushi," *Sanson seikatsu no kenkyū*, p. 544.

giant centipede. The goddess of Mount Nikkō therefore rewarded Banzaburō by giving him the right of hunting in every mountain and forest of Japan. Moreover, Banzaburō himself came to be regarded as either the ancestor or the guardian deity of the hunting tribes, and in some cases he is celebrated as the son of the Mountain Maiden (Yama-hime) and the Monkey King. This type of legend came to be associated with the mountain ascetics of the Tendai Buddhist tradition, and is widely circulated among the hunters in east and northeast Honshu.[55]

According to the third—the Shiiba type—typified by the legend transmitted in the village of Shiiba in southern Kyushu, the mountain goddess appears in the form of a helpless maiden who tests the characters of hunters. There were two brothers—the older, Ōma, who was heartless; the younger, Koma, noted for his compassion. One day when these brothers were hunting in the mountain they met a maiden who had just given birth to a child and who asked for food. The older brother, being afraid of the impurity of blood, ignored her request. The younger brother out of compassion offered his own lunch basket, whereupon the maiden, who in reality was the Divine Mother of the Mountain (Yama-no-Shinbo), promised him success and happiness.[56] There is a wide variety of legends based on this motif which have been handed down among the hunters of northeast Honshu.[57]

[55] Yanagita, "Kami wo tasuketa hanashi," *Sanson seikatsu no kenkyū*, pp. 36–38; Yanagita (ed.), *Minzokugaku jiten*, p. 484.

[56] Yanagita, *Nochi no kari-kotoba no ki* (On Hunting Traditions) (Tokyo, 1908, 1951).

[57] Sasaki, "Banji, Banzaburō no hanashi," *Tōō ibun*, pp. 56–58; see also his "Yomego-nezumi no hanashi" ("Stories of Rats and Brides"), *Tōō ibun*, pp. 86–90.

❲ Mounts Gassan and Haguro as Divine Mothers

As noted earlier, many of the mountains in Japan became centers of the activities of Shugen-dō. Chief among these is Mount Gassan, the most prominent among the three sacred mountains in Dewa, or present-day Yamagata prefecture (Dewa-San-zan), where the mountain ascetics of both the Haguro and Yudono sects practice religious austerities. Mount Gassan (literally, "Mount Moon") is worshipped by the farmers of the vicinity as an agricultural deity (Nō-gami) and as the resting place of ancestors or spirits of the dead.[58] Special Shugen-dō annual rites are performed on Mount Gassan for the four seasons: Entering the Spring Peak (Haru-no-mine), Enter-

[58] On the first day of the bon festival, a big welcoming fire (mukae-bi) is kindled by the chief abbot of the Haguro sect of Shugen-dō at a special place called Saitō-mori near the top of Mount Gassan. Then similar welcoming bon fires are lit in order from higher to lower at each place for ascetic exercises on the mountain. When the last in the sequence of bon fires has been lit on the mountain, each family in the villages at the foot lights a bon fire at the front door in order to welcome that family's ancestors. This custom seems to illustrate that the ancestor spirits arrive first at the top of Mount Gassan and then gradually come down to each family. However, from the Tokugawa period, Mount Gassan has been considered the sacred mountain of Shugen-dō. Therefore it is believed that several years after death the spirits of the dead climb up Mount Gassan, during which time they are celebrated in memorial services at particular places named Mori-no-yama ("Wood Mountain") near the villages. See Yoshio Toda, "Honpō ni okeru shi-rei-shinkō no jisshō-teki kenkyū" ("Report of Field Research on Belief in Spirits of the Dead in Japan"), Shūkyō kenkyū, No. 127 (1951); Yoshio Toda, "Mori no shinko" ("Belief and Practice of the Mori or Sacred Bush"), Shūkyō kenkyū, No. 131 (1952); Anshō Togawa, "Uzen Haguro-san no Bon-gyōji" ("On the Bon Festivals in Mount Haguro in Yamagata Prefecture"), Sendai kyōdo kenkyū, No. 158 (1948), pp. 5–7.

ing the Summer Peak (Natsu-no-mine), Entering the Autumn Peak (Aki-no-mine), and Entering the Winter Peak (Fuyu-no-mine). The autumn peak is of special interest because it features rituals that include the initiatory austerities for the novices of Shugen-dō.

The main rites of the autumn peak begin with the mystery of entering the Great Womb Store (*garbha-hukshi* or *taizō-kai*), symbolized by the special hat and sacred wooden box (*oi*) on the back of the leading mountain ascetic (*dai-sendatsu*, "great [or chief] leader") and by the ritual act of throwing down the symbolic and decorative pillar (*bonden*) in front of the main Buddha hall of Shugen-dō seminaries in Tōge-mura on Mount Haguro. These symbols and rituals are explained by the fact that all the novices, together with the leading mountain ascetic, symbolically die and enter the womb of the Great Mother, Dai-nichi-nyorai (Great Sun Buddha Mahavairocana) or enter the underworld. The religious austerities and rituals continue for about ten days at the end of August, though they are now extremely shortened and simplified from their original forms. The series of rituals and austerities is divided into three periods: severe ordeals; taboos of food, speech, and sleeping; and the *dhûta* (*zuda* in Japanese) practices. Symbolically, the novices pass through the six stages of Buddhist Hell (Jigoku), Inferno of Starvation (Gaki), the Realm of Beasts (Chikushō), the World of Asûras (Shura), the World of Humans (Ningen), and Heaven (Tenjō) into the Great Womb Store. At each step of the three periods, several mysteries and *dhûta* practices are performed. It is noteworthy that the main hall of the Kōtaku-ji temple on top of Mount Haguro, in which the novices lead a secluded life, is decorated with symbols of the Great Mother's womb. Hanging from the ceiling in the center of the hall are red and white pieces of cloth about one meter long about which twisted hemp threads are wrapped. These pieces of cloth are said to symbolize the Great Mother's blood vessels, and the hemp threads symbolize her bones. Because the religious austerities of the Autumn Peak are those of the Great Womb Store, or of pilgrimages into the Great Mother's womb, the *dhûta* practices are usually performed at the rapids, streams, or waterfalls which flow down from the mountaintop. The novices as well as the leader wear white robes, different from the normal mountain ascetic's robes of yellowish brown. The white robe corresponds to that of the deceased and the mourner. At the end of the series of initiatory rituals, each novice is led to the most sacred valley, Moto-haguro ("Original Haguro"). He makes his final confession here and purifies himself by the sacred waterfall. Then, novices go to the top of Mount Haguro and crouch together in front of the main shrine of Hagurogongen. At the signal of a loud cry by the leader, the novices spring up suddenly, shout loudly, and run downhill to the main seminary in Tōge-mura at mid-slope. The shout is called the first cry of a child at birth (*ubu-goe*). Finally, the novices must jump over the sacred fire in front of the main seminary and the main Buddha hall, where the first mystery was performed. After this, the novices are believed to be reborn as new mountain ascetics from the Great Womb Store and have conferred upon them certificates giving the mountain ascetics new names, degrees, and secret knowledge of Shugen-dō.[59]

[59] Anshō Togawa, "Haguro Shugen no nyūbu shugyō" ("On Religious Austerities in the Mountains of Haguro Shugen-dō"), *Shūkyō kenkyū*, No. 136 (1953), pp. 37–56; Togawa, *Haguro yamabushi to minkan-shinkō*

❲ Mountain as Axis Mundi

Mountains are frequently regarded not only as the divine mother but also as the symbol of the cosmic mountain, which is the *axis mundi* according to cosmologies in various parts of the world. In the shamanic cosmology, which was probably influenced by Tibetan lamaism and the ancient Bablyonian world view, the *axis mundi* is the mountain of gold which contains from seven to nine stages of heaven, the highest stage being the throne of the supreme deity of the universe.[60] A similar view has been held by the Buddhist tradition, which regards the sacred mountain of Sumeru (or Meru) as the center of the universe. In Japan, Mount Yoshino was significantly called Kinpu-sen ("Mount Golden Peak") or, more poetically, Kane-no-mitake or Mikane-no-take ("Divine Peak of Gold"). In China, Wu-tai-shan, under the influence of Buddhism, came to be regarded as the abode of Monju (Mañjuśrī in Sanskrit).[61] During the Heian period

---

(*Mountain Ascetics of the Haguro Shugen-dō Sect and Folk Beliefs*) (Tsuruoka, 1950). This was also observed in my field research on the Fall Peak (Aki-no-mine) in Haguro in 1963.

[60] S. M. Shirokogoroff, *Psychomental Complex of the Tungus* (London, 1935); Mironov and Shirokogoroff, "Śrâmana-Shaman"; Eliade, *Shamanism*; Harva, *Die Religiösen Vorstellungen der altaischen Völker*.

[61] According to Ennin's diary, *Nittō guhō junrei-kō-ki*, he (Jikaku Daishi, 794–864) arrived at the foot of Wu-tai-shan on the twenty-eighth day of the fourth month in 840. He wrote: "This then is the region of Monju (Bodhisattva Mañjuśrī). There are no trees to be seen on the rounded heights of the five summits, and they look like overturned bronze bowls. On looking at them from afar, our tears flowed involuntarily. The trees and strange flowers are unlike those anywhere else, and it is

a belief developed among Japanese Buddhists that Wu-tai-shan in China was really the paradise of the Golden Mountain of Buddhist cosmology.[62]

There is not sufficient evidence as yet to trace a causal relationship between the belief in Mount Yoshino as the peak of gold and Wu-tai-shan as the golden world of Monju. We are more certain, however, that from ancient times Mount Yoshino has been considered the symbol of the cosmic mountain.[63]

---

a most unusual region. This then is the gold-colored world of Mount Ch'ing-liang (Shōryō in Japanese, literally, "Mount Clear and Cool"), where *Monju* manifested himself for our benefit." See Ennin [Jikaku Daishi], *Nittō guhō junrei kōki*, translation with annotations, in *Kokuyaku issai kyo*, "Shiden-bu" ("Part of History and Biographies"), Vol. XXV (rev. ed., 1963), pp. 259–419; Reischauer, *Ennin's Diary*, p. 214.

[62] In the *Nihon ryōi-ki*, compiled by a Buddhist monk in the early Heian period (early ninth century), Otomo-no-Yasuko tells of his mysterious pilgrimages to the Other World after his sudden fainting; he climbed up the Paradise of the Golden Mountain and met there the late Prince Shōtoku and the Buddhist saint Gyōgi. The author of the *Nihon-ryōi-ki* commented that the Paradise of the Golden Mountain might be Wu-tai-shan. See Kyōkai, "Nihon ryōi-ki" in *Nihon koten zensho*, annotated by Yūkichi Takeda (Tokyo, 1950), pp. 75–79.

[63] We can read a very interesting description in the *Dōken shōnin meido-ki* (*Record of the Pilgrimage into the Other World by the Buddhist Monk Dōken*), which was quoted in the *Fusō ryakki* compiled in the latter Heian period. Dōken wrote: "At noon on the second day of the eighth month [of A.D. 941] when Dōken had practiced religious austerities, he suddenly felt an extreme inner heat. His throat and tongue were parched with thirst, his breathing almost stopped. . . . After a moment he was choked, and his soul left his body to roam about. . . . His soul then met a Buddhist monk who came out of a cave and gave Dōken's soul a cup of sacred water. The Buddhist monk said that he was Vajradhara [Shu-kongō-jin, in Japanese] and permanently resided in the cave in order to guard the Śakya-muni's Law. . . . From the summit he was able to observe the whole universe below. This mountain was the highest, and

The mountain beliefs in Japan, as illustrated above, show a typological similarity to shamanic beliefs of the archaic period in other parts of the world, in which such motifs as magical heat, ascension to heaven, and descent to the netherworld are prominent. In Japan, it is significant that these motifs are integrally related to sacred mountains, which are both the object of religious worship and the arena of religious practices.[64] Thus, we see that the mountain is believed to be the world of the dead; the meeting place of the living and the dead; or a passageway from this world to the next—from the profane to the sacred and from earth to heaven. The mountain is also believed to be the world of the spirits and of the deities, buddhas, or bodhisattvas, where shamans and ascetics must undergo the austerities of hell to receive the powers and blessings of paradise and where souls of the dead also must undergo initiation in order to enter paradise or Buddha's Pure Land. Shugen-dō, or mountain asceticism, was built on just these primitive but funda-

---

the ground was pure and completely flat, and a golden light shown over it. In the north there was a mountain of gold which was an altar made of seven treasures. The second virtuous monk sat on this altar and said to Dōken that he was Zaō-bosatsu, the incarnation of Śakya-muni and the main deity of Mount Yoshino, and that this world was the Pure Land of Mount Golden Peak [Kinpu]. Zaō-bosatsu gave Dōken the new name Hōzō and made him take a pilgrimage into Hell in the mountain. . . . Zaō-bosatsu also taught Dōken powerful magic, mysteries, and new knowledge, such as the cause of the disasters in this world." See *Fusō-ryakki*, in *Kokushi taikei*, Vol. XII (Tokyo, 1932), pp. 219–22; *Fusō-ryakki* was originally thirty volumes of chronological records from the earliest times to the reign of Emperor Horikawa (reigned 1086–1106) which was compiled by Kōen (d. 1169), a Tendai monk and the teacher of Genkū (Hōnen Shōnin) of the Pure Land school.

[64] See Mircea Eliade, *Birth and Rebirth* (New York, 1958), pp. 85–87.

mental common beliefs in mountains. Mount Yoshino, for example, had been regarded in the ancient Yamato dynasty as both the cosmic mountain and the Great Mother, rejuvenator and guardian of the mysteries of life. It had been an important holy site for magico-religious initiation, where the mysteries were performed to gain possession of magical power. In this connection, we should note the existence of the Nibu- (or Nifu-) Kawa-kami shrine, which was located originally at the source of the Yoshino River; later, the mountain was worshipped at this shrine as a provider of rain.[65] According to Yana-gita,[66] *niho, nifu,* or *nyū* (all of which now mean "stack of rice straw") had the original meaning of the delivery hut of the rice plant or rice child. I have already mentioned Nibu-tsu-hime, the mountain goddess of Mount Kōya, and her divine son Kariba-myōjin. Also, we can find in Japan many places named Nibu, Nifu, or Niu, which are without exception situated at river sources or water-sheds. Therefore, it seems that the mountain goddess was originally the goddess of reproduction of both plants and animals as well as human beings. These mountain god-desses were first worshipped by the hunting tribes, then by the farmers. There is some evidence that the sacred mountains occupied by mountain ascetics were exploited at first by leaders or magicians among the hunters. And there is an intimate connection between mountain as-

[65] The terms *nibu* or *nifu* in Japanese folk vocabulary mean "child-birth" or "pregnancy." Yanagita (ed.), *Sōgō Nihon minzoku goi (Synthetic Vocabularies of Japanese Folklore)* (Tokyo, 1941), III, 1148.

[66] Yanagita, "Ine no ubuya" ("Delivery Hut of the Rice Plant"), in *Niiname no kenkyū (Studies on the Harvest Festivals)* (Tokyo, 1952), I, 22.

cetics and the hunters. The hunting rituals on the mountains performed by the professional hunters were clearly formed under the influence of Shugen-dō.

Japanese mountain worship, though historically colored by Shugen-dō and Tantric Buddhism, has preserved many features of ancient shamanism which can be traced to the prehistoric period.

CHAPTER

V

Japanese Shamanism

❧❧❧Japanese shamanism has persisted throughout a long period of religious history without having been institutionalized in a strict sense, though it commingled with Shinto and Buddhism and underwent many changes.

The leading role in Japanese shamanism has been played by shamanesses. As Takashi Akiba has pointed out,[1] Korean shamanism shows a significant contrast between northern and southern Korea. There are a few male shamans in the north, while in the south (except for Saishū Island) there are almost exclusively shamanesses. In fact, generally in the southern part of Korea, the Ryukyu Islands, and many parts of Japan shamanesses outnumber shamans. In Japanese, the general term for a shamanic figure is *miko*, which means explicitly a shamaness. There is no special term for a male shaman.

[1] Takashi Akiba, *Chōsen fuzoku no genchi kenkyū* (*A Study Based on Field Researches on Korean Shamanism*) (Tenri, 1950), pp. 13–31, especially pp. 27–28.

A good illustration is seen in a folk song from the twelfth-century Ryōjin-hishō.

> Isn't there any competent Woman
> In the Eastern Province [Azuma]?
> There are male shamans there;
> Then, Deities and Spirits
> Inspire and possess the Man.[2]

According to the classification of Tarō Nakayama,[3] Japanese shamanesses are divided into two categories. The first category he calls the *Kan-nagi*, which include the *miko*, who belong to the imperial court and Shinto shrines. These shamanesses retain roles only in certain formal Shinto rituals but have lost almost all their original functions and techniques. The second category is the *Kuchiyose*, including shamanesses who settle down in their own villages or migrate from village to village in compliance with the requests of the residents. They utilize techniques of trance and engage in telepathy, mediumship, divination, and fortunetelling, employing flexible but predictable forms. Their most frequently requested service is to communicate with guardian deities or spirits or with wraiths and spirits of the dead. The most popular name for the first category is *miko* or *jinja-miko* (Shinto shrine shamaness); for the second category, *ichiko* or *sato-miko* (city or village shamaness). The shamanesses of these two categories are semi-institutionalized. The *jinja-miko* (or *kan-nagi*, using Nakayama's

[2] *Ryōjin-hishō* is a collection of folk songs and ballads of the late Heian period which was compiled about 1192 by the retired Emperor Goshirakawa. *Iwanami bunko*, No. 935 (Tokyo, 1933), II, 87.

[3] Tarō Nakayama, *Nihon fujo shi* (*History of Japanese Shamanesses*) (Tokyo, 1930), p. 4.

term) are usually chosen from among daughters of hereditary families of Shinto priests or of hereditary parishioners of particular Shinto shrines. By contrast, the *sato-miko* (or *kuchiyose-miko*, using Nakayama's term) become shamanesses through certain initiatory ordeals and training directed by a teacher or elders.

I must add a third category, which includes both male and female shamans, in order to clarify the shamanic elements of contemporary religious phenomena in Japan, such as the newly arisen religions,[4] and the functions of many independent sorcerers and magicians. I shall call this category the *jussha* (magician) or *gyōja* (practitioner) system—that is, the magico-shamanic system. The Japanese *jussha* and *gyōja* are chosen by their guardian spirit, deity, or ancestral shaman, as in the Korean *son-mootang* and the *tsusu* of the Ainu in Hokkaido. *Son-mootang* means an immature or unauthorized and non-hereditary shaman, as contrasted wth *mootang*, which means authorized and hereditary shaman. Although there are certainly frauds among these shamans, they display certain similarities to their Siberian and Mongolian counterparts.

❰ Arctic and Korean Shamanism

Shamanism has been investigated among various races and tribes, and has an extensive literature. The only work covering the whole subject of shamanism from the

---

[4] "Newly arisen religions" is a translation of the term *shinkō shūkyō* and refers to sects that appeared or came to flourish after World War II. The definition and contents of this term will be clarified in the last chapter of this book.

viewpoint of the historian of religions is Mircea Eliade's *Shamanism*.[5] According to Eliade, shamanism involves "archaic techniques of ecstasy," at the same time that it is a mysticism, a magic, and a religion in the larger sense of these words.

> *In Central and Northeast Asia the chief methods of recruiting shamans are: (1) hereditary transmission of the shamanic profession and (2) spontaneous vocation (call or election). There are also cases of individuals who become shamans of their own free will . . . or by the will of the clan. . . . However selected, a shaman is not recognized as such until after he has received two kinds of teachings: (1) ecstatic (dreams, trances, etc.) and (2) traditional (shamanic techniques, names and functions of the spirits, mythology and genealogy of the clan, secret language, etc.).*[6]

> *What it is important to note now is the parallel between the singularization of objects, beings, and sacred signs, and the singularization by election, by choice, of those who experience the sacred with greater intensity than the rest of the community—those who, as it were, incarnate the sacred, because they live it abundantly, or rather are lived by the religious form that has chosen them [gods, spirits, ancestors, etc.].*[7]

Eliade also thought it useful to limit the term "shaman" to those among the various "specialists of the sacred (medicine men, magicians, contemplatives, inspired or possessed persons) who know how to employ ecstasy for the benefit of the community.

[5] Eliade, *Shamanism*.

[6] *Ibid.*, p. 13.   [7] *Ibid.*, p. 32.

Ecstasy always involves a trance, whether symbolic or pretended or real, and the trance is interpreted as temporary abandonment of the body by the soul of the shaman. During ecstasy, the soul of the shaman is thought to ascend to Heaven, or to descend to the other world [netherworld] or to travel far away into space. . . . Since the ecstasy [trance, losing one's soul, losing consciousness] seems to form an integral part of the human condition, just like anxiety, dream, imagination, etc., we do not deem it necessary to look for its origin in a particular culture or in a particular historical movement. As an experience, ecstasy is a non-historical phenomenon; it is a primordial phenomenon in the sense that it is coextensive with human nature. Only the religious interpretation given to ecstasy and the techniques designed to prepare it or facilitate it are historically conditioned. That is to say, they are dependent on various cultural contexts, and they change in the course of history.[8]

If we cannot conclude that ancient Japan was completely dominated by shamanism, nevertheless the existence of abundant shamanic elements should not be denied. Shamanesses are still remarkably active in Japan, as in southern Korea, the Hokkaido of the Ainu, and the Ryuku Islands. According to Akiba's excellent work *Chōsen fūzoku no genchi kenkyū* (*Report of Field Researches in Korean Shamanism*),[9] the Korean shamans having the closest relationship to Japanese shamanism are divided into three characteristic types. As I have mentioned above, first there is the hereditary shaman, called

[8] Eliade, "Recent Works on Shamanism," pp. 135–54.

[9] Akiba, *Chōsen fuzoku no genchi kenkyū*, pp. 46–66.

mootang, whose career is based on formalized initiation. Second is the spontaneous *son-mootang* (unauthorized *mootang*) who has received a genuine initiatory trance or "initiatory sickness and dream." The third is the pseudo-shaman who operates solely from economic motives. Akiba adds to this classification a blind male shaman called *pansu* in the southern part and *paksu* (not blind) in the north. Usually a person who becomes a *son-mootang* manifests his shamanic tendency through behavioral abnormalities. For example, he is attacked by a kind of mental disease in his youth; he likes an unbalanced diet; he confines himself to his room, hiding from other persons. He comes to have keen eyesight in contrast to physical weakness. In his initiatory sicknesses, his face takes on a strange appearance; he suddenly rushes about in an unusually excited condition; he wanders through hills and fields, dances fanatically, speaks strange words, and falls in a faint. His awareness thus narrowed and weakened, he suddenly blurts out divine messages under the influence of hypnotism. In order to cure this initiatory pathology, one must become a shamaness or shaman, or the condition will assume a dangerous character. The future shamaness or shaman must then pass through three stages of the initiation: first, a rite for driving away the defiled or evil spirits occupying the body and mind; second, a rite to pray for the descent of the particular deity or spirit who elected him; last, a rite for the introduction of a new shaman or shamaness to all the deities and good spirits as well as to the people.[10] Akiba

[10] Hori, "Nihon shūkyō no shakai-teki yakuwari" ("Social Roles in Japanese Religion") in *Nihon shūkyō-shi kenkyū* (Tokyo, 1962), I, 50–51; Akiba, *Chōsen fuzoku no genchi kenkyū*, pp. 62–64.

concludes that the processes seen in the Korean *son-mootang* are much the same as those for the shamans of Mongolia, Manchuria, and north-central Asian tribes.[11]

(Shamanesses in Japanese Society

Korean shamanism had the closest relationship to Japanese shamanism in ancient times. The role of Japanese shamanesses changed greatly, in keeping with a socio-political change that was supposedly based on the transition from the ancient matrilineal to the patrilineal society strongly influenced by China. Having gradually ceased to play a significant political role, the Japanese shamaness was absorbed into popular folk culture and transformed her function. Consequently, Japanese shamanism is not comparable to the highly developed integral institution in Siberia.

In order to search for the original type of Japanese shamanesses, we must go back about eighteen hundred years to the shamanic and charismatic Queen Himiko or Pimiko (literally, "August Child of the Sun") of Yama-tai in the Wo (Japanese: Wa) Kingdom. (Wo was the Chinese name for "Japan" or "Japanese" in ancient times.) According to the Chinese historical document *Wo-jen-chuan* (*A History and Topography of Third-Century Japan*) in the *Wei-chi* (*History of the Wei Dynasty*), compiled by Chên-shou (A.D. 233–297), Queen Himiko ruled over more than thirty states from A.D. 180 to about 248, having unified a large part of ancient Japan into a strong united kingdom centering in Yamatai. She

[11] Akiba, *Chōsen fuzoku no genchi kenkyū*, p. 65.

exchanged envoys from time to time with the court of the Wei dynasty. There have been many heated controversies among Japanese historians, from as early as the thirteenth century to the present day, concerning Himiko's self-conception, the location of Yamatai, and its relation to Japanese historical personages. I shall limit my discussion to the religious character of Queen Himiko. We read in the Wo-jen-chuan:

> That state [Wo] was ruled by a king for 70 to 80 years. At that time, Wo was in a chaotic state as the result of which a great civil war broke out and for many years the lords of small manors attacked each other. Afterwards, the people of Wo elected a young girl as their queen who was then named Himiko. She attended and rendered service to the Deities or Spirits and had a special power that bewitched the people. She never married even in her youth, and her brother helped her administer the affairs of the Kingdom. After she was enthroned, only a few persons were able to see her. There was only one man who always attended her, served her meals, transmitted her words, and had access to her living room. Her palace, many-storied buildings and citadels were very solemn and imposing, and were guarded continuously by armed soldiers. . . . Queen Himiko died. A big tomb built in order to bury her corpse measured a hundred steps and more in diameter, and more than one hundred royal retainers and slaves killed themselves at the funeral of their Queen.[12]

There are two important suggestions from this ancient Chinese document: The first is that Himiko was en-

12 *Gi-shi Wajin den*, pp. 48, 103–4.

throned by her people at an apex of political and social crisis, when she was only fourteen or fifteen, to judge from the fact that her reign continued sixty-eight years. The second point is that Himiko's personality and character seem to be typical of the shamanic queen in the ancient Japanese theocratic ages. From the archeological viewpoint, Himiko's reign falls at the end of the Yayoi period, which spans from the introduction of agriculture to the appearance of the local kingdom, and the beginning of the Kofun period, symbolized by large mounds erected for the dead of the ruling class, and during which there was a gradual formation of the unified empire centering in the Yamato dynasty of the Tennō (or Mikado) *Trilliail* family.

It seems to me important that this highly shamanic and charismatic girl was enthroned in order to meet a social crisis presumably caused by civil war in a transitional period of revolutionary political, economic, social, and cultural changes at the juncture of the Yayoi and Kofun periods. Having compared Himiko's function and character, some historians take her to be a female local chief in Kyushu who appears in the *Nihongi*; others take her to be Amaterasu-Ō-mikami (Great Sun Goddess, mythical ancestor of the imperial family) or Yamato-totohi-momoso-hime, or take Himiko and her male attendant to be Emperor Suinin and his daughter Yamato-hime, Empress Jingū and her prime minister Takeshiuchi-no-sukune, Empress Suiko and Crown Prince Shōtoku, or Empress Saimei and Crown Prince Naka-no-Ōye (later Emperor Tenchi). It is interesting to compare the fact that the Ryukus were ruled by the Shō dynasty under a combination of a king and his sister or niece as a shamanic priestess, the latter ruling over all the shamanesses and priestesses in the kingdom, until the Meiji era.[13]

The theory of a combination of the Sun Goddess and the male deity Takagi seems unworthy of discussion since the myths of the *Kojiki* and *Nihongi* upon which it is based are obscure.[14] However, there is much evidence of shamanic activity elsewhere in these sources. For example, Emperor Sujin, the tenth emperor of the Yamato dynasty according to the *Nihongi*, was praised as the "emperor who first ruled over the state," ranking thus with the traditional first emperor, Jimmu. During Sujin's reign, many charismatic shamanesses emerged as political figures in the chaotic situation brought about by a great epidemic. Among these shamanesses the emperor's aunt, Yamato-totohi-momoso-hime, was most remarkable. She was praised as a shrewd and intelligent princess able to foresee the future. When almost half the population of the empire had died in the great epidemic, the deeply

[13] Kōei Sakima, *Nyonin seiji kō* (*A Study of the Female Rulers*) (Tokyo, 1926).

[14] According to the *Kojiki*, the Sun Goddess is described as a figure who oversees the tilling of her sacred rice field and the weaving of garments for the deities, presumably in order to offer them to her deity or deities at festivals. In the section "Descent to the Earth of the Descendant of the Sun Goddess" (*Tenson-kōrin*) of the *Kojiki*, which may be an important part of the imperial family's authoritative tradition, we can find this connection of the Sun Goddess and the deity of Takagi at several places. The name "Takagi" means literally "Lofty Tree," though Chamberlain translated it as "High-Integrating Deity," following Motoori's interpretation, since the *Kojiki* has a footnote to the effect that this deity is the same as *Takami-musubi-no-kami* ("High-Integrating Deity"). However, if "Takagi" is a "Lofty Tree Deity," it would be possible to imagine that he was a personification of a cosmic tree. See *Kojiki*, Part I, "Jindai-no-maki" ("Records of the Divine Age"); Chamberlain, *Kojiki*, pp. 115–29.

anxious Emperor Sujin prayed to be granted a revelation at a divine enclosure. The deity of Ōmono-nushi (Great Deity of All Deities and Spirits) suddenly possessed Yamato-totohi-momoso-hime to reveal the cause of the epidemic. On another occasion, she foretold an uprising by Prince Take-haniyase-hiko by explaining prophetic poems that had been sung by a mysterious girl. Later, according to the *Nihongi*, she became the wife of the deity Ōmono-nushi. However, owing to the fact that she broke a promise to her divine husband, the deity suddenly ascended to his residence, Mount Miwa (Mount Mimoro in present-day Nara prefecture), saying that she did not restrain herself but caused him shame.[15] In the reign of Suinin (successor to Emperor Sujin), Princess Yamato-hime, one of the emperor's daughters, was chosen chief priestess of the Sun Goddess at the imperial family's shrine near the capital. One day, inspired by the Sun Goddess, she started out from the shrine reverently holding up the sacred mirror, the symbol of the goddess, and traveled through various provinces in compliance with

[15] The episode was as follows: Because his visits to her were always at night, Yamato-totohi-momoso-hime could never see her husband's true form clearly. She asked the deity to stay with her until daylight. The deity willingly consented, but made her promise solemnly that she would not cry out in surprise when she saw him. However, when she looked at her divine husband's real shape, she saw a small golden snake and broke her solemn promise. Overcome with remorse, she fell down and with a chopstick stabbed herself in the pudenda and died. A large tomb for her was built by humans by day and by superhuman beings at night. It was called "Chopstick Tomb" (*Hashi-baka*). According to the *Kojiki*, she was the ancestress of the famous shamanic and priestly families Miwa and Kamo, which both exerted great influence upon Shinto as well as upon Japanese politics. *Nihongi*, Vol. V, "Records of the Reign of Emperor Suijin," Aston, *Nihongi*, I, 150–64.

the goddess' instruction, finally erecting a new shrine at Ise (present-day Miye prefecture). She was called the August Staff of the Goddess (*Kami-no-mitsuye*), and the shrine she erected became the present Ise shrine.[16] In the reign of the next emperor (Keikō), when she was still rendering service to the Sun Goddess at Ise, her nephew, the great hero Prince Yamato-takeru, visited her to bid farewell as he set out on an eastern expedition commanded by his imperial father. According to the *Kojiki*, Princess Yamato-hime bestowed on Prince Yamato-takeru the Grass-Mowing Sword (*Kusanagi-no-tsurugi*, which later became one of the Three Divine Symbols of the Japanese imperial throne). This sword had been imbued with divine and mysterious powers by Susanowo-no-kami in mythical times. The prince then achieved success in the suppression of the barbarians in the eastern provinces owing to the mysterious power of the sword. He left this sword at his lover's house at the time he tried to subjugate the evil deity of Mount Ibuki; this act was the direct cause of his tragic death.[17] It is said that the Prince Yamato-takeru's soul flew away from his corpse in the form of a swan, so that his tomb was named Swan tomb.

About Empress Jingū (Okinaga-tarashi-hime), the *Kojiki* says:

> *This Empress was at that time divinely possessed. So when the Emperor [Chūai], dwelling at the palace . . . was about to smite the Land of the barbarian Kumaso, the emperor played on his lute, and the Prime Min-*

[16] *Nihongi*, Vol. VI, "Records of the Reign of Emperor Suinin," Aston, *Nihongi*, I, 165–87.

[17] *Kojiki*, Part II, "Records of the Reign of Emperor Keikō," Chamberlain, *Kojiki*, pp. 253–67.

ister *Takeshi-uchi, being in the pure court,*[18] *requested the divine orders. Hereupon the empress, divinely possessed, charged him with this instruction and counsel. . . . Then the emperor replied . . . saying, they are lying deities; he pushed away his lute, did not play on it, and sat silent. Then the deities were very angry, and said: as for this empire, it is a land over which thou oughtest to rule. Do thou go to the one road! [Soon after this the emperor was dead.]*[19]

In the *Nihongi* the period from Emperor Sujin to Prince Yamato-takeru is full of stories which suggest the gradual unification of the empire under the endeavors of many heroes and the establishment of the hegemony of the Yamato dynasty over all Japan; Empress Jingū's reign is at the turning point of political, economic, and cultural transformation. The Yamato dynasty advanced into southern Korea and established the key position called *Nihon-fu* (Japanese Governor General) of Mimana (Jên-na, in Chinese) at the southern tip of Korea, as a result of Empress Jingū's conquest of the Silla kingdom following the divine instruction. Thereafter, a large num-

[18] The sentence "being in the pure court" follows Chamberlain's translation. However, the original text is *Takeshi-uchi-no-Sukune-no-Ōomi saniwa ni ite;* and the original characters of *saniwa* mean literally sand garden. But these characters were probably only a phonetic transliteration. *Saniwa* in old Japanese had another meaning that signified the transmitter or interpreter of the divine words. The *Nihongi* used other characters in this part to write *saniwa* as interpreter of divine words. Therefore, this sentence reading "being in the pure court" must be corrected to "The Prime Minister Takeshi-uchi, becoming or being appointed an interpreter of the divine words, requested the divine orders."

[19] *Kojiki,* Part II, "Records of the Reign of Emperor Chūai," Chamberlain, *Kojiki,* pp. 277–78.

ber of immigrants from Korea and China poured into Japan, bringing with them the advanced learning and techniques which became the direct cause of revolutionary development in Japanese culture and industry. Parenthetically, it might be added that Emperor Nintoku, a grandson of the empress, was buried at the largest terraced mound in ancient Japan, which is now compared by archeologists with the Egyptian pyramid of Khufu or the greatest Chinese tomb (that of Emperor Shih Huang Ti, the first emperor of China). It is noteworthy that such political and cultural change was brought about mainly by a powerful charismatic and shamanic empress.

For several reasons, the Japan founded on the clan system was facing immediate peril, and the whole society was falling into disorder. This dangerous situation was caused by the increased number of Korean immigrants and the elevation of their social status based upon their cultural and technical skills, and by the gradual recession of Japanese influence in Korea owing to the rise of the Sui (A.D. 589) and the T'ang dynasties (A.D. 618) in China. Under the strong influence of rationalistic Confucian ethics and universalistic Buddhist doctrines, in 645 the Taika Reform first established the empire under the strong centralized authoritarian rule of one emperor over all Japan. Many records suggest the intense activities of shamans or shaman-like personages during these critical sociocultural changes. As only one example among many, in the year before the fall of the Soga clan, which fall permitted the Taika Reform, the *Nihongi* tells us:

In this month [the Sixth Month in A.D. 644] the witches and wizards[20] of the whole country, breaking

20 The wizards and witches of Aston's translation are originally written with Chinese characters which mean "male and female shamans,"

off leafy branches and hanging them with tree fibre, watched for the time when the Ō-omi [Prime Minister Soga-no-Emishi] would cross a bridge and vied with one another in addressing to him subtle interpretations of divine words. They were in great numbers, so that they could not be heard distinctly. Old people said that this was a sign of changes . . . . Autumn, Seventh Month. A man of the neighborhood of the River Fuji in the East Country named Ōfube-no-Ōshi urged his fellow-villagers to worship an insect, saying: This is the God of the Everlasting World (Tokoyo-no-kami). Those who worship this God will have long life and riches. At length the wizards and witches, pretending an inspiration of the gods, said . . . So they more and more persuaded the people to cast out the valuables of their houses, and to set out by the roadside sake, vegetables, and the six domestic animals. . . . Both in the country and in the capital people took the insect of the Everlasting World (Tokoyo-no-mushi), and placing it in a pure place, with song and dance invoked happiness. . . .[21]

It is noteworthy that old people recognized in the shamans' unusual activities an omen of social change. Later, at moments of anxiety connected with social change or crisis shamanistic mass hysteria frequently occurred.

Empress Kōgyoku (594–661), who ascended the throne a second time as Empress Saimei after the Taika

---

and the interlinear phonetics letters in the *Nihongi* are in this case *kan-nagi*, which means a lower class of Shinto priest or priestess; however, its original meaning is probably a person who can engage and ask the deity for divine instructions. (See p. 195, above.)

[21] *Nihongi*, Vol. XXIV, "Records of the Reign of Empress Kōgyoku," Aston, *Nihongi*, II, 187–89.

Reform in 655, had a dimly shamanic and charismatic nature. In 642, when there was a great drought and all Buddhist, Yin-yang, and traditional prayers for rain were unsuccessful, the empress paid a visit to the source of the Minabuchi River, and there she knelt and prayed, worshipping towards the four quarters, and looking up to heaven. Straightway there was thunder and a great rain, which fell for five days. The peasants throughout the empire called her "an empress of exceeding virtue."[22]

After the Taika Reform, the new order of the empire and the new social system modeled on that of the T'ang dynasty, together with the new religions and ethics from abroad, made impossible the appearance of any more charismatic sovereigns such as those I have discussed. Nevertheless, magico-religious leaders as such were called upon by all levels of society in event of group, social, or national crises.

In spite of the establishment of state Buddhism and the gradual popularization of Buddhist and Yin-yang magic from the eighth century on, shamanistic tendencies spread and were assimilated by the masses, since they fulfilled their functions effectively for the psychological and social anomie of the ordinary people. Socio-religio-political disturbances followed the transfer of the capital from Nara to Kyoto in 794. The activities of popular shamans and shamanesses are recorded in several documents of this time, such as the *Shoku-Nihongi* (A *Succeeding Historical Record to the Nihongi*) and *Nihon ryōi-ki* (an early Japanese Buddhist legendary record of the eighth century). Japanese shamanism became much transformed under the influences of Buddhism and the way

[22] Aston, *Nihongi*, p. 175.

of Yin-yang, while in turn Buddhism and Yin-yang were influenced by popular shamanism. Buddhism and Yin-yang could not have been diffused among the masses without such intermingling of traditions.

From the introduction of Buddhism into Japan—or at least from the beginning of the Heian period—Buddhism and Shinto confronted each other overtly and covertly. This is seen symbolically in the frequent records of incidents in which, for example, the curse or anger of a kami revealed itself in a thunderbolt or a mysterious fire after infringement on his divine territory by the felling of sacred trees in the shrine enclosure for the building of a Buddhist temple. A shaman would announce the curse or anger of the deity. The mixture of Shinto and Buddhism meant that Buddhism gradually lowered its standards to accommodate the Shinto framework specifically to cooperate with popular Japanese shamanism. One typical example of these tendencies is the belief in goryō, which I have discussed elsewhere.[23]

Belief in goryō arose at the end of the eighth century and flourished throughout the Heian period. It was originally a belief that the spirits of persons who had died as victims of political strife haunted their living antagonists in their lifetime, and was propagated through the mouths of popular shamanesses. Buddhist priests of the Tantric Tendai (*T'ien-t'ai* in Chinese) and Shingon (*Mantrayâna; Chên-yen* in Chinese) sects, who practiced religious austerities and obtained magical virtues in the mountains, as well as the powerful Yin-yang magicians, were invited to negotiate with and exorcise these revengeful spirits.

[23] Hori, "The Concept of Hijiri," pp. 128–60, 199–232.

With the popularization of this belief, the possibility of becoming a goryō, formerly the privilege of nobles alone, was opened to the common people. Thus, the linking of popular shamanesses with the Buddhist mountain ascetics (*shugen-ja*) became more and more close. For example, during the Heian period, almost every Buddhist priest utilized a shamaness or her substitute as a medium during his exorcism in order to know the names of the revengeful spirits and their complaints and curses. On the other hand, one of the earlier social functions of the Japanese popular Jōdo school (Pure Land school) seems also to have been to transfer these revengeful spirits of the dead into the merciful hands of Amida Butsu (Amitâbha Buddha) by the repetition of his sacred name (Nembutsu), as well as to cause the believers themselves to arrive in Amitâbha's Pure Land after death.[24]

In these circumstances, the character and function of Japanese popular shamanesses took different forms: some became professional mediums dependent upon Buddhist mountain asceticism (*Shugen-dō*); others became dancers or singers; others became *kuchiyose-miko*; still others became the reciters of ballads. Japanese popular entertainment, including Kabuki, emerged in the process of the differentiation of Japanese shamanism.

Though there were significant transformations and transmutations in the history of Japanese shamanism, we must not overlook the fact that shamanic personages as well as the phenomenon of shamanic mass hysteria appeared actively among the people at each socio-political crisis or change throughout Japanese history—not only at the transition from Heian to Kamakura, or from

[24] *Ibid.*, pp. 213–28.

Ashikaga to Tokugawa, or from Tokugawa to Meiji, but also following World War II.

(Various Names of the Kuchiyose-miko System

The actual behavioral patterns of the *Kuchiyose-miko* in Japanese rural communities are significant, as are the shamanistic tendencies in the new religions which have emerged at transitional moments from the end of the Tokugawa era to the present time.

Among the various names of the *Kuchiyose-miko* system, we must notice *ichiko* and its variations: *itako* (in northeastern Honshu), *ichijo* (in Kyushu), *ita* (in the southern part of central Honshu) and *yuta* in the Ryuku and Amami islands). According to such specialists on shamanism as Takashi Akiba,[25] the origin of these words is thought to have some etymological similarity and historical connection with the names of Yakut, Buriat, Altaic, and Kirghise shamans: *udagan, utygan, iduan, üdege.*

Another local name for "shamaness" is *o-kami-n*, or *o-kami-sama.* This name is thought to have derived from *kami* ("deity," or sometimes "wife" in colloquial speech; *o* is an honorary prefix; *sama* is an honorary suffix; *n* is an abbreviation of *sama* or *san*). *Kami* has meant "god" or "deity" in Japan from ancient times to the present day; however, there is not a merely coincidental simi-

[25] Akiba, *Chōsen fuzoku no genchi kenkyū;* Taikei Kunishita (Iwai), "Shaman to yū go no gengi ni tsuite" ("Approach to the Original Meaning of the Word 'Shaman'"), *Minzoku,* Vol. II (Tokyo, 1926–27); Jōji Tanase, *Tōa no minzoku to shūkyō (People's Religions of Eastern Asia)* (Tokyo, 1943).

larity between Japanese *kami*, Ainu *kamui*, and Mongolian *kami* or *kam* for "shaman" or "shamanizing," although we cannot yet elucidate the relationship. Still another local name is *azusa-miko*, which means a "shamaness who uses a catalpa bow as a special instrument for her trance." The so-called catalpa bow (*azusa-yumi*) which the shamaness employs is a kind of one-stringed instrument, said to be used by some Central Asian shamans. Words affiliated with *azusa-miko* are *tataki*, *sasa-hataki*, and *ōyumi*. The origins of these words may be linked to the fact that the shamaness held or beat a bow, since *tataki* or *hataki* means "beating," *sasa* means "bamboo grass for beating the bow," *ōyumi* means "big bow." Finally, the local name *nonō* could have come from the Sanskrit *Namo*, a hailing or invocation of a Buddha, or from the Japanese *nōnō*, "hello." *Nōnō* supposedly suggests the impressive words spoken by shamanesses.[26]

Until the beginning of the twentieth century there were many wandering shamanesses (*aruki-miko*) in rural society and even in Yedo (the former name of Tokyo), Kyoto, and Osaka. They were called *ichiko*, *azusa-miko* as well as *Shinano-miko*, *Agata-miko* and *nonō*. *Shinano* (the old name of present-day Nagano prefecture) and *Agata* (a country name in Nagano prefecture) are from the sites of the largest headquarters of these wandering shamanesses. They visited from village to village within their territories immediately following the harvest in autumn, traveling in groups of five or six. Their main functions were: communication with spirits, deities,

[26] Nakayama, *Nihon fujo shi*, p. 14; Yanagita, "Fujo kō" ("A Study of Female Shamans in Japan"), *Kyōdo kenkyū*, Vol. I, Nos. 1–12 (1913).

wraiths, and the dead; divination and fortunetelling through trance; prayers for recovery of the sick; and purification of new buildings, wells, stoves, and hearths. They might give their own fetish to a parishioner's child so that he would grow up in good health; sometimes they held memorial services for a parishioner's ancestors. Some were said to have practiced clandestine prostitution, especially in the urban societies.[27]

⟦ Initiation of Kuchiyose-miko

These wandering shamanesses have almost disappeared in present-day Japan, though many settled village shamanesses belonging to the *kuchiyose* system are still active in various provinces, notably in the Tōhoku (northeastern) area of Honshu. In the Tōhoku area they are not genuine shamanesses in the strict sense, not having been elected or chosen by their deity or spirit but rather, voluntarily or involuntarily, adopted by an elder shamaness master and bound to her in the relationship of master and apprentice. In the Tōhoku area almost all the shamanesses are blind. Blind girls in this area have usually become the apprentices of the older shamanesses who lived near their native village. The novices undergo training disciplines such as cold-water ablution, purification, fasting, abstinence, and observance of various taboos. They are taught the techniques of trance, of communication with superhuman beings or spirits of the dead, and of divination and fortunetelling; they also learn the melody and intonation used in the chanting

[27] Hori, *Wagakuni minkan-shinkō-shi no kenkyū*, II, 655–68.

of prayers, magic formulas, and liturgies, and the narratives and ballads called *saimon*. After three to five years' training, they become full-fledged shamanesses through the completion of initiatory ordeals and an initiation ceremony which includes the use of symbols of death and resurrection.[28]

When the novice has completed her training, she is initiated into the shamanic mysteries by her mistress. Before the initiation ceremony, as preliminary preparation, the novice puts on a white robe called the death dress and sits face to face with her mistress on three rice bags. Several shamaness elders assist in the ceremony. They chant and utter the names of deities, buddhas, and several magic formulas in unison with the mistress and the novice. In this mystical atmosphere, the novice's joined hands begin to tremble slightly. Observing carefully the novice's change of behavior, the mistress perceives the climax of inspiration and suddenly cries in a loud voice to the novice: "What is the name of the deity that possessed you?" Immediately the novice answers: "So-and-so deity (or sometimes buddha or bodhisattva) possessed me." When the mistress hears this answer, she throws a large rice cake at the novice, and the novice falls off the bags and faints. Sometimes the elders dash water on top of the novice's head 3,333 times at a wellside or at the seashore. The novice in a dead faint is warmed by the body heat of shamaness elders who share her bed, and finally regains consciousness. The novice is said to be newborn and is then initiated. She changes her white death dress to a colorful so-called wedding dress and performs the ceremony of the traditional

[28] *Ibid.*, p. 662.

wedding toast by exchanging nine cups of *sake* with her mistress. This exchange of cups is the most important part of the traditional wedding ceremony of Japan. After ritually practicing the first communication with her ancestral spirit and other spirits of the dead, the novice is given a large feast to certify her proficiency as an independent shamaness. Her mistress, shamaness elders, parents, brothers and sisters, relatives, and friends are all invited. After a week or ten days' isolation at her tutelary shrine as a rite of recovery or *agrégation*, she becomes a professional shamaness.[29]

The formulas for inquiring of spirits of dead persons are great in variety, though somewhat formalized. For example, I have heard a shamaness in Aomori prefecture say:

> *Hear me! Hear me!*
> *I call for today's water;*
> *What water may I call for?*
> *I call for the water on the young spray.*
> *[The spirit] comes with its sleeve bathed in tears.*
> *[The spirit] comes with its skirt full of dewdrops.*
> *We can only hear its voice, not see its form;*
> *We can but hear its sound, not see its figure;*
> *[The spirit] comes on seven or eight rapid currents;*
> *[The spirit] comes down to play in dancing;*
> *And [the spirit] comes to give us an account.*

Another shamaness in Akita prefecture said:

> *Coming along the seashore in paradise,*
> *We hear the songs of plovers,*

[29] *Ibid.*, pp. 662–63.

The plovers are proud of their voice,
By singing and singing;
By what cause and condition can [the spirit] come
    up to this world?
By a cup of tea and pure water for the service.

Or, finally, in Aomori prefecture:

In the dark night
When I hear the voice of a crow
Who never sings;
What kind of fruit would grow
On a spray of the mysterious tree named zuiki?
There would grow the Six Characters
Of Na-Mu-A-Mi-Da-Butsu.[30]

Another formal feature is the use of particular terms for the given names of relatives and others at the séance. For example, the spirit of the dead calls the eldest son the "first treasure" (ichi-no-takara); the married daughter the "outer-door treasure" (kabe-no-soto-no-takara); the husband the "high headgear" (taka-eboshi); the eldest brother and sister "first row" (ichi-no-narabi); the native house the "old fire" (furu-bi). The shamaness usually carries a black case on her back in which talismans, fetishes, written formulas, and Buddhist sutras may be found; she also has a rosary which is made of 180 wooden or stone beads strung together with several polished skulls and fangs of badger, fox, sable, bear, or antelope, as well as several old coins. This rosary is called irataka-no-juzu and is said to have originated in Buddhist asceticism and Shugen-dō.[31]

[30] *Ibid.*, pp. 663–64.
[31] *Ibid.*, p. 664.

⟨ *Social Functions of the Kuchiyose-miko*

The shamanesses of the Tōhoku area are usually requested to communicate with and transmit the will of
superhuman beings and the spirits of the dead. They
are often invited to visit a family in mourning, because
the first communication with the spirit of the newly dead
person is thought to be an important part of the funeral.
They call it the *hotoke-no-kuchiake* ("opening of the dead
person's mouth"). *Hotoke* originally meant "Buddha,"
but in colloquial speech now indicates any dead person.
Especially when a person has met an unnatural death or
died in difficult childbirth, the ceremony of opening the
dead person's mouth is the most important service for
the salvation of his soul. The relatives collect a sum of
money and rice from seven neighboring villages and invite a shamaness to perform a special and complicated
service called *nana-kura-yose* (séance together with the
seven divine seats). This seems to be a survival of the
ancient belief in *goryō*.[32]

One interesting custom is the large gathering of shamanesses held once a year, on the day of *Jizō-bon*,[33] at

[32] *Ibid.*, pp. 667–68; "Nihon shūkyō no shakai-teki yakuwari," in
Nihon shūkyō-shi kenkyū, Vol. I, pp. 192–93.

[33] *Jizō-bon* is a mixture of the belief in Jizō-bosatsu (the Buddhist
bodhisattva Kshitagarbha) and the *bon* festival that is still the most popular annual festival, including memorial services for the spirits of the dead
as well as for the ancestors of each family. The *Jizō-bon* is held on the
festival day of Jizō in the sixth month of the lunar calendar, while the
bon festival is held from the thirteenth to fifteenth days of the seventh
month in almost all rural societies in the Tōhoku (northeastern Honshu) area.

several sacred mountains and temples in northern Honshu, such as Mount Osore, the Jizō hall in Kanagi-machi in Aomori prefecture, Hachiyō-ji temple in Fukushima prefecture. *Jizō-bon* is a festival for the bodhisattva Kshitigarbha, whose Japanese name is Jizō (Ti-tsang in Chinese). Jizō, popular bodhisattva among the Japanese since the tenth century, is believed to be a savior of spirits of the dead, who otherwise would be suffering tortures in hell, as well as a guardian deity of children.

Mount Osore is a dormant volcano and is believed to be the Other World[34] by the inhabitants of the area, who believe that there is a terrestrial paradise as well as a terrestrial hell on the mountaintop with its crater lake. From early morning on the twenty-fourth day of the sixth month of the lunar calendar—the festival day of Jizō—old men and women from various villages climb Mount Osore carrying special rice dumplings to offer at each of the stone statues of Jizō and stupas and mounds along the mountain paths. Since ancient times the common people have believed that dead children are required to heap up small stones to build a stupa, goaded by the ogres of hell, if they died without having offered any service to their parents or community. Accordingly, any woman who has lost a child heaps small stones in the shape of a stupa as a substitute for her child on this day.

More than thirty shamanesses also climb the mountain

[34] Several sacred mountains in Japan are believed to be the Other World. For example, according to folk legends in the Heian period, Tate-yama, Haku-san, Kimpu, Nachi, and others were believed to be mountains which dead persons climbed and where they lived as ghosts. These mountains afterward became sacred for mountain asceticism (Shugen-dō). Mount Osore is one survival from ancient times of such mountains of the dead.

for the festival and occupy a special corner near the main
hall of the temple in order to fulfill the worshippers'
requests. Old women who have been deprived of husband, son, daughter, or grandchild ask one of the shamanesses to communicate with this spirit as a part of the indispensable memorial service. They sit on the ground
around a shamaness and listen with rapt attention to the
voice of the dead relative who speaks through the shamaness. From morning till midnight these shamanesses
fall into trances to communicate with departed spirits
upon each request. A shamaness's income on that day
alone might amount to more than eight thousand yen
(approximately twenty-five dollars) at the rate of a hundred (about thirty cents) for each request. Each trance
for a single spirit continues for five or ten minutes on the
festival day; on ordinary days, it lasts an hour or more.[35]

We can recognize some peculiar characteristics which
distinguish the *kuchiyose-miko* from the general type
common to northern Asia. First, *the kuchiyose-miko* does
not suffer a psycho-mental disorder or initiatory disease
before her initiation. She is transformed into a shamaness by human means, not by a psycho-mental process or
by divine calling and election. Second, during her trance,
she does not invoke a particular deity who has elected her
as its mouthpiece. Instead, she usually invokes the guardian deity or tutelary deity, or the buddha or bodhisattva,
of her client. She falls into a trance and relates the divination or the invocation as if she herself had become a
deity or a spirit of the dead through her own power, not

[35] Hori, "Minzoku-gaku kara mita Nihon-jin no reikon-kan ni tsuite"
("Soul Concepts of Japanese Peoples from the Viewpoint of Folklore
Studies"), *Nihon shūkyō-shi kenkyū*, Vol. I (Tokyo, 1962), 173–75;
Wagakuni minkan-shinkō-shi no kenkyū, II, 661–62.

through the medium of her own deity or spirit. Finally, communication with spirits of the dead may be exceptional in northern Asian shamanism. For example, the shamanesses whom I met among the Ainu in Hokkaido are, without exception, loath to communicate with spirits of the dead, even though they have come to accept this practice following the Japanese custom, mainly in order to get money. They say that by doing so they would fall under their guardian deity's displeasure, because they might be defiled by coming into contact with a new and unpurified spirit. When they do listen for the voice of a departed relative, in order to beg forgiveness to their deity they require the client to offer a special *inao* (an offering to the deity made of wood carved like a flower, peculiar to the Ainu) in addition to the normal one.[36]

⟨ *Shamanesses and the Folk Arts*

In concluding this chapter, I should like to call attention to the particular techniques of *kuchiyose-miko*, such as the *saimon, uta-nembutsu,* and *etoki. Saimon* means a written address to the deities; however, the *saimon* as a folk art is a kind of ballad, a distortion of its original meaning. Two varieties of *saimon* ballad are: the *yamabushi-saimon,*[37] mainly distributed in the Tōhoku area by *yamabushi* of the Haguro sect; and the *sekkyō-saimon,* originally transmitted by *yamabushi* of the Kumano sect. Probably under the influence either of *Haguro-yamabushi* or *Kumano-yamabushi,* shamanesses in the

[36] Hori, *Wagakuni minkan-shinkō-shi no kenkyū,* II, pp. 664–67.

[37] *Ibid.,* pp. 174–75.

Tohoku area still hand down their peculiar ballad named *oshira-saimon. Oshira* is the name of a guardian spirit enshrined with each main family of the village. It is called *oshira-sama* or *oshira-gami* (in some places, *ohira* or *ohina,* supposedly because of the connection with *hina,* a doll, or paper cut in the shape of a human figure), and is thought of as a pair of deities. The *oshira-sama* are symbolized by two small sticks made of the branches of a special kind of mulberry tree carved into various shapes. Each stick is covered with cloth. *Oshira-sama* are worshipped mainly by housewives, organized on the basis of *dōzoku* groups, small territorial groups, or groups of relatives, usually around the vernal equinox. On the festival night, a village shamaness is invited to each family where the *oshira-sama* are enshrined, to perform a séance in order to pray for the good health, good harvests of crops, and silkworms of the associated families. After a formal ceremony, the shamaness recites the *oshira-saimon,* holding and moving the two divine dolls in both hands as she recites the ballad. This is called *oshira-asobase* (literally, "to entertain the *oshira-sama*"), but it is said to be a survival of the ancient word *kami-asobase* ("Shinto dancing and music").[38]

[38] It is very interesting as well as puzzling that the story told by the *oshira-saimon* ballad first appeared in a Chinese book of legends named *Sou-shên-chi* (compiled by Kan-pao about the fourth century A.D., in the Tsin dynasty. This legend is classified by folklorists as the "horse-headed-maiden" type (*ma-tou-lan* type in Chinese). The Japanese variation of it which has been preserved by the blind shamanesses in the Tohoku area is as follows: Once upon a time, there was a beautiful daughter in a wealthy family, but she had love only for the fine family horse. Her father, angered by this passion, killed and skinned the horse. His beloved daughter was deeply grieved by this. On the next day the horse's skin was hanging on a tree, and the daughter robed herself with it. In this guise she marvelously soared higher and higher into the sky, scorn-

The *etoki* or holy picture is one of the earliest examples of historical diversification of the shamanic function. *Etoki* literally means "explanation by means of a picture." Historically, this form originated among shamanesses belonging to the Kumano *Shugen-dō* and afterward was practiced professionally by wandering women of the lower classes[39]—called *Kumano-bikuni* ("Buddhist nuns of Kumano").[40] In medieval times, especially during the Ashikaga period (1338-1573), the mountain ascetics (*yamabushi* or *shugen-ja*) of Mount Kumano sometimes married shamanesses and wandered with them from village to village throughout Japan. Because the *Kumano-shugen-ja* had been controlled by Mantrayâna Buddhist Tendai and Shingon sects, the wives of *shugen-ja*

---

ing the parent's distress. A few days later, many silkworms descended from the sky to the mulberry tree in the garden and spun cocoons. Her parents believed that the silkworms were incarnations of their daughter and her horse husband, and reared them carefully. This was said to be the origin of silkworm culture in Japan. Villagers who engage in silkworm culture have come to enshrine daughter and consort as *oshira-sama*, in accordance with this legend. Yanagita, *Kyōdo kenkyū*, Vol. I, pp. 397–408.

It is still unclear how the blind shamanesses in rustic northeast Honshu, far from cultural centers, received and transmitted this legend. Perhaps it was through some unknown educated *yamabushi* or Buddhist priest who interpreted the origin of silkworm culture by borrowing a Chinese legend. However, as the result of the distribution of the *oshira-saimon*, *oshira-sama* are worshiped by villagers as guardian deities of silk culture, while there still survives their original function as guardian of the household. See Yanagita, "Oshira-gami-ko" ("A Study of the Oshira Deity"), *Yanagita Kunio shū*, XII, 267–431; Hori, *Wagakuni minkan-shinkō-shi no kenkyū*, II, pp. 661–63, 667, 694.

[39] Hori, *Wagakuni minkan-shinkō-shi no kenkyū*, II, pp. 699–700.

[40] *Bikuni* originated from the Sanskrit term *bhiksuni* ("nun"). See *ibid.*, pp. 144, 180–81, 698–703, 754.

were colloquially called nuns (*bikuni*). They traveled from village to village to preach the way to salvation in the Pure Land of Amida Buddha and the moralistic theory of causality, designating as *etoki* boards on which pictures of paradise (*Jōdo*) and hell were painted. They lived on offerings from the villagers.

In the early Tokugawa period (1603–1867) the *Ise-bikuni* appeared, functioning in the same manner as the *Kumano-bikuni*, and are thought to have been directly influenced by the *Kumano-bikuni*. In this period both *Kumano-bikuni* and *Ise-bikuni* completely lost their shamanic functions and qualities and became merely ballad singers and reciters from lower-class or outcaste groups. They developed several religious folk arts, such as the *uta-Nembutsu* (sung *Nembutsu*), the *uta-zaimon* (sung *saimon*), and the *sekkyō-saimon* (sermon ballads). These arts may be considered historical transformations of the original shamanic techniques of ecstasy and trance.[41]

Such wandering popular artisans have almost completely disappeared, but their influence survives in artists or entertainers of today. Even such highly developed music and drama as Kabuki, Jōruri, or the Bunraku puppet shows may have originated from, or have been associated with, special techniques of shamanic ecstasy in the seventeenth and eighteenth centuries. The shamanesses in the Tohoku area should be observed as unchanged examples of the coexistence of shamanic and artistic functions.[42]

[41] *Ibid.*, pp. 37, 45, 422–23, 698–99, 754.

[42] "Aruki-miko to uta-bikuni" ("Migrating Shamanesses and Singing Nuns"), *ibid.*, pp. 651–707.

CHAPTER
VI

---

*The New Religions
and the Survival of
Shamanic Tendencies*

🙚🙚🙚O̲ne of the most significant religious phenomena in Japan after World War II has been a sudden
rise of new religious movements. Sprouting up like mush-
rooms after a rain, they amounted to more than seven
hundred sects at the peak.[1] The *Shūkyō benran* (*Manual
of Japanese Religions*), issued by the Department of Education (Monbu-shō) in 1954, gives the statistics in the
accompanying tabulation.[2]

[1] Hori, "Minshū-seikatsu to shūkyō" ("Folk Life and Religion") in
Nihon shūkyō-shi kenkyū, Vol. I, pp. 141–44. See also Section I: "Gen-
dai Nihon no shūkyō-teki jinkō" ("Religious Population of Modern
Japan").

[2] Monbushō shūmu-ka (comp.), *Shūkyō benran* (*Manual of Japanese
Religions*), compiled by the Bureau of Religious Affairs in the Department of Education (Tokyo, 1954), pp. 530–31.

This phenomenon should be understood as a response to the acute anomie into which the Japanese people were thrown by defeat and occupation. The established religions in Japan had supported the old regime and had accorded it ultimate meaning and value, and understandably were not able to minister to people confused in the face of the collapse of state and society in 1945. The cultural value system that had previously controlled the conduct of individuals was broken by the occupation as well as by the political, economic, and social disasters of

RELIGIOUS ORGANIZATION

	INCORPO-RATED	UNINCORPO-RATED OR-GANIZATIONS	TOTAL
Shinto affiliation...........	204	54	258
Buddhist affiliation	220	46	266
Christian affiliation	38	12	50
Others	85	66	151
Totals................	547	178	725

NUMBER OF SHRINES, TEMPLES, AND CHURCHES

	OFFICIALLY AFFILIATED	INDEPENDENT	TOTAL
Shinto (in origin)..........	120,608	984	121,592
Buddhist (in origin)........	82,798	645	83,443
Christian (in origin)........	3,737	82	3,819
Others	4,994	79	5,073
Totals................	212,137	1,790	213,927

NUMBER OF RELIGIOUS PROFESSIONALS (PRIESTS, MONKS, NUNS)

	MALE	FEMALE	TOTAL
Shinto affiliation...........	110,293	60,290	170,583
Buddhist affiliation	122,570	59,976	182,546
Christian affiliation	4,117	4,217	8,334
Others	9,596	4,394	13,990
Totals................	246,576	128,877	375,453

defeated Japan. At this point, religious sects that had been oppressed by the militaristic government revived, and new religious movements endeavoring to answer to this acute anomie sprang up. Actually, the complete destruction of traditional Japanese social, cultural, and political structures was averted by the rise of the new religious movements.[3] This can be understood in terms of Merton's theory of anomie,[4] which states that ritualism denies the cultural end of a given society but approves institutionalized means as a response to anomie.

H. Neil McFarland has pointed out the five factors which caused the emergence of messianic cults in primitive societies, such as the Ghost-Dance religion of the American Indians and the Cargo cults of New Guinea, and has compared them with the Japanese new religions phenomena. He says:

These cults are examples of a socio-religious phenome non which, for over a half-century, has been reasonably well understood by anthropologists. Among such cults,

[3] Hiroo Takagi, *Shinkō shūkyō* (*Newly Arisen Religions*) (Tokyo, 1958), pp. 212–42, especially section on "Shinkō shūkyō no shakai-teki kinō" ("Social Functions of the Newly Arisen Religions"), pp. 228 ff. See also his *Nihon no shinkō shūkyō* (*Newly Arisen Religions of Japan*) (Tokyo, 1959).

[4] R. K. Merton, *Social Theory and Social Structure* (rev. and enl. ed.; Glencoe, Ill., 1957). See especially Chapter IV, "Social Structure and Anomies," pp. 126–40; Chapter V, "Continuities of the Theory of Social Structure and Anomie," pp. 161–75. See also Merton, "Social Structure and Anomie," in *The Family, Its Function and Destiny*, ed. Ruth N. Anshen (New York, 1949); and "The Social-Cultural Environment and Anomie," in *New Responsives for Research on Juvenile Delinquency*, ed. Helen L. Witmer and Ruth Kotinsky (Washington, 1959), pp. 24–50; and Talcott Parsons, *Social System* (Glencoe, Ill., 1951), pp. 256–57; 322–25.

wherever they have been discovered, there is discernible a remarkably standard pattern of development in which at least five factors are recurrent: (1) social crisis intensified by an intrusive culture; (2) a charismatic leader; (3) apocalyptic signs and wonders; (4) ecstatic behavior; and (5) syncretic doctrine. The milieu from which they arise, described in the words of anthropologist Margaret Mead, is the "ferment of half-abandoned old and half-understood new."[5]

(General Tendencies of the New Religions

Iichi Oguchi has analyzed the general tendencies of the new religions as follows.[6] The founder is always somewhat critical of established religions in theoretical matters, but the criticisms never attack organized religion as such, since the new order is still modeled on established precedents. The theories of the new religions are dynamic in comparison to the formalized theologies of the traditional sects; but while they reject the doctrines and dogmas of the older religions, their own message is not based on new or creative insights. The founders know, however, how to relate a simple message to the frustration and fragmentation of the general populace. Underlying the new religions is an age-old shamanistic element transformed into a modern shape and coupled with residual features of traditional ancestor worship.

[5] H. Neil McFarland, "Japan's New Religions," in *Contemporary Religions in Japan*, I, No. 4 (December, 1960), 60.

[6] Iichi Oguchi, *Nihon shūkyō no shakai-teki seikaku* (*Social Characteristics of Japanese Religion*) (Tokyo, 1953), pp. 74–75, 102.

According to Hiroo Takagi,[7] the ethos of the new religious movement is in effect pre-modern; that is to say, all the new religions have the following characteristics: elements of Japanese folk beliefs; inter-human relations based on a pseudo parent-and-child system; anti-social and yet life-affirming attitude; and, finally, astute organizational ability and commercialism. For the most part the new religions promise to solve the problems of the masses by means of magico-religious formulas without undercutting the framework of the old social order. This means that what these new religions provide is a subjectivistic, temporary "solution" of people's problems, so that converts are made to feel that they can start their lives afresh in the midst of a troubled world and enjoy better human relations within the context of their newly acquired religious groups. However, these new religions have made no attempt to address themselves to the larger issues of social evils and injustice. In addition, many of the founders or organizers of these new religious groups seem to have charismatic personalities. Almost every one of them was born as the second or third child of a poor landowner, peasant, fisherman, or small merchant, and had firsthand experience of poverty and the difficulties of the downtrodden. In spite of, or indeed because of, all this they found a deeper meaning of life in their religious faith.[8] This may account for the fact that they are such effective communicators and teachers to the men and women of the lower strata of Japanese society.[9]

[7] Takagi, *Shinkō shūkyō*, pp. 86–241; see especially pp. 86, 101, 102, 122, 228, and 241.

[8] *Ibid.*, pp. 142–209.

[9] Following Oguchi's and Takagi's analyses, Clark B. Offner and Henry van Straelen, in their work *Modern Japanese Religions*, have

⟮ The Three Periods of the Emergence of New Religions

The leading new religions in present-day Japan must be divided into three groups or periods in accordance with their origin and development. The first group appeared and developed in the last period of the Tokugawa shogunate before the beginning of the Meiji era—that is,

---

pointed out twelve characteristics of the new religions: (1) The particular teaching, emphases, ceremonies, and sacred writings of each are considered to have been divinely revealed to the founder. (2) The founders of the new religions do not seem to excel in humility. Some refer to themselves as saviors of the present age or equate themselves with Moses, Christ, Buddha, Confucius, or certain Japanese emperors. (3) The majority of the new religions are syncretistic to a greater or lesser degree. They freely incorporate the teachings and practices of various other religions or philosophical systems. (During their whole history the Japanese have shown a pronounced undogmatic tendency together with a great flexibility and adaptability of mind. They link together quite contrary views, a characteristic which goes together with a distaste for absolutes. They can easily worship at Buddhist temples and at the same time at Shinto shrines or Christian churches.) (4) Doctrinally and ceremonially the new religions tend to be simple—almost superficial. Many have little concrete doctrine of their own. Their doctrinal bases are often Buddhist or Shintoist with certain peculiar emphases. Simplicity of doctrine is one obvious reason for their popularity among the masses. (5) Related to doctrinal simplicity is the primary emphasis upon "this worldly" benefit. The new religions are more concerned with meeting man's material needs in the present than with giving hope for the future or speculating about the nature of another world. One result of the "this worldly" emphasis is the important and almost indispensable part played by physical healing. (6) Most of the new religions have a strong eschatological character. They point to a bright and cheerful life sometime in the future in this world. (7) The enthusiasm and individualism of the new religions contrast with the established faiths and may also be con-

from the beginning to the middle of the nineteenth century, just at the time of the great change from the pre-industrial feudal system to modern industrial Japan. In this period many independent religious movements arose. However, the Tokugawa shogunate prohibited the establishment of any new religious sects beyond the thirteen Buddhist sects already authorized. After the Meiji Restoration, these movements were permitted to establish themselves as thirteen Shinto sects. Some of them were the institutionalizations of nationalistic Shinto, such as

---

sidered characteristic. One enters a new religion by individual faith, rather than simply by virtue of family or geographical accident. Having become a believer by choice, it is normal for one to become an enthusiastic proponent of his faith. (8) Many of the new religions have rejected any traditional hierarchical organization which distinguishes between clergy and laity. Most of the believers are entitled to perform sacred functions, and this lay character seems to stimulate missionary activities among the members. Nevertheless, lack of a priesthood does not mean lack of organization. Great care is taken to assure liaison with the denomination's headquarters. (9) Despite pretensions on the part of some to be world religions, the new religions are definitely Japanese faiths. Thy are rooted in Japan and make their appeal to the Japanese. Their "newness" is found in certain emphases or enthusiasms rather than in major differences from traditional Japanese thought. (10) As a movement among the masses, the new religions are usually tainted to a greater or lesser degree with superstition. Shamanistic features are prominent in many. In some cases this is because ancestor worship played an important role in their foundation. (11) Along with this tendency toward superstition and shamanism, there are other elements in the new religions which evidence a more modern outlook. An obvious new respect for women is seen both in the number of women founders and in the large proportion of women preachers, teachers, and believers. (12) Finally, an outstanding characteristic, even the raison-d'être of certain new religions, is faith healing. It is also one of the main attractions of these religions. See Offner and van Straelen, *Modern Japanese Religions,* pp. 28–37. See also Maurice A. Bairy, *Japans neue Religionen in der Nachkriegszeit* (Bonn, 1959).

the Misogi (Purification), Shinri (Divine Doctrine), Shinshū (Divine Learning), Taisei (Divine Completion), and Shūsei (Practice and Becoming) sects; others were reorganizations of those popular religious associations based especially on mountain asceticism or Shugendō, such as the Jikkō (centering in the worship of Mount Fuji), Fusō (the same), Mitake (worship on Mount Ontake in Nagano prefecture), and others. Finally, and most important, were Kurozumi (from the name of the founder), Tenri (Heavenly Truth), Konkō (Golden Light), and other sects which had been established by founders who were elected or possessed by their own kami through the medium of Buddhist ascetics called *shugen-ja* (magico-religious mountain ascetics).[10]

The second group appeared from the end of World War I to the Manchurian Incident in 1931, a period of oppression brought on by serious economic depression and the rise of militaristic totalitarianism. The Ōmoto (Great Foundation) and Hitonomichi (Way of Mankind) sects sprang up and rapidly flourished among the lower classes of townspeople, while the Tenri sect and the Konkō-kyō sect generally gained in influence among the peasant, laboring, and merchant classes. However, Ōmoto-kyō in 1935 and Hitonomichi in 1937 were attacked and completely crushed by the government under the pretext of offenses against the law for maintenance

[10] I. Oguchi and Shigeyoshi Murakami, "Kindai-shakai seiritsu-ki no shin shūkyō" ("New Religions Emerged in the Period of Establishment of Modern Industrial Japan"), in *Nihon shūkyō-shi kōza* (*Lectures on the History of Japanese Religions*), ed. Oguchi, Iyenage, Saki, and Matsushima, III (Tokyo, 1959), 217–20; Takagi, *Shinkō shūkyō*, pp. 36, 44, 47, 50, 55–56; see also D. C. Holtom, *Modern Japan and Shinto Nationalism* (New York, 1963).

of the public peace and *lèse-majesté*. However, they have been revived since World War II.[11]

The third group appeared immediately after World War II in the throes of political, economic, and cultural ruin. Ōmoto-kyō was revived as Ōmoto-Aizen-en (Great Foundation Love of Goodness Garden) and Hitonomichi as the P L Kyōdan (Perfect Liberty sect). Sekai-kyūsei-kyō (World Messianic Association), the Reiyū-kai (Spiritual Friends' Association), the Seichō-no-Iye (House of Growth), Risshō-Kōsei-kai (Integrative Becoming, a group following the Nichiren Buddhist line), Sōka-gakkai (Creating Value Academy, following the Nichiren Buddhist line), and other small sects suddenly flourished.[12]

[11] Oguchi and Murakami, "Kindai-shakai seiritsu-ki no shin shūkyō"; Takagi, *Shinkō shūkyō*.

[12] It is noteworthy that the Seichō-no-iye and the Sekai-kyūsei-kyō are large religious bodies which separated from the Ōmoto-kyō sect. The Reiyū-kai, Risshō-kōsei-kai, and the Sōka-gakkai sects are the three largest and most active religious bodies in the line of the Nichiren Buddhist sect. The Tokumitsu-kyō sect and its branch, Hitonomichi (now revived as P L Kyōdan), originated from the Mitake-kyō (a popular association promoting mountain asceticism based on Mount Ontake). However, it is also significant that the founder of the Ōmoto-kyō sect, Nao Deguchi, was once a believer and later a teacher of the Konkō-kyō sect during her religious roamings. The Konkō-kyō's influence on the Ōmoto-kyō sect is evident in terminology, teaching, and practice. The personal histories of Bunjirō Kawate, the founder of the Konkō-kyō sect, and Nao Deguchi of the Ōmoto-kyō sect will be described later. But it is now sufficient to note that Nao was possessed by Konjin (the Kami of Gold, sometimes called Ushitora-no-Konjin ["Kami of Gold in the Direction of the Northwest"]), who is also the principal deity of Konkō-kyō.

On the other hand, of the three big Nichiren-related religious bodies, Risshō-kōsei-kai sect separated from the Reiyū-kai sect. It is also noteworthy that among the various Buddhist sects the Nichiren sect has had a unique situation in the field of new religious movements. Actually the

❲ Survivals of Shamanic Tendencies

Returning to our theme, I should like to discuss the relationship between the new religions and Japanese shamanism. From this viewpoint, we must discuss the shamanic character of the founders of these new religions which without exception have appeared during critical periods of social, economic, and political changes within modern Japan.

Among ten major founders seven were chosen or possessed by a kami, and all had experiences of mystical inspiration and religious initiation. If we include other founders of smaller sects, such as Jikōson, the founder of the Jiu-kyō sect, which was prominent in the newspapers about thirteen years ago, or Sayo Kitamura of the so-called Dancing Religion (Odoru-shūkyō or Tenshō-kōtai-jingū-kyō), the shamanistic character of these persons would be even more remarkable.

For example, Sayo Kitamura calls herself the Ō-gami-sama (Great August Kami) and believes that the Tenshō-kōtai-jingū (Divine Palace of the Heavenly Shining Great Kami) actually exists in her body. Nami Orimo, the founder of the Dai-hizen-kyō (Great Sun Teaching) sect, claims that the highest kami of the universe

---

Nichiren-related new religions now represent more than one-third of all the new religious bodies in Japan. Their theology, sacred books, and the objects of worship are superficially based on those of Nichiren Buddhism, though of course there are many varieties and transformations in the teachings, interpretations, practices, and activities. (See Takagi, *Shinkō shūkyō*, pp. 55–56.)

has descended upon her. Itoko Unigame, the founder of the Shintō-shin-kyō (Shinto New Religion) sect, was possessed by Konjin (Kami of Gold, the kami of the Konkō and Ōmoto sects) and Ame-no-minaka-nushi-no-kami (Lord of the Heavenly Center).

Now let us consider in more detail the lives of several founders, in order to clarify their shamanic and charismatic as well as their mystic character. We will confine ourselves to founders who have transmitted their mystical and initiatory experiences in their own writings and who have exerted great influence by becoming models for new religious movements: Munetada Kurozumi, of Kurozumi-kyō; Bunjirō Kawate, of Konkō-kyō; Miki Nakayama, of Tenri-kyō; Nao Deguchi and Onisaburō Deguchi, both of Ōmoto-kyō; Mokichi Okada, of Sekai-kyūsei-kyō; Masaharu Taniguchi, of Seichō-no-Iye.

❨ *Munetada Kurozumi*

Munetada Kurozumi, the founder of the Kurozumi-kyō sect, was born into the family of a hereditary Shinto priest in 1780 in present-day Okayama prefecture. He is said to have been well educated, but had a sensitive, introspective nature from childhood. In his youth, in the transitional period before the Tokugawa shogunate gave way to the Meiji Restoration, he had been impressed by the unusual mass-hysteric movements of pilgrims to the Ise shrine, with their chanting, dancing, and begging (*okage-mairi*). He himself made a pilgrimage to Ise at the age of twenty-four. The Ise shrine is dedicated to Amaterasu-Ō-mikami, the Sun Goddess, believed to be

REPRESENTATIVE NEW RELIGIONS

Sect[a]	Founders	Social Status of Parents	Education	Age at Conversion	Nature of Conversion
KUROZUMI	Munetada Kurozumi (M)	Shinto priest	Home	35	Mystical experience of union with the Sun Goddess (Amaterasu-Ō-mikami)
TENRI	Miki Nakayama (F)	Ruined landowner	Home	41	Chosen and possessed by ten kami which were later systematized under the control of Tenri-Ō-no-mikoto (Supreme Kami of Heavenly Truth)
KONKŌ	Bunjirō Kawate (M)	Poor farmer	Self-taught	45	Inspired and possessed by Konjin or Konkō-Daijin (Great Kami of Gold)
ŌMOTO	Nao Deguchi (F) Onisaburō Deguchi (M)	Poor carpenter Poor peasant	None Educational certificate	56 27	Chosen and possessed by Konjin Fell into trance ard called by Ko-matsu-no-mikoto (Kami of a Small Pine Tree)
HITONO-MICHI	Tokumitsu Kaneda (M) Tokuchika Miki (M)	Small-scale merchant Small-scale merchant	(Formerly a mountain-ascetic of the Mitakekyō) (Formerly a Buddhist novice of Ōbaku Zen sect)	52	Inspired by the Rising Sun to believe that kami is one not many

[a] Shigeyoshi Murakami, Kinsei minshū shūkyō-shi no kenkyū (A Study of the Popular Religions of Modern Japan) (Kyoto, 1957); Murakami, "Bakumatsu ishin ki ni okeru minshū shūkyō no sōshō" ("The Emergence of Popular New Religions during the Later Tokugawa Regime and the Meiji Restoration"), in Nihon shūkyō-shi kōza (1959), II, 197–276; T. Inui, I. Oguchi, A. Saki, and A. Matsushima. Kyōso—shomin no kami-gami (Founders of the New Religions—Kami of the Masses) (Tokyo, 1955).

REPRESENTATIVE NEW RELIGIONS—*Continued*

Sect[a]	Founders	Social Status of Parents	Education	Age at Conversion	Nature of Conversion
REIYŪ-KAI	Kimi Kotani (F)	Poor peasant	Primary school	25	Chosen and possessed by kami and spirits. In the tradition of the Nichiren sect
SEKAI-KYŪSEI	Mokichi Okada (M)	Small-scale merchant	Primary school	45	Chosen and possessed by kami and spirits, especially Kannon. Separated from the Ōmoto sect
SEICHŌ-NO-IYE	Masaharu Taniguchi (M)	Farmer, afterward owner of small factory	Waseda Univ., not graduated	38	Inspired by divine revelation. Separated from the Ōmoto sect
RISSHŌ-KŌSEI-KAI	Myōkō Naganuma (F)	Poor laborer	Primary school	50	Chosen and possessed by the spirit of Nichiren and other Buddhist deities
SŌKA-GAKKAI	Tsunesaburō Makiguchi (M) Jōsei Toda (M)	Farmer Fisherman	Normal school	59	Formerly a primary schoolmaster. Monotheistic theology and movement based on Nichiren doctrine. Actual organizer of Sōka-gakkai

the mythical ancestress of the imperial family as well as a personification of the sun. As the result of his pilgrimage he became a pious believer in Amaterasu-Ō-mikami. In 1812, he lost both his father and mother within ten days in an epidemic. Heartbroken at this unexpected misfortune, he soon contracted tuberculosis. His condition became critical in 1814. While in a desperate state, he suddenly arose and prayed with his whole heart that he might become a kami after his death in order to save all human beings who were suffering from sickness. (We may observe here one typical example of survival of ancient belief in *goryō* or *reijin*). In the early morning of the winter solstice of 1814, as he piously worshipped the rising sun, he suddenly felt the unification of his whole life with Amaterasu-Ō-mikami. This mysterious experience made Munetada awaken to his own mystical power. The experience was later called by him "Tenmei-jikiju" (direct initiation by heaven's decree or calling). After his conversion he gradually recovered from his illness. He then endeavored to preach the divine power of Amaterasu-Ō-mikami, at first to lower *samurai* and neighboring small landowners. He composed more than one hundred and twenty Japanese poems called "Go-shin-ei" (Divine Poems), published together with his letters under the title *Go-ka-mon-shū* (*Collection of Divine Poems and Letters*).[13]

[13] Gendō Yano, *Kurozumi Munetada-ō den* ("Biography of Munetada Kurozumi"), in *Shintō sōsho* (Tokyo, 1897); Murakami, *Kinsei minshū shūkyō-shi no kenkyū* (1957), pp. 88–97; see also Holtom, *Modern Japan and Shinto Nationalism*, p. 160.

⟨ Bunjirō Kawate

The Konkō-kyō sect was founded in October, 1859, by Bunjirō Kawate (1814–1883), a poor farmer in present-day Konkō-machi near Okayama. In this area there existed an old and strong Shugen-dō tradition, centering especially in the Kojima-yamabushi (or Kojima-gorū-yamabushi). Their headquarters were close to Okayama and Konkō-machi. (They were under the influence of the Ishizuchi-yamabushi centering in Mount Ishizuchi in Shikoku.) Superstitious beliefs and practices based on Onmyō-dō flourished among the masses, since the yamabushi utilized them to appeal to the common people. Among the various kami and buddhas Shugen-dō venerated, the most fearful was Konjin, who brought evil on any who violated the direction in which, in his regular circuit of the heavens, he was residing. Konjin's curses (called shichi-satsu, "seven-murders") were extremely awe-inspiring to the common people.

Bunjirō was a timid, cautious, and pious person from his youth. As with Munetada, Bunjirō was much impressed by the okage-mairi movements, and he also made a pilgrimage to the Ise shrine together with neighboring peasants. Furthermore, he made a pilgrimage to the eighty-eight Shingon Buddhist temples in Shikoku (Shikoku-henro or Hachijū-hakka-sho-junrei) when he was thirty-three years of age. He was also very much in fear of the curse of Konjin. In spite of his diligent farm work, misfortunes befell his family. It is said that he had to build seven tombs for his dead children as well

233

as for his domestic animals in a short period. At forty-two years of age he himself became seriously ill and asked a *yamabushi* to pray for his recovery. As expected, the *yamabushi* told him that his illness was the result of the curse of Konjin. After he had made amends to Konjin, his illness was completely cured. He became an even more ardent believer in Konjin as well as in various other kami and buddhas.

In 1857 his younger brother was suddenly possessed by Konjin. This deeply impressed Bunjirō, and he became the first follower of his brother's religion. In the next year, when Bunjirō was forty-five years of age, he himself was possessed by Konjin directly. The god said to him:

> You must obey my orders and worship me as the one true kami. . . . I will register your name before all the Japanese kami as my ujiko ["parishioner"] so that you will be able to receive my messages. Up to today you have had misfortunes and sufferings. However, from now on, you must pray to me with your whole heart, so that I can make you into a powerful person who needs neither medical doctors nor magicians.

This revelation was written down by Bunjirō himself. Together with successive mysterious experiences and teachings, it was published under the title *O-oboe-gaki* (*Divine Memorandum*). Konjin as revealed to Bunjirō seems to be quite different from the deity of popular belief. This Konjin was the one true kami, who is the ancestral kami of the earth, and who loves those who trust him, much as good parents love their children. This is in sharp contrast to the Konjin of popular belief, who brings misfortune to people. During the two years after his first revelation, Bunjirō continued to work diligently as a farmer and preached his Konjin to neighboring peasants. In 1859 he decided to establish a new religion upon the kami's request, and completely abandoned farming. Konjin was renamed by him Tenchi-kane-no-kami (Kami of Gold in Heaven and Earth), and Bunjirō himself became a kami named Bunji-daimyōjin.[14] His focus of evangelization was mainly on farmers, rural merchants, and artisans.

It is noteworthy that Bunjirō insisted on human equality and the rejection of magical healing. He called his followers the kami's *ujiko* and taught cooperation between the kami and the *ujiko*. He strongly denied superstitious belief in direction, day, and place, teaching rather: "Wherever, whenever and what direction it may be, it is a good place, good day and good direction, if the person be good." This seems an interesting example of religious rationalization from superstition to metaphysic, paralleling the socio-cultural modernization of nineteenth-century Japan. In 1868, when the Emperor Meiji proclaimed the establishment of a reformed modern state, Bunjirō renamed himself "Ikigami-Konkō-daijin" (Living Great Kami Light); he continued his religious activities until his death in 1883. The influence of the Konkō-kyō sect and belief in Konjin is clearly seen in the theology of the Ōmoto-kyō sect and of its founder, Nao Deguchi, whose shamanic initiation I shall describe later.

[14] Delwin B. Schneider, *Konkokyo: A Japanese Religion* (Tokyo, 1962); Murakami, *Kinsei minshū shūkyō-shi no kenkyū*, pp. 97–112.

❨ *Miki Nakayama*

Miki Nakayama was born in 1798, the daughter of a landowner in present-day Tenri in Nara prefecture. She has said that as a child she had been a moody girl who disliked crowded places, preferring to stay alone in her room to practice handicrafts, sewing, and calligraphy. But she also liked to go to Buddhist temples to chant the name of Amida-Butsu. She received a religious certificate (*gojū-sōden*) from the Jōdo sect (Pure Land School) in her nineteenth year. At the age of thirteen she was married to Zen'emon Nakayama, a landowner of a neighboring village, and gave birth to one son and five daughters. The first half of her life covered the period of continuous extraordinary social anxiety caused by both the great famine which reached its peak in 1836 and the political disturbances of the last stage of the Tokugawa shogunate. In 1837, Heihachirō Ōshio, a famous Confucian and Shinto scholar, started a rebellion in Osaka against the shogunate after having severely criticized its maladministration. The Nakayama family gradually declined throughout this period.

In 1837, Miki's eldest son Shūshi became seriously ill. Miki, pregnant at the time and overcome with anxiety over her son's illness, would become mentally deranged at times. She wrote later that after she became forty-one years old she sometimes felt as if she were mad. Her body would sway; frequently she would faint while occupied with her domestic duties. Several times she asked Ichibei, a mountain ascetic (*yamabushi*) who lived in a neighboring village, to perform a special incantation and faith cure (usually called *yose-kaji*) for Shūshi's recovery. Ichibei used a female medium in the course of his faith cure in order to learn the cause of his patient's disease. On the night of the twenty-fourth of the Tenth Month in 1838, Miki took the place of Ichibei's own absent medium. Miki, after a cold-water purification, took two sacred staffs in her hands. Suddenly, during Ichibei's incantation, Miki fell into a trance, and the Great Heavenly Generalissimo (Ten-taishōgun) and nine other kami descended and possessed her, proclaiming: "Miki's mind and body will be accepted by us as a divine shrine, and we desire to save this three-thousand-world through this divine body. Otherwise, and if you all refuse our desire, the Nakayama family shall completely cease to exist. . . ."[15]

After her husband died in 1853 and the Nakayama family had fallen into the depth of poverty, Miki began to perform incantations and faith cures for the neighboring peasants. Around 1864, a small kō association was established by her followers. In 1867, Miki received the title of Tenri-ō-myōjin (Kami of the Heavenly King of Truth) from the orthodox Shinto family Yoshida in Kyoto. She composed twelve *mikagura-uta* poems, which she and her followers recited as a substitute for the Shinto

[15] *Tenri kyōso den* (*Life of the Founder of the Tenri-kyō Sect*), compiled by the Tenri-kyō dōshi-kai (Tenri, 1913); Bunichi Okutani, *Tenri kyōso den kōwa* (*Lectures on the Biography of the Founder of the Tenri-kyō Sect*) (Tenri, 1924); Murakami, "Bakumatsu ishin ki ni okeru minshū shūkyō no sōshō," in *Nihon shūkyō-shi kōza*, II, 208–24; Inui et al., *Kyōso* (1955), pp. 16–28; H. van Straelen, *The Religion of Divine Wisdom* (Kyoto, 1957); Tenri-kyō Honbu (ed.), *A Short History of Tenrikyō* (Tenri, 1960).

Norito ("prayers"). Her preaching gradually became messianic under the direct influence of the political changes of the time. After her seventy-first year, she began to dance and sing her *mikagura-uta* songs in front of the kami's altar. From 1869 to 1882, Miki extemporaneously composed 1,711 *waka* poems following divine revelations or inspirations. These poems were compiled under the title *Ofude-saki* (literally, *The Tip of the Writing-brush*), and became the sacred teachings of the Tenri-kyō sect. She died in 1887 at the age of ninety, leaving twenty-one churches and more than fifteen thousand followers.[16]

(*Nao Deguchi and Onisaburō Deguchi*

Nao Deguchi was born in 1826, a daughter of a poor carpenter in a small town in present-day Fukuchiyama in Kyoto prefecture. She had to serve an apprenticeship as a nursemaid from her eleventh year because of the poverty of her home. Nao married at seventeen years of age, and became the mother of three sons and five daughters. According to her biography, before her marriage she suddenly disappeared from her house for a few days, and after returning home she said that she had practiced religious austerities on a mountain. When she was nineteen, Nao fell into a critical condition because she was possessed by the spirit of one of her aunts who had committed suicide.

In 1890 and 1891, the third and eldest daughters of

16 *Ofude-saki* was compiled in seventeen paper-bound volumes. The original handwritten manuscript by Miki herself is treasured at the headquarters of the Tenri-kyō sect.

Nao in succession became mentally deranged after childbirth. The unexpected madness of her two daughters
gave Nao the severe shock which became the overt cause
of her shamanic activity. On the tenth of January, 1892,
just one month after her eldest daughter was stricken,
Nao was suddenly possessed by a kami after having
dreamed several times that she was in the divine world.
Her first initiatory symptoms continued for thirteen days,
during which Nao was convinced that some invisible
being had entered her body. She performed a cold-water
purification, as the invisible being had instructed; she
groaned with tension, jumped up, and roared violently
from deep in her abdomen. It is said that during this
first violent attack the following dialogue occurred between Nao and the invisible being in her abdomen.

Invisible Being: "I am a kami named Ushitora-no-
Konjin [Kami of Gold in the Direction of the North-
west]."

Nao: "I do not believe what you say; you deceive
me, don't you?"

Invisible Being: "I never lie, for I am a kami."

Nao: "Oh! Such a great kami you are! But, aren't
you a fox or badger deceiving me?"

Invisible Being: "I am neither a fox nor a badger. I
am a kami who wants to re-create and rebuild this
Three-Thousand-World to become the world of Konjin
at once, just as plum flowers open suddenly. Without
me this world would not be rebuilt. . . . Though it
may be a high ambition, I will endeavor to make the
eternal divine world, and roll this Three-Thousand-
World into one."

Nao: "Is it true what you are saying?"

Invisible Being: "I, the kami, could not do so if I told a lie."[17]

From this year to the next, violent shamanic attacks (*otakebi*, "courageous shout" or "divine roar") visited her intermittently. Nao also performed incantations and faith cures for the neighboring peasants or townsmen and gained several followers. She began to write her *Ofude-saki*, though she had been illiterate. Immediately after her first shamanic attack, Nao visited the branch church of the Konkō-kyō sect in Kameoka near Fukuchiyama and later became a teacher of this sect. Nao was also influenced by the Tenri-kyō theology. This is the reason why Nao's ideas have remarkable similarities to those of both Konkō and Tenri. In 1896 Nao separated from the Konkō-kyō sect and tried to form an independent sect, though unsuccessfully because of pressure from government police as well as from the Konkō-kyō headquarters.

Eventually, Nao was visited by Kisaburō Ueda in 1897. This was the turning point for the independent development of Ōmoto-kyō. Kisaburō Ueda, twenty-eight years old at that time, became an active associate and later the successor and the son-in-law of Nao Deguchi. Later, he changed his name to Onisaburō Deguchi. The Ōmoto-

[17] Nao Deguchi, *Keireki* (*My Life Story*) (Ayabe, 1902); *Kōhon Ōmoto kyōso den—kaiso no maki* (*Manuscript of the Biographies of the Founders of the Ōmoto-kyō Sect—Section on the Founder*), compiled by the Ōmoto kyōgakuin (Ayabe, 1957); Shizuo Hattori, *Ōmoto kyōso Deguchi Nao den* (*A Life of Nao Deguchi, the Founder of the Ōmoto-kyō Sect*) (Ayabe, 1921); Murakami, *Kinsei minshū shūkyō-shi no kenkyū*, pp. 117–29; Inui et al., *Kyōso*, pp. 59–67. *Ōmoto Movement: Its Origin, Aims, and Objects* and the *Universal Love and Brotherhood Association* (Kameoka, 1952); Tōjūrō Murai, *What Is "Ōmoto"?* (Kameoka, 1957).

kyō sect calls Nao the Kyōso (Foundress) and Onisaburo the Sei-shi (Holy Teacher).

Onisaburō Deguchi, the great organizer of the Ōmoto-kyō sect, possessed a weak body in his early days, and was frequently haunted by apparitions of his departed grandfather. He listened to magico-religious teachers and was also influenced by his grandmother's father, a local scholar of nationalistic Shinto who advocated the study of magical formulas (*koto-dama*). Blessed with an exceptional memory and intelligence, Onisaburō took a rebellious attitude toward the world, which because of his limited opportunities seemed to him full of inequality and vexation. It is said that even in his adolescence Onisaburō had frequent hallucinations. In 1898 he was beaten by some village gamblers for troubles involving women, and barely escaped with his life. Severely reprimanded by his mother, Onisaburō invoked the aid of the kami with regret and suffering. On that same night, according to his report, he was led from home by a divine messenger. He wandered about Mount Takakura for about a week and was granted mystical experiences. After he returned home he announced to his family that he had gone to practice religious austerities, having been led by a kami. It is said that then, owing to exhaustion, he was unable to speak for several days. This experience of wandering and of religious austerities became the basis of later memoirs entitled *Reikai-monogatari* (*Story of the World of Spirits*). He tells us that his soul had wandered about the spiritual realm, his religious mission was revealed, and he gained occult powers and received several divine revelations. The name of the kami who elected him was revealed two and a half months after his first initiation.

Some scholars are skeptical about Onisaburō's story of his experience on the mountain, holding that it was probably his own arbitrary action and not a real initiatory election. Even supposing this to be true, we must say that it followed a stereotyped pattern peculiar to shamanism.

During World War I, after Nao had retired, Onisaburō was active in the messianic movement: he published a bulletin named *Shikishima-shinbun*; he organized the religious military system; he proclaimed that he was not only the Holy Teacher but an incarnation of Miroku (the bodhisattva Maitreya, believed to be the future Buddha who will descend from Tusita Heaven to save the human race; this belief had frequently been the touchstone of agrarian revolts in Japanese history). Onisaburō also performed a peculiar faith cure termed *chinkon-kishin* (unification with the kami through meditation or repose of one's own soul). There was occasionally a revivalistic atmosphere in his large kami hall. Onisaburō also gave his followers objects called *mite-shiro* (substitutes for the divine hands). They were dipper-shaped pieces of wood with sacred characters written on them, and were believed to be magical means of healing. From 1917 to 1921, Onisaburō published the Ōmoto-kyō bulletin *Shinrei-kai* (*Spiritual World*). Masaharu Taniguchi, the founder of the Seichō-no-Iye sect, was one of its editors in his youth. Several intellectuals became Onisaburō's followers.

The movement was attacked in 1921 by government

police, and the messianic divine hall (Miroku-den) and all its other buildings and institutions were destroyed in 1935. Onisaburō died in 1948 at the age of seventy-eight, having reconstructed his sect as Ōmoto-aizen-en after World War II. His *Reikai-monogatari* reached eighty-one volumes and is now the sacred book of the sect. He also composed many poems.[18]

From this rough sketch of the biographies of the founders of representative new religions, we can recognize that there still survive some of the fundamental elements of genuine Arctic shamanism, though with many artificial and historical embellishments, alterations, and transmutations. These persons displayed unusual features or abnormalities in their personalities—they were constitutionally weak, loved solitude, were introspective, and had visions and auditory hallucinations. They experienced initiatory mental disorders in the context of personal crises. They were possessed or visited by a kami during their first trance. They felt a reintegration of personality after initiation, which took the form of the development of shamanistic techniques and self-control. They created such apocalyptic literature as the *Go-shin-ei* of Munetada Kurozumi, the *O-oboe-gaki* of Bunjirō Kawate, the *Ofude-saki* of Miki Nakayama and Nao Deguchi, the *Mikagura-uta* of Miki Nakayama, and the *Reikai-monogatari* of Onisaburō Deguchi.[19]

[18] *Kōhon Ōmoto kyōso den—seishi no maki* (*Section on the Holy Teacher*), compiled by the Ōmoto kyōgakuin (Ayabe, 1957); Onisaburō Deguchi, *Waga hansei no ki* (*Story of Half My Life*) (Ayabe, 1935); Murakami, *Kinsei minshū shūkyō-shi no kenkyū*, pp. 140–48; Inui et al., *Kyōso*, pp. 70–75.

[19] Hori, *Nihon shūkyō-shi kenkyū*, I, 50–52.

❲ *Seichō-no-Iye, Sekai-kyūsei-kyō, and Sōka-gakkai*

In concluding this chapter, I must add a few words about the peculiar characteristics of the Seichō-no-Iye, Sekai-kyūsei-kyō, and Sōka-gakkai sects.

Masaharu Taniguchi (1893–   ), the founder of the Seichō-no-Iye sect, first became an Ōmoto-kyō believer, and served on the editorial staff of the bulletin of the Ōmoto-kyō headquarters, *Shinrei-kai*. Educated at Waseda University in Tokyo, Taniguchi was interested in Buddhist and Christian theories as well as in Christian Science and Spiritualism. He also was interested in such Western intellectuals as Schopenhauer, Tolstoi, Oscar Wilde, and Nietzsche. It is said that he was most impressed by F. L. Holmes' *Love of Mind Action*, which he translated into Japanese. After the great earthquake struck Tokyo in 1923, Taniguchi heard mysterious voices more frequently than before. He practiced *chinkon-kishin*, the technique of ecstasy or trance mentioned above. According to Taniguchi's memoirs, during this exercise he once heard a voice from an invisible being: "Arise now! Now is the time. It is a mistake to think of waiting until you have sufficient money or time before beginning your work of enlightenment." Despite Taniguchi's protests, the voice came back: "There is no such thing as material appearance. Do not be tricked by things that do not exist. . . . You are reality. You are Buddha. You are Christ. You are infinite. You are inexhaustible."[20] Suddenly Tani-

[20] Masaharu Taniguchi, *Seimei no jissō* (*Reality of Life*) (Tokyo, 1958), XX, 163 ff.; see also Taniguchi, *Divine Education and Spiritual*

guchi picked up his pen and began writing the work which was published under the title of *Seimei no jissō* (*Reality of Life*).

His literary gift and his knowledge of metaphysics, philosophy, and mysticism as well as his concern for Spiritualism, his practice of the Ōmoto-kyō's *chinkon-kishin*, and his own doctrine inculcating spiritual reality as the basis of social reformation, led Taniguchi to a unique venture in philosophical writing. After his first revelation at thirty-eight years of age, he wrote a great number of articles which were later compiled into voluminous books. His principal work is the *Seimei no jissō*, which has now reached more than forty volumes.

Some similarities to Taniguchi's mysterious experiences are seen in those of Mokichi Okada (1882–1954), the founder of the Sekai-kyūsei-kyō. Both Taniguchi and Okada began in the Ōmoto-kyō sect. Unlike Taniguchi, Okada was the son of a small merchant and suffered from poverty and sickness. After the great earthquake in 1923, overwhelmed by sickness, financial crises, and his wife's death, he sought spiritual help in the Ōmoto-kyō sect. During practice of the *chinkon-kishin*, he began to have various mysterious experiences. According to the *Guse no hikari* (*Light of the Savior*), he was possessed in December, 1926, by a divine being named Inanome-no-kami, who was revealed to be a form of Kannon, the Buddhist goddess of mercy. Kannon told him that she wanted to use Okada's body to perfom a great work of salvation for all mankind. Okada wrote: "From the first year of Shōwa [1926] Kannon-sama constantly possessed my body,

---

Training of Mankind (Tokyo, 1960); Inui et al., *Kyōso* (1955), pp. 97–135.

taught me many things, gave commands, and used my body with perfect freedom. She simply used me as a vehicle to save all men. . . ."[21] He also proclaimed that the Buddha, Christ, and Mohammed were mere preachers of the kami's will; however, Okada believed that he himself was a man truly united with the kami.

Okada's method of evangelization is somewhat different from Taniguchi's, though both have been deeply influenced by Onisaburō's Ōmoto-kyō practices such as *chinkon-kishin*. Okada developed his own method for treatment of the sick, but borrowed from Onisaburō's *mite-shiro*, which is similar to that of many folk magico-religious movements.

The Sōka-gakkai sect is the most vigorous, dogmatic, exclusivistic, belligerent, and self-confident group in contemporary Japan, and is the fastest growing.[22] This sect is closely associated with Nichiren-shō-shū, one of the denominations of the Nichiren sect. Though the Sōka-gakkai sect proclaims that it spreads the real teachings of Nichiren over the world, strictly following the special theology and authority of the Nichiren-shō-shū, it has its own special theory—value creation (*sō-ka*). This theory was revealed by Tsunesaburō Makiguchi (1871–1944), the founder of this sect. The sect has engaged in socio-religious activities but has also made rapid progress by the traditional method of *shakubuku* ("browbeating into submission") advocated by Nichiren (1222–1282), the historical founder of the Nichiren sect.

21 Yoshiko Okada, *Guse no hikari* (*Light of the Savior*) (Atami), cited by Offner and van Straelen, *Modern Japanese Religions*, pp. 78–79; Inui et al., *Kyōso* (1955), pp. 171–206.

22 Offner and van Straelen, *Modern Japanese Religions*, p. 98.

Originally, Nichiren-shō-shū was only a small society. After Makiguchi and Jōsei Toda converted to it in 1928, that faith was united with their theory of value creation and became an impelling force. In 1930 Makiguchi published a series of books entitled *Sōka-kyōiku taikei* (*A System of Value-Creation Education*), setting forth the Sōka-gakkai theory of education, value, and religion. In 1937, Makiguchi and Toda established the Sōka-kyōiku-gakkai (Society for Value-Creation Education) with some sixty members. Makiguchi died in 1944 under strong pressure from the military and the police. After Makiguchi's death, through the dynamic leadership of his successor and co-founder, Jōsei Toda (1900–1958), Sōka-gakkai advanced with great strides. Toda published the monthly *Dai-byaku-renge* (*Big White Lotus*) and the newspaper *Seikyō-shinbun* (*Holy Teachings*). These publishing ventures, like those of Onisaburō and Taniguchi, appealed to both intellectual young people and to laborers who felt the postwar anomie.

Toda utilized vividly the method of *shakubuku* or forced conversions which he expounded in his book *Shakubuku-kyōten* (*Scripture of Conversion by Force*). Toda created a strict, military-like organization. Giving a vital strength to the movement are the youth organizations, structured on a military model. These groups sing spirited marching songs urging them to battle and victory.[23] The young people's divisions now total some quarter of a million members, a driving force behind the sect's political successes. At present *Sōka-gakkai* (under the guise of the Kōmei-kai party) is the third largest political body in the upper house of the Japanese Diet.

[23] *Ibid.*, p. 103.

Curiously, Sōka-gakkai denies that it is an independent religious body, insisting it is merely a lay association within the Nichiren sect. But its rapid growth, its penetration into labor unions, its recent successes in political activities, and its offensive methods of gaining converts have all forced national attention upon it. Offner and van Straelen regard it as one of the most important socioreligious groups in present-day Japan, and recognition of it, whether as a religion or not, is unavoidable in any study of modern religions.[24]

Finally, I should like to point out again that the religious interest of the founders, Miki Nakayama, Nao Deguchi, Taniguchi, and Okada, resulted from frustration, disappointment, and experiences in which they were completely helpless. These conditions were caused by social, political, economic, cultural, or socio-psychological instability which were keenly felt by a person of especial religious sensitivity, particularly of the charismatic or shamanic type.

Though these founders may proclaim themselves messiahs and teach the possibility of paradise in this world, they never became practical social reformers. They have given frustrations, disappointments, and experiences of helplessness an individual outlet in individual salvation. Therefore, the new religions in Japan have played a conservative role, serving to help maintain the status quo and to prevent social revolution. This role is due also to their magico-religious or folk religious tendencies. The charac-

[24] Akio Saki and I. Oguchi, *Sōka-gakkai, sono shishō to kōdō* (*Sōka-gakkai Sect: Its Thought and Activity*) (Tokyo, 1958); Kyōtoku Nakano, *Shinkō shūkyō no kaibō* (*Analysis of the Newly Arisen Religions*) (Tokyo, 1954); Hiroo Takagi, *Shinkō shūkyō*; Sōka-gakkai Honbu, *The Sōka Gakkai* (Tokyo, 1960).

teristics indicated above are not unique to Japanese new religions and their founders. If one carefully examines modern American cults and minority religious movements,[25] one can find many similarities to those of Japan, as well as to new religious movements in Africa, Indonesia, and other places in the world.

[25] Charles Samuel Braden, *These Also Believe: A Study of Modern American Cults and Minority Religious Movements* (New York, 1951); J. P. Williams, *What Americans Believe and How They Worship* (New York, 1952). See Offner and van Straelen, *Modern Japanese Religions*, pp. 29–30.

SELECTED BIBLIOGRAPHY

(*Subject Bibliography*

JAPANESE RELIGION AND CULTURE

Adams, Charles J., ed. *A Reader's Guide to the Great Religions*. New York: Free Press, 1965.

Anesaki, Masaharu. *Japanese Mythology* (Vol. 8 of *The Mythology of All Races*, ed. C. J. A. MacCulloch). Boston: Marshall Jones, 1928.

――――. *History of Japanese Religion*. London: Kegan Paul, Trench, Trubner, 1930. A standard work, although dated.

――――. *Religious Life of the Japanese People*, rev. Hideo Kishimoto. Tokyo: Kokusai Bunka Shinkokai, 1961.

Aston, William George, trans. *Nihongi: Chronicles of Japan from Earliest Times to A.D. 697*. 2 vols., London, 1896; 2 vols. in 1. London: George Allen & Unwin, 1956.

Bunce, William K. *Religions in Japan: Buddhism, Shinto, Christianity*. Rutland, Vt.: Charles E. Tuttle, 1955. Deals with the modern period.

Chamberlain, Basil Hall, trans. "Ko-ji-ki: Records of Ancient Matters," *Transactions of the Asiatic Society of Japan* 10 (supplement, 1882).

Florenz, Karl. *Japanische Mythologie. Nihongi, "Zeitalter der Götter."* Tokyo: Hobunsha, 1901.

――――. "Die Japaner." In *Lehrbuch der Religionsgeschichte*, ed. Chantepie de la Saussaye, pp. 262–422. Tübingen: Mohr, 1925.

Griffis, William Elliot. *The Religions of Japan: From the*

Dawn of History to the Era of Meiji. New York: Charles Scribner's Sons, 1901.

Gundert, Wilhelm. *Japanische Religionsgeschichte: Die Religionen der Japaner und Koreaner in Geschichtlichen Abriss Darstellt.* Stuttgart: Gundert, 1943.

Haguenauer, Charles M. *Origines de la civilization japonaise: Introduction à l'étude de la préhistoire du Japon,* Part I. Paris: Imprimerie nationale, 1956.

Harada, Toshiaki. "The Development of Matsuri." *Philosophical Studies of Japan.* Vol. 2, pp. 99–117. Tokyo: Japanese National Commission for UNESCO, 1961.

Hearn, Lafcadio. *Japan: An Attempt at Interpretation.* New York: Macmillan, 1904. An eccentric and romantic work, but also informative.

Japanese Association for Religious Studies and Japanese Organizing Committee of the IXth International Congress for History of Religions, eds. *Religious Studies in Japan.* Tokyo: Maruzen, 1959.

Japanese Classics Translation Committee. *The Manyōshū: One Thousand Poems Selected from the Japanese.* Tokyo: Iwanami Shoten, 1940.

Japanese National Commission for UNESCO. *Japan: Its Land, People and Culture.* Tokyo: Printing Bureau of the Ministry of Finance, 1958.

Lowell, Percival. *Occult Japan or the Way of the Gods.* New York: Houghton Mifflin, 1895.

Matsumoto, Nobuhiro. *Essai sur la mythologie japonaise.* Paris: Geuthner, 1928.

Numazawa, Franz Kiichi. "Die Weltanfänge in der japanischen Mythologie." *International Schriftenreihe für soziale und politische Wissenschaften, Ethnologische Reihe.* vol. 2. Freiburg, Switzerland: Paulusverlag, 1946.

Ōbayashi, Taryō. "Die Amaterasu-Mythe im alten Japan und die Sonnenfinsternismythe in Sudostasien." *Ethnos* 25 (1960): 20–43.

Philippi, Donald L., trans. *Norito: A New Translation of the Ancient Japanese Ritual Prayers.* Tokyo: Institute for Japanese Culture and Classics, Kokugakuin University, 1959.

Reischauer, Robert Karl. *Early Japanese History.* 2 vols. Princeton: Princeton University Press, 1937.

Sansom, Sir George B. *Japan: A Short Cultural History.* New York: Appleton-Century-Crofts, 1931; rev. ed., 1962.

———. *A History of Japan to 1334.* Stanford: Stanford University Press, 1958.

———. *A History of Japan, 1334–1615.* Stanford: Stanford University Press, 1961.

———. *A History of Japan, 1615–1867.* Stanford: Stanford University Press, 1963.

Satow, E. M. "The Mythology and Religious Worship of the Ancient Japanese." *The Westminster and Foreign Quarterly Review* 54 n.s. (1878): 27–57.

———. "Ancient Japanese Rituals." *Transactions of the Asiatic Society of Japan* 7 (part I, 1879): 97–132. 9 (1881): 182–211.

Slawick, Alexander. "Kultische Geheimbünde der Japaner und Germanen." *Wiener Beiträge zur Kulturgeschichte und Linguistik* (Salzburg-Leipzig) 4 (1936): 675–764.

Smith, Robert J., and Beardsley, Richard K., eds. *Japanese Culture: Its Development and Characteristics.* Chicago: Aldine, 1962.

Tsunoda, Ryūsaku, Bary, W. Theodore de, and Keene, Donald. *Sources of Japanese Tradition.* New York: Columbia University Press, 1958.

FOLK RELIGION

Foster, George M. "What Is Folk Culture?" *American Anthropologist* 60 (part I, no. 2, April–June, 1953).

Leslie, Charles, ed. *Anthropology of Folk Religion.* New York: Vintage Books, 1960.

Redfield, Robert. *The Primitive World and Its Transformations*. Ithaca, N.Y.: Cornell University Press, 1953.

———. *The Little Community* and *Peasant Society and Culture*. 2 vols. in 1. Chicago: University of Chicago Press, 1956.

SHINTO

Aston, William George. *Shintō: The Way of the Gods*. London: Longmans, Green, 1905. Still a useful introduction, although his classification of Shinto deities and his naturalistic interpretation of religion are questionable.

Holtom, Daniel C. *The National Faith of Japan*. London: Kegan Paul, Trench, Trubner, 1938.

———. "Shintoism." In *The Great Religions of the Modern World*, ed. Edward J. Jurji, pp. 141–77. Princeton: Princeton University Press, 1946.

Katō, Genchi. *A Study of Shintō: The Religion of the Japanese Nation*. Tokyo: Zaidan-Hojin-Meiji-Seitoku Kinen Gakkai, 1926.

Muraoka, Tsunetsugu. *Studies in Shintō Thought*, trans. Delmer M. Brown and James T. Araki. Tokyo: Japanese Ministry of Education, 1964.

Ponsonby-Fane, Richard A. B. *Studies in Shintō and Shrines*. Kyoto: Ponsonby Memorial Society, 1942. A great wealth of useful information, but no visible organization.

Revon, Michel. *Le Shintoisme*. Paris: Leroux, 1907.

Satow, E. M. "The Shinto Shrines of Ise." *Transactions of the Asiatic Society of Japan* 1 (1874): 99–121.

———. "The Revival of Pure Shin-tau." *Transactions of the Asiatic Society of Japan* 3 (part I, supplement, 1875; rev., 1882): 1–87.

Schwartz, W. L. "The Great Shrine of Idzumo." *Transactions of the Asiatic Society of Japan* 41 (part IV, October, 1913): 493–681.

Selected Bibliography

Underwood, A. C. *Shintoism: The Indigenous Religion of Japan.* London: Epworth Press, 1934.

BUDDHISM

Eliot, Sir Charles. *Japanese Buddhism.* London: Edward Arnold, 1935. A standard work on the subject in English.

Hori, Ichirō. "Buddhism in the Life of the Japanese People." In *Japan and Buddhism,* ed. The Association of the Buddha Jayanti, pp. 19–67. Tokyo: Tokyo Budda Jayanti Association, 1959.

———. "Self-Mummified Buddhas in Japan." *History of Religions* 1 (no. 2, Winter, 1962): 222–42.

Kamimura, Shinjō. "Buddhist Worship of the Masses." Research Papers (mimeographed for the IXth International Congress for History of Religions), pp. 15–20. Tokyo, 1958.

Reischauer, August Karl. *Studies in Japanese Buddhism.* New York: Macmillan, 1917.

Suzuki, Daisetz Teitarō. *Manual of Zen Buddhism.* Kyoto: Eastern Buddhist Society, 1935.

———. *Zen and Japanese Culture.* New York: Pantheon Books, 1959.

Takakusu, Junjirō. *The Essentials of Buddhist Philosophy.* Honolulu: University of Hawaii Press, 1947.

CONFUCIANISM AND OTHER CHINESE RELIGIOUS ELEMENTS

Armstrong, Robert C. *Light from the East: Studies in Japanese Confucianism.* Toronto: University of Toronto Press, 1914.

Frank, Bernard. "Kata-imi et kata-tagae: Étude sur les interdits de direction à l'époque Heian." *Bulletin de la Maison Franco-japonaise* 5 n.s. (nos. 2–4, 1958). A thorough monograph on directional taboos and good introduction to Onmyōdō (the way of yin and yang) in Japan.

257

Saunders, E. Dale. "Koshin: An Example of Taoist Ideas in Japan." *Proceedings of the IXth International Congress for History of Religions*, pp. 423–31. Tokyo: Maruzen, 1960.

〔 *Chapter Bibliography*

CHAPTER I

Buchanan, Daniel C. "Inari, Its Origin, Development, and Nature." *Transactions of the Asiatic Society of Japan* 12 (second series, 1935): 1–191.

Buckley, Edmund. *Phallicism in Japan*. Chicago: University of Chicago Press, 1895.

Casal, U. A. "The Goblin, Fox and Badger and Other Witch Animals of Japan." *Folklore Studies* 18 (1959): 1–94.

Dorson, Richard M. *Folk Legends of Japan*. Tokyo and Rutland, Vt.: Charles E. Tuttle, 1962.

———, ed. *Studies in Japanese Folklore*. Bloomington, Ind.: Indiana University Press, 1963.

Eder, Matthias. "Figürliche Darstellungen in der japanischen Volksreligion." *Folklore Studies* 10 (1951): 197–280.

Holtom, Daniel C. "Some Notes on Japanese Tree Worship." *Transactions of the Asiatic Society of Japan* 8 (second series, December, 1931): 1–19.

———. "The Meaning of Kami." *Monumenta Nipponica* 3 (no. 1, 1940): 1–27. 3 (no. 2, 1940): 32–53. 4 (no. 2, 1941): 25–68.

Hori, Ichirō. *Wagakuni minkan-shinkō-shi no kenkyū* (A Study of the History of Japanese Folk Religion). 2 vols. Tokyo: Sogensha, 1953; 1955.

———. "Japanese Folk-Beliefs." *American Anthropologist* 61 (no. 3, June, 1959): 405–24.

Ishida, Eiichirō. "The Kappa Legend." *Folklore Studies* 9 (1950): 1–152.

———. "Mother-Son Deities." *History of Religions* 4 (no. 1, Summer, 1964): 30–52.

Matsumoto, Nobuhiro. "Notes on the Deity Festival of Yawatano, Japan." *Southwestern Journal of Anthropology* 5 (Spring, 1949): 62–77.

Numazawa, Franz Kiichi. "The Fertility Festival at Toyota Shintō Shrine, Aichi Prefecture, Japan." *Acta Tropica* 16 (supplement, no. 3, 1959): 197–217.

Opler, Morris E. "Japanese Folk Beliefs concerning the Cat." *Washington Academy of Science Journal* 39 (1945): 269–76.

Ouwehand, C. *Namazu-e and Their Themes: An Interpretative Approach to Some Aspects of Japanese Folk Religion.* Leiden: Brill, 1964.

Revon, Michel. "Ancestor-Worship and Cult of the Dead (Japanese)." *Encyclopedia of Religion and Ethics,* ed. James Hastings. New York: Charles Scribner's Sons, 1917.

Takatsuka, Masanori, trans. *Folklore Dictionary,* ed. Folklore Institute of Japan. Lexington, Kentucky: Kentucky Microcards no. 18, 1958.

Tsukakoshi, Satoshi, trans. *Konjaku: Altjapanische Geschichten aus dem Volk zur Heian-Zeit.* Zurich: Niehans, 1956.

CHAPTER II

Beardsley, Richard K., Hall, John W., and Ward, Robert E. *Village Japan.* Chicago: University of Chicago Press, 1959.

Befu, Harumi, with Edward Norbeck. "Japanese Usages of Terms of Relationship." *Southwestern Journal of Anthropology* 14 (no. 1, Spring, 1958): 66–86.

Bellah, Robert N. *Tokugawa Religion.* Glencoe, Ill.: Free Press, 1957.

Benedict, Ruth. *The Chrysanthemum and the Sword: Pat-*

terns of *Japanese Culture*. Boston: Houghton Mifflin, 1947.

Cornell, John B., and Smith, Robert J. *Two Japanese Villages: Matsunagi, A Japanese Mountain Community; Kurusu, A Japanese Agricultural Community.* (Center for Japanese Studies, Occasional Papers, no. 5.) Ann Arbor, Mich.: University of Michigan Press, 1956.

Eder, Matthias. "Familie, Sippe, Clan und Ahnenverehrung in Japan." *Anthropos* 52 (1957): 813–40.

Embree, John F. *Suye Mura.* Chicago: University of Chicago Press, 1939.

———. "Some Social Functions of Religion in Rural Japan." *American Journal of Sociology*, no. 47 (1941), 284–89.

Harada, Toshiaki. "The Origin of Community Worship." In *Religious Studies in Japan*, ed. Japanese Association for Religious Studies, pp. 213–18. Tokyo: Maruzen, 1959.

Hulse, Frederick S. "A Sketch of Japanese Society." *Journal of the American Oriental Society* 66 (no. 3, July–September, 1946): 219–29.

Kitagawa, Joseph M. "The Buddhist Transformation in Japan." *History of Religions* 4 (no. 2, Winter, 1965): 319–36.

Norbeck, Edward. "Pollution and Taboo in Contemporary Japan." *Southwestern Journal of Anthropology* 8 (no. 3, Autumn, 1952): 269–85.

———. "Yakudoshi: A Japanese Complex of Supernaturalistic Beliefs." *Southwestern Journal of Anthropology* 11 (no. 2, Summer, 1955): 105–20.

CHAPTER III

Coates, Harper H., and Ishizuka, Ryūgaku. *Hōnen the Buddhist Saint.* Kyoto: Society for the Publication of Sacred Books of the World, 1925.

Fujiwara, Ryōsetsu. *Nembutsu shisō no kenkyū (A Study of the Nembutsu Ideology).* Kyoto: Nagata Bunshōdo, 1957.

———, trans. and annot. *The Tanni Shō: Notes Lamenting Differences.* Kyoto: Ryukoku University Translation Center, 1962.

Hori, Ichirō. "On the Concept of Hijiri (Holy-Man)." *Numen* 5 (no. 2, April, 1958; no. 3, September, 1958): 128–60; 199–232.

Inouye, Mitsusada. *Nihon Jōdo-kyō seiritsu-shi no kenkyū (A Historical Study of the Development of Pure Land Buddhism in Japan).* Tokyo: Yamakawa, 1956.

Lloyd, Arthur. *Shinran and His Work: Studies in Shinshū Theology.* Tokyo: Kyobunkwan, 1910.

Visser, Marinus Willem de. *The Bodhisattva Ti-Tsang (Jizō) in China and Japan.* Berlin: Oesterheld, 1914.

———. *The Bodhisattva Akasagarbha (Kokuzō) in China and Japan.* Amsterdam: Koninklijke Akademie van Wetenschappen, 1931.

CHAPTER IV

Earhart, H. Byron. "A Religious Study of the Mount Haguro Sect of Shugendō: An Example of Japanese Mountain Religion." University of Chicago: unpublished Ph.D. dissertation, 1965.

Hori, Ichirō. "On the Concept of Hijiri (Holy-Man)." *Numen* 5 (no. 2, April, 1958; no. 3, September, 1958): 128–60; 199–232.

———. "Mysterious Visitors from the Harvest to the New Year." In *Studies in Japanese Folklore,* ed. Richard Dorson, pp. 76–106. Bloomington, Ind.: Indiana University Press, 1963.

Neumann, Nelly. "Yama no Kami—die japanische Berggottheit." *Folklore Studies* 22 (1963): 133–366.

Renondeau, G. "Le Shugendō; Histoire, doctrine et rites des anachorètes dits Yamabushi." *Cahiers de la Société Asiatique* 17 (1965).

Slawick, Alexander. "Zur Etymologie des japanischen Terminus *marehito* 'Sakraler Besucher.'" *Wiener Völkerkundliche Mitteilungen,* second yearbook, no. 1 (1954): 44–58.

CHAPTER V

Eder, Matthias. "Shamanismus in Japan." *Paideuma* 6 (no. 7, May, 1958): 367–80.

Fairchild, William P. "Shamanism in Japan." *Folklore Studies* 21 (1962): 1–122.

Kitagawa, Joseph M. "Kaiser und Shamane in Japan." *Antaios* 2 (no. 6, March, 1961): 552–66.

Nakayama, Tarō. *Nihon fujo-shi* (*History of Japanese Female Shamans*). Tokyo: Ookayama Shoten, 1930.

Slawick, Alexander. "Kultische Gereimbünde der Japaner und Germanen." *Die Indogermanen- und Germanenfrage: neue Wege zu ihrer Lösung, Wiener Beiträge zur Kulturgeschichte und Linguistik* 4 (1936): 675–763.

Yanagita, Kunio. "Fujo kō" ("A Study of Female Shamans in Japan"). *Kyōdo kenkyū* 1 (nos. 1–12, 1913).

CHAPTER VI

Bairy, Maurice A. *Japans neue Religionen in der Nachkriegszeit.* Bonn: Röhrscheid, 1959.

Deguchi, Nao. *Scripture of Ooomoto.* Kameoka: Oomoto-kyo Headquarters, 1957.

International Institute for the Study of Religions. "Sōka Gakkai and the Nichiren Shō Sect (I)." *Contemporary Religions in Japan* 2 (no. 2, March, 1960): 55–70.

Kishimoto, Hideo, ed. *Japanese Religion in the Meiji Era,* trans. John F. Howes. Tokyo: Obunsha, 1956.

Kitagawa, Joseph M. "The Contemporary Religious Situation in Japan." *Japanese Religions* (Kyoto) 2 (nos. 2–3, May, 1961): 24–42.

———. "Religious and Cultural Ethos of Modern Japan." *Asian Studies* 2 (no. 3, December, 1964): 334–52.

Kohler, Werner. *Die Lotus-Lehre und die modernen Religionen in Japan.* Zurich: Atlantis, 1962.

McFarland, H. Neill. "The New Religions of Japan." *The Perkins School of Theology Journal* 12 (no. 1, Fall, 1958): 3–21.

Offner, Clark B., and Straelen, Henry van. *Modern Japanese Religions.* Leiden: Brill, 1963.

Schneider, Delwin B. *Konkōkyō: A Japanese Religion.* Tokyo: International Institute for the Study of Religions, 1962.

Tenrikyō, The Headquarters of. *A Short History of Tenrikyō.* Tenri: Headquarters of Tenrikyō Church, 1956.

Tenshō-Kōtai-Jingū-Kyō. *The Prophets of Tabuse.* Tabuse: Tenshō-Kōtai-Jingū-Kyō Headquarters, 1954.

Thomsen, Harry. *The New Religions of Japan.* Tokyo and Rutland, Vt.: Charles E. Tuttle, 1963.

Van Straelen, Henry. *The Religion of Divine Wisdom.* Kyoto: Veritas Shoin, 1957.

Yashima, Jirō. *An Essay on the Way of Life.* Tondabayashi: P L Kyodan Headquarters, 1950.

INDEX

Index